MAMASKATCH

MAMASKATCH

A CREE COMING OF AGE

Darrel J. McLeod

MILKWEED EDITIONS

Published 2019 by Milkweed Editions
Printed in the United States of America
Cover design by Mary Austin Speaker
Cover photo courtesy of Darrel J. McLeod
Author photo by Ilja Herb
Interior design by Mary White
. 19 20 21 22 23 5 4 3 2 1
First US Edition

Milkweed Editions, an independent nonprofit publisher, gratefully acknowledges sustaining support from the Ballard Spahr Foundation; the Jerome Foundation; the McKnight Foundation; the National Endowment for the Arts; the Target Foundation; and other generous contributions from foundations, corporations, and individuals. Also, this activity is made possible by the voters of Minnesota through a Minnesota State Arts Board Operating Support grant, thanks to a legislative appropriation from the arts and cultural heritage fund. For a full listing of Milkweed Editions supporters, please visit milkweed.org.

Library of Congress Cataloging-in-Publication Data has been applied for.

Milkweed Editions is committed to ecological stewardship. We strive to align our book production practices with this principle, and to reduce the impact of our operations in the environment. We are a member of the Green Press Initiative, a nonprofit coalition of publishers, manufacturers, and authors working to protect the world's endangered forests and conserve natural resources. *Mamaskatch* was printed on acid-free 30% postconsumer-waste paper by Thomson-Shore.

MAMASKATCH

This book is dedicated to all my relations,
including those in the spirit world,
and to those who have chosen to walk alongside me
for so many years, in particular Milan.

Freedom is what we do with what is done to us.

—Jean-Paul Sartre

Contents

Spirals

I AM SUSPENDED in purgatory—that no man's land between full sleep and wakefulness—when I hear her voice: "Darrel! I need to talk to you. Come down now. Puh-leeze..."

One o'clock in the morning on a Monday, a school day ahead. All of the records have played through and my mother, Bertha Dora, has turned on the transistor radio in the kitchen. My nostrils twitch from the fumes of a freshly lit cigarette, and the smell of stale beer hangs in the air. Great. Provincial exams today.

I catch snippets of the radio announcement: *Janis Joplin heroin overdose.* A driving rhythm on the bass guitar contrasts with Janis's shrill and throaty voice as she exhorts someone she loves to rip out another piece of her heart.

"Come 'n turn the records over, Son," Mother yells. "I love this woman's voice, but they're sayin' she died."

I know what will happen next if I don't go. She will pound the broom handle on the first of the twelve stairs up to our bedroom, causing another restless night for my little sisters and brother. But I wait a few minutes more, hoping she will pass out or get distracted, and I pray the kids will sleep through it. They hate listening to me when I'm trying to get them ready for school: *Gaylene and Holly, brush your hair. Travis, brush your teeth and put on your good clothes; you can't wear those raggedy jeans and old runners to school. Gaylene, put the Cream of Wheat on, and be sure to stir it this time.* It's even worse when they're tired too.

Then the agonizing starts. Oh my God, oh my God—I was wrong to talk Mother into bringing them out of the foster home. They were better off there, with the Milots. Three years we were apart: 1967 to 1970. But now it's too late—we can't send them back, and they've already seen so much. Gaylene and Holly cried every night of their first two weeks here, scared by the drunkenness and loud voices of partying strangers. They don't know it was because of me Mother got them back, that I hounded and nagged her to take me for a visit, to go to court so they could live with us here in Athabasca. Well, it worked, and now here we all are in this shack behind the pool hall.

"Darrel! Come here. Please, Son. I need to talk to you."

Damn, she isn't giving up. Her voice, which is usually a lilting alto, squeaks when she tries to force volume. I think of Tituba from *The Crucible*, which we studied recently in my Grade Nine drama class. Yes… this is like a play—think of it as a play—a cyclical drama with the scenes taking place in our living room or kitchen, with new characters every weekend. Last week it was Eddie Mullins—Mother called him Dad, then launched into a long explanation after seeing the puzzled looks on our faces. The props are altered in each scene, along with the costumes. Like that buckskin jacket that I love. Fantastic plots and intrigues—like last night at eight o'clock, Uncle Andy on all fours thinking he was an astronaut crawling on the moon after a successful Apollo mission. The play even has special effects: overwhelming new odours, a blue haze, the darkness of a power failure, the occasional flash of lightning and cats shrieking nearby.

Mother's cigarette smoke is getting to me. Her hoarse voice wails in unison with Janis Joplin's, pleading earnestly with the Lord to buy her a Mercedes Benz. I doubt if Mother has even seen a Mercedes or a Porsche—I know *I* haven't. Somehow it doesn't matter. She loves this song and tries to outsing Janis. Mother's rasp is almost as dramatic, but she can't get the volume. Will she turn off the radio, get out the guitar and try it on her own?

I sneeze, pull off the covers, roll out of bed and pull up my loose underwear. Grab a shirt, a pair of pants and socks to protect against the cold floor. My round thirteen-year-old face in the scratched hallway mirror—thick black hair sticking out every which way and faint purple bags under my eyes. I spit into my hands, slick my hair down and rub my eyes with closed fists. Where will her stories and songs take us tonight, and how many hours will pass before I can go back to bed? I trudge downstairs, turn off the radio and flip the records.

Johnny Horton comes on first. "Whispering Pines." Oh boy, that'll make her cry, but I don't dare change it. I take my place in the kitchen chair opposite her. Mother lights yet another Rothmans tailor-made cigarette and sets it down in the clear glass ashtray. The bright red spark gradually burns up the tobacco to make a long grey ash that holds together until she picks it up. Then she starts.

"That priest, Father Jal, came to see us a couple of months after your dad died, you know, just after you were born. It was a Saturday evening and you kids were asleep. We were staying with your great-grandfather, Mosom Powder, in his trapping cabin near Spurfield. There was nowhere else to go. No widow's pension in those days, Son. One afternoon, there was a knock on the door. I opened it, and there he stood. He was in Spurfield to cel'brate mass the next day and said he wanted to see if we were okay. I was so impressed that he would come to console us, to pray for me, and for you—the new baby. I asked him to come in. He smiled and asked how we were doing, but before I could answer he stepped in closer. I thought he was going to pray—put his hands on your forehead or on mine. But a strange look came over him, and he turned toward me, put his back to you. I thought he was raising his arm to make the sign of the cross—to bless us and the cabin, but instead, he opened his hand wide, and he fondled my breast. With the other hand he started feeling me up."

Jesus! I took catechism with Father Jal! I gasp at the image of the short and balding priest touching her like that with his pudgy hands. I clench my teeth. I breathe deeply to calm myself—afraid to get emotional. My eyes meet Mother's for a second, but neither of us can handle the intensity of what we see. I wonder if the other priests I have known would have done the same—I only admire one of them, Father Fornier. After hearing this story, I understand why Mother cried the day I told her I wanted to be a priest when I grew up. We go quiet for a few minutes and stare at the kitchen floor.

That night she tells me again about going to a residential school run by the Catholic Church at Grouard. About being taken from her mother when she was only six years old, having to sleep in a dorm with thirty-nine other little girls. She tells me about being forced to learn English along with her sisters. Then how her sisters Margaret and Agnes, her auntie Helen and several other aunties who were teenagers at the time escaped. Merle Haggard warbles the last line of "The Fightin' Side of Me."

The next record falls from the stack. The needle sets itself down and there is static. Elvis's voice launches into "There Goes My Everything." Oh no, Mother sings that song almost every time she gets out her guitar. Will she go on again, telling me how it makes her think about Daddy dying, or my sister Debbie getting married at age fifteen?

The pattern of my mother's stories is different from the ones I hear at school. The timelines are never linear. Instead, they are like spirals. She starts with one element of a story, moves to another and skips to yet a different part. She revisits each theme several times over, providing a bit more information with each pass. At first I find it hard to follow, but I've learned that if I just sit back and listen without interrupting, she will cover everything and make each story complete.

"Auntie Margaret and I grew up on the trapline. We moved around every season and camped in large canvas tents to be closer to the animals and birds. In the evening, we sat around the fire, Auntie Margaret across from me, sometimes cutting sheets of moose meat to make *kakiwak*—dried meat—other times scraping moose or beaver hides for tanning. I always sat right beside Mother, your Cucuum Adele. Oh, she used to get so upset when I had to go pee. It was a big deal. She had to walk in the bush with me till we found a fallen tree that I could sit on and hang my behind over."

I smile inside at the notion of my strong mother with her man-hands being a dainty little girl. The detail in her stories and the intensity of her look as she tells them holds my attention, but the way she speaks as if it all took place yesterday or the day before troubles me. We both know that it happened years ago, and that it's part of our family history that will soon be forgotten.

"Auntie Margaret had her first baby, Chiq-iq, there on the trapline, you know. I loved that baby. There were no soothers then, so she would suck on my bottom lip between feedings—fall asleep that way.

"The birds are messengers, Son. Sometimes they told me things that would happen in our family. *Âhâsiw, mikisiw, ôhô* and *wiskipôs*— crow, eagle, owl and whisky jack. They'll help you—guide you through life. Watch them, talk to them."

She chuckles nervously and watches for my reaction. I laugh too. Her bloodshot brown eyes are an exact replica of my own. In these moments she is so sincere, so real. I love that she thinks she can communicate with birds. Will I ever have that gift myself?

"I learned to be tough, Son. My brothers were rough, and I had to learn to defend myself or get beaten up play-fighting. I learned to whip the boys and come out on top."

Then she remembers something else, and she tells the next story while moving her hands as if she were now the play's director. With the mention of each character she raises her hand and points to where they are in the scene that's so vivid in her mind.

"Auntie Helen was sitting there. My mother, Cucuum Adele, was over there, and your dad was sitting over that way. Your dad and I played guitar and harmonized for your *cucuum*. People invited us to sing at parties all around Slave Lake, Spurfield and Smith. Sometimes the neighbours let us take their Model T. Your dad made me drive, because he was drinkin'. I didn't drink then. I started after your dad, Cucuum Adele and my brother Louis died, even though that ain't no excuse."

I block the wave of emotion that comes over me about Daddy's death, about Granny and Uncle's deaths. I lost the three of them before I even had them. How could I fathom that scale of loss—that I would never be kissed by my father; that Cucuum would never sing to me in Cree, never rock me or tickle my belly with her vibrating lips; that Uncle Louis would never teach me to snare rabbits or hunt.

The effort to suppress my feelings leaves me with a pulsating headache. I lean back as far as I can, cross my arms and stretch my legs out in front of me. Mother stares at me. I wonder what she sees, and in my weakened state I wonder if she can read my mind, if she knows that I too have a dark story to tell.

Mother continues on, and every half hour or so I pull myself upright. I feel guilty about my dreariness and impatience. It is in these nocturnal sessions that I learn about our family history. Dead family members come to life and find their place in my heart. The seasonal dwelling sites and hunting areas she describes so clearly take shape in my head.

After a few hours she starts to slur her words and nod off. I take advantage of her sleepiness to put a few LPs that I like on the metal peg of the turntable—Creedence Clearwater Revival, Roy Orbison and Elvis Presley—turning the volume down at the same time, but I don't get away with it. She shakes her head and sits up straight.

"Play Johnny Horton again. Or put on Johnny Cash. Merle Haggard. Please, Son. I need to hear country. Turn it up, can't hear it." Her tone is gentle, but it's a demand, not a request.

The Johnny Cash album slides down the peg first; the arm moves over to the edge of the 33⅓ album and sets itself down.

Call him drunken Ira Hayes, he won't answer any more...

"Yes, that song, Son. I love that song."

Not the whisky drinking Indian, nor the marine that went to war.

I finally get to bed around four in the morning. I roll onto my side and rest my head in the crook of my elbow, careful not to awaken my little brother. Sometimes after these sessions I can fall asleep, but other times I lie there thinking about what Mother has told me. Why does she pick me to tell her stories to, and why does she only tell them when she's drinking? She knows I have school in the morning and that I never miss a day—she must think what she's recounting is important. Does she want me to repeat her stories to others, my sisters and brothers, her grandchildren—someday, somewhere?

I know I could never share stories the magical way she does. The structure of our language, Cree, is hard-wired in her brain, and English is still a challenge for her. She sees the world differently from the way they teach us in school. Rocks are alive—she calls them our grand-fathers. The markers for *I* and *you* are attached as extra syllables to the verb forms. The second-person pronoun is always more important, so it comes first, whether it's the subject or the object. Unlike in English, *I love you* and *you love me* both start with the marker *ki*, for *you*. The third person is split into two parts; this distinguishes important characters in a conversation from secondary ones. The gendered pronouns *he* and *she* don't exist in Cree. Mother has told me this more than once, laughing at herself for getting the two mixed up.

Is that why my older brother, Greg, and my uncle Danny could play at dressing up as girls so often without Mother getting upset? Is that why my uncles aren't as hairy as the Métis or white guys around? What about me? Will I be a regular Cree guy, like most of my uncles, or more like Danny and Greg, who grew up mimicking Mother, my sister Debbie and our aunties? If I spoke Cree, would I see the world the way Mother does and have the answers to these questions? Would I be less afraid?

AS I TOSS in bed, it occurs to me that Mother is preparing me for a life that terrifies her—a world that is foreign and hostile. She wants to warn me about the Catholic church, about the priests and the nuns, and to remind me that we have other ways of being spiritual. We have our ancestors, medicine men, ceremonies and sacred herbs. She wants me to know that for help and guidance, they are the ones to call upon. Them and the birds. *Âhâsiw, mikisiw, ôhô* and *wiskipôs.*

Hail Mary, Full of Grace

Hey Mareh? —full of grease
Lart in yer tea
Blasst artaow munst wimmin
an blasst arfroot ah yur woun
Cheezus.

BERTHA REHEARSES THIS new prayer kneeling on the linoleum floor beside her cot, which is lined up with the thirty-nine others in the dormitory. Her skin itches in the stiff nightgown. She feels so small and alone in the big room. No familiar aroma of wood smoke or wild peppermint tea. The room is musky and damp, which makes it hard to concentrate.

It's her second year at the residential school, but she still has no idea what the words she pronounces mean. She struggles to remember the sounds and intonation of each line. Tomorrow she will have to recite the entire prayer in front of the nuns and all the other girls, even the older ones. She doesn't want everyone to laugh at her as they have at the other girls her age. She glances around. Annie, who sleeps in the next cot over, is watching her and giggling. Bertha squeezes her eyes shut to ignore her.

Annie could be Bertha's older sister or first cousin: the same smooth brown complexion and deep brown eyes; the same jet-black hair hacked into an inverted rag mop, just grown out a bit. Like most of the girls in the school, Annie speaks Cree, or *Nehiyaw*. She has been in St. Bernard's Indian Residential School at Buffalo Bay for a few years already and although she speaks English quite well, she often whispers and sings to herself—in Cree—smiling pensively each time she stops.

Annie remembers how hard it was to learn the Hail Mary prayer, but she mastered it some time ago. She recited the prayer by heart earlier today in front of a gaggle of gloating nuns and noticed Bertha watching her in amazement. Annie also sang a version of "God Save the King" and capped it off with the date: "Todayh 'his 'hwenesdeh sectembur twunee forth   nihn-t'in fortih wun." Bertha, listening in wonder, had no idea what the song meant, let alone that extra string of strange sounds at the end.

Suddenly Bertha senses a warm presence. She opens her eyes. Annie is kneeling directly in front of her. Bertha grasps Annie's outstretched hands and wraps her fingers and thumb around them to complete the connection. Annie pronounces each line slowly and carefully. Bertha watches her lips intently, then repeats after her:

> *Hail Mareh, full of grace,*
> *The lort is with thee.*
> *Blesset art thou 'mongstall wimmen.*
> *And blesset is the fruit of thy womb,*
> *Cheezus.*

BERTHA IS AT the school with her older sister Margaret, her aunties, already in their early teens, and dozens of cousins. Daily she struggles, being away from her mother, her home and the younger kids. She craves the food her mother, Mosom and Cucuum feed her: stewed moose ribs, fried whitefish, the marrow of moose thigh bones, thinly sliced deer meat, boiled potatoes and carrots, sweet red willow shoots and dried or stewed berries. This evening, just after suppertime, kneeling there on the hard floor, the memory of good food makes her especially sad. While the others ate real food, she nibbled stale bread and washed it down with a glass of water. She knows that Margaret will have done the same.

Early that morning, just before breakfast, they were caught *again*—talking Cree. Bertha had found herself alone, one-on-one, with Margaret and whispered to her fervently for a few moments. They huddled to one side of a statue of the Virgin Mary, which sat on a pedestal at the end of the main hallway.

"*Ninohte Nigawi, ninohte Nigawi*," Bertha mumbled over and over, squinting to hold back tears. Margaret cooed as she ran her fingers through her sister's hair.

> *N'sims, mahti poni mahto.*
> *Mahti poni mahto n'sims.*
> *Kiyam.*

Suddenly, they heard footsteps and a *swoosh*. Bertha clenched her jaw, and her hands trembled. Her eyes moved up to the black robe and cape, then to the pink and white face—the forehead covered by a stiff white strip attached to an oval frame. Black hood. Bertha's terrified gaze stayed on the headscarf for a moment. Was there hair under there? So many times the older girls had debated this—some saying, "Well, of course they have hair, they're human, you know," and others saying, "They hate hair—look what they done to ours. They probably shave their heads." Sister Pierrette bent down low, and Bertha watched with fascination the shiny metal cross dangling at mid-chest, as if by magic.

The girls recognized Sister Pierrette's particular bouquet—unwashed hair and the ripe sweat accumulated in her robes. They jerked their heads back as they felt her sour breath on their tiny round faces, gaping at her bushy eyebrows and faint black moustache. She spoke in a unique blend of Cree, French and broken English.

"*Pahagat-h'own*," Sister Pierrette said in lilting Cree. "Speak Hing*lish*! Come into de class*room*. h'Astum. Qwee- ah-h*oh*! Come here! *Vite*! hur*ry*! Sister Marguer*ite*! Viens ic*itte*. Dese two sau*vages* were speak*ing* dair lang*uage* h'ag*ain*. What do you tink we should do wit *dem*? De terd time dis week—*qu'est-ce qu'on fait d'elles, donc*?"

The girls looked down the hallway in horror. Another dark figure moved in their direction: Sister Marguerite. This nun never smiled, and her face looked as though it were on fire: bright red with white scaly patches. Her arms shuffled awkwardly in her heavy robe so that she appeared to float across the floor—a surreal black-and-white mannequin.

It was hard for Bertha not to stare; Sister Marguerite's nose stuck out even farther today. She carried the scent that some of the Sisters had at certain times of the month—a smell the girls had never noticed at home—though today her essence was partially masked by the incense fumes from morning mass. Her gaze was gentler than that of Sister Pierrette. She hustled Bertha and Margaret into the empty classroom nearby, then sighed.

"Ah—pas en*core*, les filles! Not h'ag*ain*! You have ta learn, girls. Here—no *Cree*—Hing'*lish* h'on*lee*!"

"Me, I tink dey should wear der moca*siiin* roun der neck fer two *day*!" Sister Pierrette growls.

"*Oui, oui—mais aussi—du pain sec* and h'wat*er* h'on*ly* for two day, *non*?"

As the nuns watched, Margaret and Bertha took off their moccasins, tied them together and hung them around their necks. All day they walked barefoot on the cold floors of the classrooms, dorm, dining room and chapel.

NOW, ONE LAST time Bertha repeats after Annie: "Blesst is the fruit of thy womb, Cheesus," with a convincing "ah-*min*." Then she climbs back into her bed. But once everyone is asleep she tiptoes past four cots to Margaret's, gets in and cuddles close. At home Bertha usually slept with her mother, her older sisters, an auntie or a *cucuum*; until this school, she had never slept alone. Slowly, she calms with the help of her sister's warmth and delicate fragrance. She tries hard not to fall asleep, knowing she has to get back to her own bed before morning.

"*NIGAWI, NIGAWIIIII! NIMAMAAAA! Namoya!... Moyaaaa!*" Bertha cried this out as soon as she understood that the strange men at the door had come for her, as they had for Margaret two years earlier. Bertha's mother had always been affectionate and attentive, but now she turned her back on her daughter.

"*Wiyawi-i-i Ndans*," she commanded. She waved her arm high, motioning for Bertha to leave the large canvas tent. Usually her mother only did this when she was fed up with the racket and wanted the kids to go and play. Bertha had wondered why some of her clothes had been packed into a cardboard box that had sat by the door for two days.

"Waaaaaaa *namoya... Nigawi!*" Bertha's piercing voice.

The boat ride down the river was fast—the white poplars and Jack pines a blur. Then the car ride over a dusty and rough dirt road. She sat in the back seat sobbing, her head cradled in her hands. The physical distance was only thirty miles, but Bertha was transported into another world.

Bertha and her captors arrived at the three-storey red-brick building. It looked enormous to Bertha, who had only seen the summer tent houses and the whitewashed log cabins where she and her family took shelter for the winter months. A grassy meadow led down to the reedy bay of the lake. Bertha fixed her gaze on the water, which went on forever.

It all had happened so fast, yet now things were moving in slow motion. The group of new girls was lined up. They gazed at the floor, glancing up only as each girl moved to the front of the line to have her braids cut off.

Bertha peeped around whenever she dared, trying to spot Margaret and her aunties Helen, Mable and Eva. She didn't see them. Her eyes became fixated on that mound of raven-black braids on the floor around the chair. One nun, her face strangely framed with stiff white canvas, held each girl by the arms and placed her onto the chair. Another nun, shorter but dressed identically, chopped off the braids just below the ears with large steel scissors. It took just four or five rapid snips. Strange-looking girls got up from the chair, hair cut flat all around with bangs that stopped inches above their eyebrows. Puffy eyes—faces stunned with shock.

Next, the assembly line led them to a giant white enamel basin.

Each girl in turn stood in the bathtub while two nuns scoured her body with a scrubbing brush designed for wooden floors. Hair was shampooed with a liquid that stunk like diesel, and then dried vigorously with a white towel that smelled like bleach. The last nun forced flour-sack dresses over their heads.

BERTHA AWAKES IN a panic but is confused about why. First she rubs her belly to soothe the aching emptiness, then cringes as she realizes she's still in Margaret's bed. She tiptoes back to her bed, climbs in, covering herself with the thin sheet and scratchy wool blanket. She feels dazed, but her thoughts are clear. She knows her *nigawi* and her *mosom* would never let her go hungry—not her nor any child. In their home, the little ones—*awasisuk*—always ate first, savouring delicacies as the adults looked on. Bertha knows what she has to do. She will find a way to talk to Auntie Helen, her mother's second-youngest sister, to ask for guidance.

Mid-morning, when Bertha and Margaret muster with the other girls to do their gardening chores, they spot Helen in the doorway. Even in the peculiar school uniform she is beautiful, with her smooth, dark complexion, deep-set eyes and confident gaze.

Bertha coughs to get Helen's attention.

"Mar-*gret*," Helen calls, mock-glaring at the two girls. "Put on your moccasins 'fore you go outside! Why ya wear dem aroun your neck hanaways?"

Margaret glances around to see if there are any nuns close by. Oh no! There is the unmistakable tall silhouette, just behind Helen. By lifting her chin slightly and protruding her lips, Bertha points behind Helen. Helen goes silent and lifts her hand to her forehead as if to make the sign of the cross. The nun strides past them and down the hallway without saying a word. The three girls sigh.

"Nuns heard us talking Cree," Bertha whispers.

"*Mah... sosquats.*"

"They make us do this." She touches the leather strand around her neck. "And jus' eat *papwesagun*—drink *nipiy*." Her bottom lip is sticking out, trembling—her face is screwed up. *"Whuh waah! Sos-quats!"* Helen turns red as her breathing becomes audible.

Then they catch the flash of a crucifix against a black robe, see the black headscarf with its white frame. It is Sister Marie-Ange, who works with the older girls. The girls have seen her crying in the chapel after evening prayers. Bertha and Margaret do a volte-face, brush past a cluster of girls, then dart in opposite directions.

Helen watches the two little pairs of bare feet shuffle down the hallway. Fury flashes from her eyes in the direction of the nun.

"*Wah waw!* They're doing it again. Punishing kids jus' for talkin' Cree! *Sosquats!* Damn!"

THAT AFTERNOON IN the chapel, Helen focuses on the statue of the Virgin Mary. The Sisters don't know, but she has hidden a medicine bundle her mother gave her inside the hollow of the statue. Now she never feels sad when she kneels in front of it, and she prays to it for hours on end, repeating endlessly the Hail Mary prayer.

She walks over to the statue and reaches inside. Yes, the amulet is still there. She picks it up and caresses its rough leather surface. Its smoky aroma reminds her of home.

I've had enough, she thinks. *It's one thing what they done to me and my sisters, but now they're picking on the younger ones.*

She remembers the time that Sister Pierrette slapped her because she choked on her supper, eating dry porridge for the third time in one day. She recalls being caught speaking Cree to her sister Mable. They locked her in a musty, dark closet in the basement. For two days Helen sat on a thin mattress placed on the cement floor, hearing only the shuffle of feet above her. Cold mush, dry bread and water. She was ten then.

But what infuriates her most is the recollection of waking to feel hands moving over her body, first along her thighs, then up to her chest, then to the spot that the Sisters had taught the girls they themselves were never supposed to touch. She knew the huddled figure by the bed was Sister Pierrette, recognized her smell. Every time it happened Helen lay awake for the rest of the night, overcome with anguish and shame.

Helen startles at footsteps just outside the chapel. She knows the cadence of the steps. Bolting upright she dashes to the door, coming face to face with Sister Pierrette.

"Hay-layn. I wanna talk with you. *Astum.* Let's go back into *la chapelle, chère.*"

As Pierrette steps in close, Helen jerks away. Her mouth is parched. She stumbles backwards, almost falls. Pierrette slides past and stands in the aisle, turning her back to the dramatic crucifix suspended behind the altar. Helen swallows hard, then shuffles back into the chapel. Her gaze shifts to the statue of the Virgin Mary. She catches her breath and stands up straight, confused for a moment by the calm coming over her—a balm on her forehead. She hears her *mosom*'s drum: *boom BOOM boom BOOM boom BOOM boom BOOM*. Or is it her own heartbeat pounding in her head? Then she sees them.

First her *cucuum*, then her *mosom*, and their parents too. Then her aunties and uncles who have moved on into the spirit world. They're all there around her, filling the chapel. She's overwhelmed and trembling, but strong. She forces a breath, raises her eyebrows and moves closer to Pierrette.

"Yeah, I wanna talk to you, *too*!" Her gaze is solid now, unwavering. "What you doin' to Bertha and Margaret? They're goin' aroun' barefoot and not eatin' in the dinin' room for two days!"

"*C'est pas de tes affaires*! Not your biz*ness*."

"*Scanak*! I'm their auntie; they're my relations! Did you hit them too?"

"*Arrête*! Shut h'*up* now, or you go downstair. Maybe for *h'a* long time!"

Helen inches closer, toe to toe with Pierrette. "You send me down there again, and I will tell what you done to me at night! I will tell everythin'!"

The white frame around Pierrette's face is a stark contrast with her crimson cheeks and purple lips. The putrid vapour of her breath has intensified—or is it just that she's breathing so much harder now? She has clenched her fists, and Helen girds herself for a blow. Instead, Pierrette beams her hatred through her beady blue eyes. Is she trying to instill terror in Helen's soul? She exhales forcefully, spraying Helen with droplets of saliva, then turns and stomps out of the chapel.

Helen goes quickly to the front pew, where she kneels, drinking in the presence of her ancestors. She glances at the special statue, then closes her eyes and whispers *hai-hai hai-hai* over and over until the pounding in her head stops. As her breathing slows, she contemplates the Virgin Mary and a plan takes shape in her mind.

HELEN HAS ORGANIZED a few secret sessions with the older girls over the last few months, discussing how they can help each other. She knows the Sisters' schedules and behavioural patterns. And the girls trust her. Many are first, second or third cousins. Even girls who aren't related come to these secret meetings. Every single one of them has a sister, a brother or a cousin who hasn't survived. Each month a few more die.

Early one morning Helen managed to peek at the class register to check the name of a missing cousin. What she saw confirmed the rumours:

> Name: Mary Gladue
> Date of Birth: May 9th, 1927
> Attendance: Absent
> Reason: Dead – TB

She scrolled down the page frantically—the word *dead* was printed beside the names of others who were missing. TB was written by two others, but for most, no reason was given.

OVER THE NEXT two days, with Helen leading, the girls have urgent Cree conversations in different hiding places: Friday afternoon in the basement laundry room. Saturday morning outside, behind the chapel, while pretending to play freeze tag.

Helen knows she has to be cunning. There are cliques in the group of older girls. Some of the Sisters have even groomed a few girls to be their stool pigeons. The nuns' brainwashing about the wickedness of being Indian, speaking Cree and using their Indian medicine in heathen ceremonies has worked on these girls. They get special privileges, candy and open affection from the Sisters.

A plan is hatched. They'll strike Sunday afternoon. This is when most of the nuns leave the school grounds and only two are on duty.

SUNDAY MORNING ARRIVES. Helen, Bertha, Agnes, Margaret, Annie and the other girls walk to the church for eleven o'clock mass. At the entrance, each dips her right hand into the holy water and makes the sign of the cross. They genuflect to the crucifix behind the altar. They stand, sit, kneel, then stand, sit, kneel at all the right times.

The priest calls, "*Dominus vobiscum.*" In perfect unison they utter the response: "*Et cum spiritu tuo.*"

They line up for communion as usual, kneeling before the priest, closing their eyes and sticking out their tongues so he can place the sterile white Host on it.

"*Corpus Christi.*"

The girls who have been meeting glance at Helen, unsure whether they should swallow the Host, today of all days—afraid they might choke. They pucker—the dry Host sticks to the roof of their mouths; they let it disintegrate there.

During the final procession from the altar to the exit, the pungent smoke of burning incense reminds them of sweetgrass and sage.

NOW HELEN AND Agnes hasten from the church to the schoolhouse. They conceal themselves on opposite sides inside the entrance, pressing up against the wall so they can't be seen. Helen glances at the crucifix above the door—the near-naked man with the crown of thorns on the cross. Is He on their side, or will He help the Sisters who wear His gold ring and claim to be His brides?

When Helen closes her eyes, her heart thumping, an image of the Virgin Mary appears in her head, just above the centre point of her eyes. Mary is so clear, a serene figure cloaked in an emerald-green mantle, but the face Helen sees has a deep-brown complexion and beautiful, prominent cheekbones. Her hooded almond eyes project pure love.

She thinks about genuflecting or making the sign of the cross. But this Mary—her *cucuum*, her mother, her auntie, her sister—doesn't require that.

Girls are trooping past Helen and Agnes and into the school. Helen peers outside through the open door. Aspens line the road away from Buffalo Bay and Grouard, their delicate leaves dancing with excitement. So many times Helen has longed to wander into the forest to greet her animal friends and commune with them once more. She longs to stroll to the lakeshore—wade in slowly to wash away her sorrow and anguish, and then find her way home.

Helen's heart begins to thunder again. If this doesn't work, she, her sisters and all her cousins will suffer. Punishment will be swift and severe. The fiery images the nuns show them every day flash through her mind— tortured faces burning in a lake of fire while the Devil hovers above with his spiked trident in hand, peering down with sadistic glee. She glances over at Agnes, positive that she must be having similar thoughts.

Agnes's flushed face is a stone sculpture, her breathing short and fast. But when Helen catches her eye, she smiles. By nighttime, if all goes well, they could be home in their own beds.

That's it. The last girl is in. Mable is always the last. Helen and Agnes hold their breath, then hear the familiar pattern of the Sisters' footsteps on the school stairs. Their eyes meet. Helen nods. Agnes nods in reply.

What unfolds next happens so fast it will forever be a blur in the girls' minds. And the sequence of events will differ each time Bertha, Helen, Margaret or Agnes tells the story. Each of them will emphasize certain points and leave out others. But Bertha's version—my mother's version—is the one I know best.

Helen jumps in front of Sister Marguerite, pushing against the nun's chest with all her strength. Marguerite struggles to stay on her feet, shuffles forward, back, and then tumbles down the stairs leading to the entrance. She lies at the bottom, her stunned red face framed by her displaced headscarf. Then Agnes shoves Sister Pierrette with all her might. Pierrette falls backwards too, sliding headfirst to the bottom. Helen scurries down and pounces onto Marguerite's stomach. Agnes, with lightning speed, lands hard on Pierrette's stomach, taking the nun's breath away.

"Au secours... Au secours!" Sister Marguerite screams. "Girls, please help us!"

BERTHA STANDS IN the doorway, trembling, Annie by her side. The sun is shining; the songbirds trill in full force. A breeze makes the leaves on the poplar trees dance more feverishly than ever. The nuns are crying for help, but Bertha doesn't go. Instead, she looks over to her big sister Margaret. As though giving a signal, Margaret removes her moccasins from around her neck and slips them on. With extended lips she motions toward Bertha, and Bertha steps into her own moccasins, hands shaking as she struggles to fasten the leather laces.

A cluster of girls pushes through the doorway and down the stairs, forcing Bertha and Margaret aside. "FIGHT FIGHT FIGHT FIGHT. *Pagamahow. Pagamahow.*" They have witnessed many fights, mostly between boys or men, but also between their aunts and female cousins. This time, even the crows caw loudly.

Margaret leads Bertha down the stairs. Through the crowd they see Helen straddled across Sister Marguerite's chest. The starchy head-scarf is off, and Helen is pulling the nun's hair. Bertha sighs at the sight of it. It's just like Cucuum's hair—thick, shoulder length and wavy, coal black with white strands.

Helen lifts and pounds Sister Marguerite's head on the cement as hard as she can. A thin stream of blood flows from Marguerite's nose down to her collarbone. If Helen had been a man, Bertha thought, Sister Marguerite would be dead. The nun rolls onto her side, covering her head with her hands, her crucifix now on the ground beside her, upside down, her rosary tangled in knots beside it.

Bertha watches, breathless, as Agnes mimics the pounding Helen is delivering. She hears Sister Pierrette moaning and muttering incomprehensible words. It seems that a blinding fury has come over Agnes too.

Bertha has to act. If you hurt someone for any reason, by hitting, teasing or tormenting them, it will come back to you. *Seven times worse,* her *cucuum* had told her. And killing, the nuns had taught her, is a mortal sin. You'll burn in hell.

"*Astum.* Come on. *Semak*—NOW," Margaret shouts at Bertha. "*Kwee ah hu!* Hurry! Before the others get back." But Bertha scrambles over to Agnes, grasps her wrists to wrestle them away from Pierrette's head. Blood from Agnes's hands smears onto Bertha's.

"Agnessss… *EKOSI… Astum!* Come on—*kwee ah hu!*"

"Run! Run! Go! Go! *Kiwek*—go home! Now—hurry! *Kwee ah hu!*" Helen yells. "We'll catch up."

Bertha and Margaret flee, running toward the welcoming birds and poplar trees that will guide them home.

"*Scanak!* Mean bitss!" Helen rams Sister Marguerite's head into the ground again. "Mean. Mean. Why you so mean to us?" She is both yelling and pleading at the same time. Then Agnes is plucking at the back of Helen's uniform with bloody hands.

"*Ekosi maga!* Let's go, Helen. C'mon. *Astum.*"

Helen jumps up, feeling the wetness on the back of her blouse. She, Agnes, Mable and their nieces take off running, screaming, "*Mamaskatch!* We're free!"

Bertha hears their voices in the distance and yells back a response: "*Tapwe! Mamaskatch. MAMASKATCH!*"

The last time Bertha, my mother, told me this story, it was in the wee hours. As she came to the end, she opened her eyes wide. "Word spread fast about the escape, Son. Especially 'bout how our aunties beat up those nuns. I don' know if it was because the nuns were scared, or because so many kids died in that place, but the *simaganisak,* the bulls, never took us back there like they had other kids. I stayed home with Mother and slep' in her bed every night, till I was eighteen and married your dad. Agnes never came home. They say she hitchhiked to the West Coast and married a fisherman."

She looked into my eyes and attempted a smile.

Macimanitowi: Devils

THIS HAPPENS WHEN I am a baby. There is a knocking at the door of Mosom Powder's trapping cabin—three sharp raps, then a tense male voice. "Bertha McLeod. It's Mr. Jones—Alberta Social Services. I know you are in there. Can you please open the door?"

"Leave us alone."

"There's been a report of drunkenness and partying with children present. I need to see the children."

My mother hears the man recede down the wooden plank, which forms a ramp up to the base of the porch, then his steps, returning.

"I know why you're here," she calls. "There ain't no party. I play guitar and sing to the kids sometimes. Ain't nobody drinkin'. The kids ain't here now anyways. They're visitin' my sister-in-law in Kinosew."

"I have it from a good source that there's been partying here. Children are being neglected."

"I don't know who coulda told you that. There ain't no party. Leave us alone."

"I need you to open the door. I have the authority to do a home inspection, and that is what I intend to do. I need to see your children."

"*You* are going to make sure my children are safe? That's my job. You take people's kids away—send them to white families. Everyone knows what you do! You're not taking my kids. Get outta here *now!*"

"Bertha, I have the proper authority to do this. If you don't co-operate, I will have to come back with the police. It took a great deal of effort to get here. Please open up, so I can inspect and be on my way."

"I can't. You'll have to wait until Mosom gets home. There ain't nobody else around now. Don't trust men like you. The kids ain't here! There ain't nothin' for you to see." Standing right at the door, she yells, "You can't snoop around here! Just leave—now!" She leans over and grasps the handle of the axe Mosom uses for splitting logs and pulls it closer. She can manoeuvre it to defend her kids if she has to. Then she turns to her two small children. "Hide the baby—*kwee ah hu*—hurry. Climb out the window. Go hide in the woodshed like I showed you."

From where she guards the door, Mother watches my sister Debbie wrap me snugly, a scowl of intense determination on her face. Debbie sets me inside the cloth-lined basket, places it on the chair and climbs through the back window. Greggie strains to lift and pass the basket through, praying I won't make a peep. Then he climbs onto the chair and struggles to pull himself up and out.

Bertha moves back into the enclosed porch, right in front of the door. She stands tall, her hands trembling. Her worst nightmare is happening. She can't open the door—she has to stall for a time. Thankfully, today is the day Mosom is supposed to return from his week-long hunting trip.

Mr. Jones paces the plywood landing outside—then not a sound. Has he gone to peek through the windows of the front room? Oh God, is he going to go around behind the cabin to the woodshed? Bertha holds her breath, listens intently. She hears the platform in front of the porch creak. Good—he's staying out front.

Trying not to make a sound, she sits on the kindling box in the porch and leans back against the wall. She'll wait him out. After all, what's he going to do—break down the door? Well, he might try. She gets the large butcher knife from the kitchen and jams it into the door-frame—at least it would be one more obstacle should he try to break in.

She had been praying daily that the government worker, Mr. Jones, would never find his way to the tiny trapper's cabin that Mosom, her grandfather, had set her up in outside of the tiny village of Spurfield.

She and Mosom both knew that she had to hide deep in the woods with Debbie, Greggie and baby Darrel—Lapatak.

Like her ancestors, Bertha spent her whole life in the bush around Lesser Slave Lake. After the recent sudden deaths in her family—her husband, Sonny; her mother, Cucuum Adele; her cherished older brother, Louis—she knew that the land, the rocks, the rivers and streams, the trees, plants, animals and birds would heal her family, help them to carry on with life. But she also knew that as a widow— with no money, no home and nowhere else to go—she would become a target. They would come for her children, just as they had come for her. She and Mosom had discussed the stories they had heard about poor Indian families whose kids were taken away, never to be seen again. But now, in the late 1950s, not all of the kids were brought to residential schools. Instead many were given—or even worse, sold— to *Moniyawak,* white people, for adoption. Nobody understood why this was happening, apart from the fact that the mothers were poor and usually single. There were rumours that hundreds of kids had been taken away to other provinces, to the United States and even overseas.

It didn't help that Mable McLeod, the mother-in-law who had scorned Bertha from the beginning, was angry that she'd gone into hiding with *her* grandkids. Bertha even wondered if it was Mrs. McLeod who had sent Mr. Jones after her.

Sitting on the kindling box, she feels a chill at the thought of losing Lapatak. He was a parting gift from Sonny. She loves doting on him—cuddling him, making him giggle by planting her lips on his belly and blowing, chanting to him in Cree and pushing an engorged brown nipple between his puffy lips at the slightest whimper. Before each feeding, she tries to clear her head of sadness and anger by doing a smudging ceremony with sweetgrass and sage. And even through the haze of three burials, sleepless nights of grief, rotating visits of condolence, then giving birth alone and having to move her little family, she makes sure her milk is rich. She forces herself to eat plenty of the wild foods Mosom gathers and hunts.

Wah wah! Hasn't she survived enough in the last six months without facing the wicked Mr. Jones? For the past year, the bird messengers she relies upon to warn and guide her have been twittering, squawking and cawing. Ravens and crows dive-bomb her head every time she steps outside. A sparrow has flown into the cabin not once, but twice. Many days, in the wee hours, woodpeckers drum on the cabin's south wall. She has become more anxious with each new sign. How could there be so many at once? But the birds have never misled her. Day after day, she is on edge—vibrating, wary of what will happen next.

Tears form in her eyes as she recollects watching Mosom sitting in his homemade rocking chair, holding Lapatak—his thick white moustache and beard brushing against the baby's soft skin. She knows that Mosom's fragrance—a blend of peppermint tea, Drum tobacco, wood smoke and a gentle, clean, manly odour—is as comforting to her children as it has been to her from as early as she can remember.

They can't separate us now, she thinks. We are just starting to settle in with Mosom.

THUMP THUMP   THUMP THUMP

Oh God, now he's pounding with his fists.

As Mr. Jones rattles the door, Bertha sees the black latch on the inside moving.

"Bertha Dora McLeod, I know you're in there. I've been waiting here twenty minutes already. I can't go until I've seen the children and spoken to you. Open the door *now*."

When she hears him stepping away, she is convinced he's going to check all around the house and clearing. She has to get outside to distract him—keep him away from the woodshed. She jumps up, pulls the knife out of the door frame and sets it on the kindling box—within her reach. She turns the simple lock and pulls the door open.

There he stands, Mr. Jones—a cross between an undertaker and a Catholic priest, with his sallow complexion, stiff black suit, bleached white shirt and black tie. His silhouette in the open doorway contrasts sharply with the autumn leaves covering the ground and fluttering on the maple and poplar trees behind him. He reaches into the inside pocket of his suit coat and pulls out some folded papers.

MOSOM HAS BEEN stalking a huge bull moose for six days now, following its tracks, observing where it goes to drink and to graze. He has been observing the other animal tracks too, making sure that he himself isn't being stalked. He knows the bull's every move. Now it is about a quarter of a mile ahead of him, on its daily route. He is ready to take it down, but as he stands immobile under a tall Jack pine, waiting, he senses that something is wrong at home. The birds are behaving oddly, warning him of danger. And Bertha is there alone with the three kids—no men and no rifle. He knows he has to get home *cemak.* The moose can wait until next week. He picks up the cluster of rabbits he has snared and the bundle of fireweed, cranberries, rat root and wild mint he has gathered, and strides the two miles back toward his cabin.

From the edge of the forest Mosom sees a dark figure standing in his doorway. He grasps right away who the man is and why he is there. The man's right hand is raised and he is waving some papers in the air. Mosom coughs.

Mr. Jones jerks his head back and looks behind him.

Mosom casts a striking figure; he has the leathery, wrinkled face of an elder now, but is still a bold presence—a warrior. Calm and confident. His hunting rifle is slung loosely over his shoulder. This latest scourge infuriates him. First the *Moniyawak* moved into their territory uninvited, making empty promises and offering beads and trinkets in exchange for land, furs and food. They spread the flu and smallpox through infected blankets, causing the deaths of thousands of *Nehiyawak.* Then they slaughtered the buffalo, causing widespread starvation. Every fall they still take *awasisuk* from their parents' arms and send them to live in residential schools, often with cruel priests and nuns, for months or years at a time—and now this: poor *Nehiyaw* children being sold or given away.

"*Kigwaaey ntawayataman?*" Mosom's deep voice through clenched teeth.

The man in black takes two steps toward Mosom and tries to force eye contact. "Sir, you cannot interfere with my work. I must proceed. I need the children.   Ahh…   Ah-wah-siiii-suk—and the baby."

Mosom stares right through Mr. Jones—slides his hunting rifle into his hands and jams the butt up against his shoulder. A twitch of his right hand, then a rapid *click-click* sound. Mr. Jones jumps to one side. He raises both arms to shield his chest. Then he raises one hand and waves it frantically as he jerks up onto his tiptoes and shouts, "Don't shoot! Please. I'll go."

"*AWAS! KWEE-AH HU! Atimochisk!*" Mosom shouts. "*Macimanito,*" he mutters as he and Bertha watch Mr. Jones's *whitikiw* figure shrink into the distance.

"*Tapwe,*" Bertha thinks. "The Devil."

Bertha calls out to Debbie and Greggie to bring Lapatak around from the woodshed. Debbie carefully carries me to where our mother is standing and hands me over. Bertha undoes the top of her blouse to give her baby a soothing feed of warm milk. Debbie and Greggie wrap their arms around her legs and press in as close as they can.

THE NEXT MORNING Bertha is anxious—disturbed by her dreams. In one dream, she was living in a larger and more modern house. A baby girl stood in a crib wailing, and there were toddlers running around—one of them was blonde and pretty. Sonny's older cousin Ned—what was he doing there? The house was a shambles, with garbage and broken glass all around. Where would she start with the cleanup? Debbie was gone—but where to?

In her second dream Lapatak was a mature man. He was handsome like Sonny, but had Bertha's darker complexion and eyes. Wavy locks of silver framed his beaming face. He was sitting on the deck of a house that looked a lot like Mosom's cabin—a grey, weather-worn wooden exterior. The house was surrounded by giant spruce trees, ten times grander than the largest trees Bertha had ever seen.

Why was Lapatak alone? Where were his kids and grandkids? They must have been playing in the forest or at the lake.

Her son was perched on a high stool at a makeshift wooden table. It was a sunny day; there was a gentle breeze. He looked out over a vast oasis-blue sea. Birds were chirping and whistling—towhees, blue jays, red-winged blackbirds and hummingbirds, buzzing and flitting in all directions. High overhead, barely visible, an eagle circled. On the table in front of him sat a goblet full of scarlet wine. High in front of his head he held a white wafer, split in two—one half placed precisely over the other to form the shape of an owl—just like the priest did. He was chanting in a blend of Cree, some other Indian tongue, and English:

> *Ha-iy   ha-iy Mosomwa, Cucuumwa,*
> *Hytchka siam. Ha-iy   ha-iy.*
> Thank you grandfathers and grandmothers.
> For making me the high priest of my own life, now and
>   forever.
> Amen.
> *Ha-iy   ha-iy. Ha-iy   ha-iy.*

Suddenly Bertha was there with him, off to one side and a few steps back. Smiling, she moved in closer—trembling. Her right arm was folded behind her back, some hard object in her hand. She brought it around and glanced down. She gasped. Mosom's sharpest hunting knife.

One Little Indian Boy

HAD BEEN practising for this day for years. Countless hours of playing school, with Debbie and Greggie taking turns being the teacher, Gaylene and I the pupils. We sang, coloured, laughed, cut things out with scissors, glued things together, told stories and played games. Now here I was, at long last, walking along the only sidewalk in Smith with my older brother and sister, heading to Grade One.

I shivered with excitement at the thought of seeing my favourite Indian cousins from Spurfield every day of the week, as I had when we'd lived in that tiny settlement with Mosom. I couldn't wait to make friends with more white kids, too. Other than our neighbours, the O'Neils, my only contact with white kids so far had consisted of fighting, throwing rocks or shouting insults.

As we approached, cousins from both sides of the family were converging on the school grounds. The Indian cousins from Mother's side had just arrived by bus and were huddled in a scrum. My fairer cousins from my father's side all lived in Smith. We had been to their houses with Mother and our stepfather, Ned, on family visits, but those kids were never keen to play with us. Today, at school, they strutted around talking and guffawing—showing off their new clothes, shoes and haircuts. Debbie and Greggie continued their back-and-forth banter.

"Miss Long is mean," Greggie warned.

"Well, whaddaya expect?" Debbie sputtered. "She's an old maid. They say she's been livin' alone here for thirty years. Always wears them poofy white blouses and that navy blue skirt—says her hair colour is South Sea blue. Tucks a kleenex inside the cuff of her sleeve. Never smiles. But she wasn't as mean to me as she was to our cousins, Luh-pi, Beaver and Chicken."

These last-minute warnings were scary. I felt my eyebrows furrow; the smile I had planned for that day, practising in the mirror, wouldn't materialize.

The morning had been hectic. I paced the kitchen while Mother pulled Debbie's hair into tight French braids and straightened the hem of her ruffled red dress. She reminded Greggie to pick out decent clothes—trousers without patches and an ironed shirt. And for my first day of school, an intense inspection: shirt tucked in, teeth brushed, hands washed, fingernails scraped and trimmed, face scrubbed and shoes polished. The stiff black oxfords already hurt. Mother had bought them for my First Communion, and I hadn't worn them since. "Just for the first day, my boy, then you can wear your canvas runners." I winced as she laced them up. She let me put a dab of Brylcreem in my hair to slick it back and make a little wave. A red sweater with black stripes along the zipper covered my short-sleeved dress shirt.

I had a swirl of confusing emotions as I stepped into the cool autumn air. Yes, I was off to school, but till now I had loved having Mother to myself all day—going shopping at LaFrance's General Store, getting the mail at the tiny post office run by the Wrays, baking bannock or making Boston cream pie, sneaking treats for just the two of us. I loved snuggling with Mother in her bed for afternoon naps when she took a break from the gruelling daily routine of cooking, baking, hanging clothes outside, ironing, waxing the floors by hand, sewing and minding the baby—Travis. I was amazed at how she took apart man-sized pants from the thrift store, cut them to size and made them fit me—as if by magic.

I had also enjoyed going with Mother to visit my great-grandmother, Cucuum Lennie, Auntie Francis and Granny McLeod. I stood right by Mother's side to listen to the Cree conversation. Even when one of them switched to English, Mother answered in Cree.

I hung on every word, trying to figure out what they were saying. Eventually she would chase me outside to play, saying *wyowi*—waving her hand high in the air. When we got home I would ask her, what does *anoch* mean? What does *miyosin* mean? She would tell me, but then wag her strong index finger in my face and lecture me about how I had to speak English.

I spent time outside in my little sandbox, building castles, moulding mountains and grooving streams, lost in an imaginary world, until one afternoon I noticed that I was surrounded by giant black crows. Their persistent *caw caAW CAW*s got louder. Cottony clouds layered over the sun, leaving me in the shadows. I ran into the house trembling, seeking Mother's calming embrace.

ASPEN POPLARS AND maple trees lined the street in front of the school. Mesmerized, I watched as one orange maple leaf after another fluttered toward me, then away, twirling in rapid spirals down to the ground. I had butterflies fluttering in my stomach and weak knees at the thought of being in Miss Long's class.

"Pretty soon you'll be able to read comics on your own, Dades"—Greg's nickname for me. "You won't need me and Deb to read 'em for you. You can't hog 'em, though—you're gonna have to get more Archie comics so I kin trade you for the Superman ones you like so much."

"Ha! Look who's talking! It's you who hogs the comics. Half that big stack you have is mine." Deb reached over my head to poke Greggie's shoulder. "And you'll be able to count your own pennies too, Dades, so *he* can't cheat you out of 'em anymore."

"Huh, you're always sneaking Mother's *True Romance* magazines. Whaddaya need comics for when you kin read all that girlie love stuff? And it's none of your business about the pennies." Greggie pushed Debbie back—hard, making her step off the sidewalk into a puddle.

A flutter of joy as I spotted the merry-go-round, teeter-totters and swings just past the wide cement stairway. We'd had so much fun playing there in the summer months. A few of my cousins now stood on the ladder of the tall blue slide, yelling for the kids above them to hurry up so they could have their turn. A couple of them waved and I waved back. Deb walked me to my classroom, holding my hand until we got to the doorway. Then she pivoted and walked away. I stumbled through the doorway, glancing around.

Green metal desks with lacquered wooden tops so far beneath the vast white ceiling. Mind-numbing fluorescent lights, gleaming tiled floor, green chalkboard with white lines at the front of the room—mysterious yellow shapes etched onto it.

I found a desk in the middle of the room, sat down and hunched my shoulders. There, at the front of the classroom behind the big desk, Miss Long.

Her wrinkled face was masked by makeup, but it didn't look like the fragrant Maybelline that Mother and my aunties used or that Greggie and Uncle Danny stole and applied when they were playing house. Miss Long had dabs of red on her cheeks, and her lipstick was purple. I stared. Why had she come all made up to school? It wasn't like she was going to the bar.

Miss Long slid her index finger down the class list. "Not another McLeod!" she burst out. "*Darrel McLeod*, where are you?"

I raised my hand, but she didn't look up from the class register.

"Well, speak up. Where are you?"

"Here," I answered meekly.

"Oh, I see, we have two Darrels. McLeod and Brown. McLeod—you'll be Darrel Two, Brown, Darrel One. Ahhh. Stormy O. You're *back*. Let's see if you can pass this year. You'll need to work harder!"

I looked over at Stormy. His gangly legs were stuffed under the small metal desk. We had just become neighbours—our mothers were good friends. He caught my gaze and smiled mischievously. I looked away.

My cousin Teddy, with his dark-brown complexion and thick, coal-black brush cut, sat in the next row, one desk up from me. He was as tall as Stormy and had to tilt his knees together and stick his feet out to the sides so he could fit into his desk. His torso was stiff and straight. He was shaking and muttering something under his breath. Since Teddy had hardly ever seen white people, and the stories we had heard about them weren't good, I guessed what he was saying: *Moniyawak*—white people—all these white people. He turned his head to look through the huge windows above the cubbyholes that held our boots and coats. I turned too and saw the billowy grey clouds gliding across the arctic-blue prairie sky. I knew that Teddy could also hear the magpies and crows squawking loudly, summoning us both back where we belonged. I usually saw my cousin kneeling in a meadow picking berries, or running down to the creek through the poplar trees, stopping to peel white bark to give to his dad, Uncle Charlie, to help get a fire going in the cook stove. My heart sank. What were we doing *inside* with all these strangers? Why hadn't Debbie and Greggie told me it was like this? I wished I was in Spurfield playing with Teddy and all my other Indian cousins. I could stay with any of my aunties or uncles there—just had to show up at their door.

A cough—Miss Long. I sat up straight and looked around the room.

Miss Long had focused on my cousin. "Charles Twin, why are you so upset? We sent you home last September on account of your whining! You will not moan and groan for two weeks this year. Stop it, Charles! I'll have no babies in this class—*especially* boys. We'll have a bigger desk brought in this afternoon."

Why was she calling him Charles? His name was Teddy— Teddy Bear.

Chalk dust and stale air hung in the room. A tickle in my nose and then a sneeze. This drew an annoyed glance over the reading glasses perched on Miss Long's nose.

Now *I* was trembling. The other kids sat quiet, staring at the walls, ceiling or floor while she fumbled with the class register.

"Oh, for Lord's sake! Darrel Two, go sit with your cousin. Maybe that'll help him settle down. And don't *you* start acting up."

I squeezed in beside Teddy, and put my hand on his back. His body was quivering. He folded his arms on his desktop and rested his head on them.

Oh my God. What was he so scared of? What did he see that I didn't?

AFTER FINISHING THE roll call, Miss Long handed out supplies—over-sized pencils, scrapbooks, glass bottles of translucent Lepage's glue with their pink, angled rubber tops, boxes of wax crayons and blue-lined scribblers.

I glanced about. Scowling white faces surrounded me. There were two exceptions—Janice Curruthers from the black colony of Amber Valley and my Chinese buddy Perry Mah, whose family ran the Smith Hotel Café. We'd gone there as a family for ice cream cones the previous Sunday after church, and I'd played outside with Perry. My mother and his dad, Jack, stood on the steps of the café and laughed, agreeing that we looked like twins.

At recess, a natural sorting occurred. The Indian kids clustered together while the white kids formed a few distinct groups: rich kids, farmers' kids and mill workers' kids. Perry and Janice stood by themselves, watching wistfully from the sidelines. At lunchtime I started out playing with my Spurfield cousins, then joined some of the poorer white kids, and later tried to join the rich kids. The rich kids turned and ran away from me, being sure not to spill their pouches of Lik-M-Aid or gummy bears.

AFTER THE FIRST week of school, I became fixated on one thing: what could I do to get Miss Long to like me? My grandmothers, aunties and older cousins all raved about what a good kid I was. Some of them, including my great-grandmother Cucuum Philomine, even singled me out to tell me so, and to give me a quarter or some candy. When printing my name in my scribbler, I shaped my letters perfectly, keeping squarely within the sets of solid blue lines. When counting, I made sure I got all the numbers right. I was extra loud every morning when we sang "Jesus Loves Me." I recited the Lord's Prayer exactly, sounding out every word and hoping Miss Long would notice that I had memorized it quickly. I even volunteered to water the plants at lunchtime.

Some weeks into the fall, Miss Long made an announcement that quickened my pulse. We were going to sing "Ten Little Indians." She would have to be impressed with me now! I knew the melody from singing it with Deb and Greg at home. I was, after all, the only Indian boy in the class. Teddy hadn't returned after the first day.

"Grade One—please form a large circle and hold hands. Cindy, you will be the first to go inside the circle. Those of you behind Cindy will follow her into the circle one by one, until we get to ten. Once you're in the circle, remember to do the nice little Indian dance we practised—bend forward, backwards, then jump and turn around and skip forward into single file. When we bring you back into the circle, do your best Indian hoot while you pat your mouth with your right hand. The last little Indian has to sit cross-legged in the middle of the circle while we sing to him. Remember, we start slowly, then go faster and faster towards the end. Let's go."

One little, two little, three little Indians
Four little, five little, six little Indians
Seven little, eight little, nine little Indians
Ten little Indian boys.

Ten little, nine little, eight little Indians
Seven little, six little, five little Indians
Four little, three little, two little Indians
One little Indian boy.

I smiled as we sang, thinking the whole class was chanting about me. And lo and behold, I was the last one in the circle. I did my best Indian call—while patting my mouth as the other kids circled me, going faster and faster until they were flying. When the song ended, I lingered, savouring the moment, waiting for a word from Miss Long. But when I glanced up at her, her look back gave me a jolt. Her eyes were narrow slits and her mauve lips were pursed off to one side.

A WEEK OR so later, on a Friday, I was at my desk colouring, happy because Stormy was chattering to me. I must have stopped paying attention to what I was doing, or pressed my blue wax crayon too hard, because all of a sudden it snapped. I peeped around, to see if anyone had seen it happen, then slid the crayon back into the bright orange Crayola box—stashed it.

"You're dismissed, class. Outside for recess, please."

As we headed out the door to the playground, Stormy stopped beside Miss Long. She leaned over, and he whispered something in her ear.

Darrel's mother, Bertha, poses for an unknown photographer at age seventeen, a year before she would marry Darrel's father, Clifford (Sonny). 1949

Greggie (left), Bertha (centre) and Debbie (right) sit on the steps of Mosom Powder's trapping cabin near Spurfield while Mosom displays a set of snowshoes he crafted himself. This photo was taken by a visiting anthropologist. c. 1958

Auntie Agnes, Bertha, Great-Aunt Eva and Auntie Margaret pose with their eldest children in a meadow near Mosom's trapping cabin. Bertha is holding one of Auntie Margaret's children. c. 1959

Cousins from several families in Darrel's settlement in Spurfield gather for a group photo. Cousins were close like siblings—and they were numerous. Debbie is in the centre with Darrel (in the stroller), and Greggie is on the far left. 1959

Debbie would spend countless hours caring for Darrel. 1959

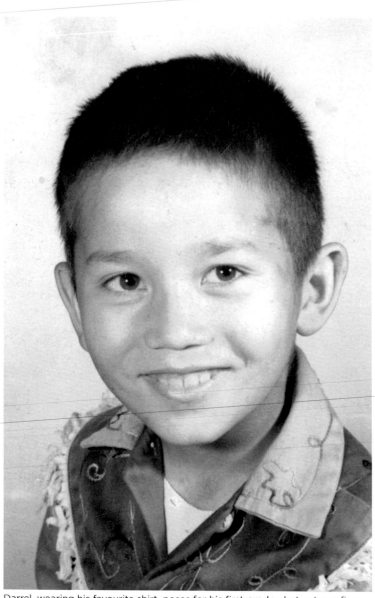

Darrel, wearing his favourite shirt, poses for his first-grade photo at age five. 1963

Debbie married Rory to escape home life at age fifteen. Bertha catered the wedding single-handedly. 1966

To try out her new camera, Bertha called Holly, Travis, Gaylene and Darrel (left to right) in from playing outside so they could pose for her. 1967

Debbie and her boyfriend, John (right) arrive in Athabasca for a summer visit with Bertha and Swede (left). c. 1971

The McLeod family (minus Darrel, who took the photo) sits down in Athabasca to what would be its last Christmas dinner intact. 1971

Just months before passing away, Debbie dances at Gaylene's wedding. 1981

Darrel sets the stage to perform Bette Midler's "The Rose" for Debbie, Trina, Gaylene and Milan. 1981

Pictured here with Bertha (left) and Darrel (right), Debbie's son, Joseph, had just spent his summer vacation with Darrel in Vancouver. 1982

After recess, the class stayed outside for a spinning game.

Little Sally Saucer sitting in the water,
Cry, Sally, cry.
Wipe the tears from your eyes.
Turn to the east and turn to the west,
Turn to the one you love best.

I got to go third. With a few jerks of her pale hands, Miss Long tied the blue kerchief with white polka dots over my eyes. It felt so tight. I was sure that my forehead must be all crumpled. I couldn't wait until my turn was over. But in spite of the annoyance, I hoped that when Miss Long pulled the blindfold off I would be pointing at the one blond girl in the class, Cindy Stelter, at Perry Mah or at Stormy.

Around the edges of the blindfold, I glimpsed Cindy's silky flaxen hair. I tingled with excitement. As I drew closer, I noticed she smelled like candy or some exotic fruit I hadn't yet tasted. I made sure I was pointing at her when the blindfold came off.

Then we trooped inside. After we completed our lesson of printing numbers and letters, Miss Long announced that she had a surprise for us.

"Darrel Two," she commanded, "please come to the front of the class and face me."

"Me?" I looked around the room. "Me?"

"Yes, Darrel Two, you. Now!"

She was holding one hand behind her back.

The other kids started to giggle. Usually, at the slightest noise, Miss Long would yell, "Grade One, be quiet!" This time she allowed their laughter.

"Darrel Two, I understand you broke your blue wax crayon."

I faced her, shuddering. "It was an accident," I stammered. "I was colouring and pressing too hard. It just broke." Out of the corner of my eye I noticed the smirk on Stormy's face.

"Well, we don't break our crayons in this class. I warned you. You have to do better than your brother and sister. But you're already doing worse."

She thrust her right hand forward, revealing a narrow strip of black tire rubber. So that was the strap Debbie and Greggie had talked about.

"Class, should I give him five straps on each hand, or more?"

"MORE, MORE!" they shouted.

"TEN, or more?" Miss Long's lips curled into a smile. Her cheeks were bright red.

"MORE. MORE!" Even more boisterously. Stormy was now standing beside his desk, yelling louder than the others and pumping his fist into the air. I bit my bottom lip until it hurt. Cindy Stelter was standing beside her desk too, but she wasn't cheering.

"Class—you're enjoying this too much. We'll do ten on each hand. Darrel Two, hold out your left hand."

That was my sore hand. Surely she would see the fresh scab and skip it, go to the other hand. Miss Long placed her warm hand sideways under my sore one and pulled it forward, but didn't look down. She was gonna do it. She really was gonna do it.

"Okay, class, count with me to ten, slowly. Darrel Two, you have to participate."

Her other hand flew over her head.

"ONE." *Whack*. Ouch! That stung. "Darrel Two—keep your hand out, please. Hold it steady."

"TWO." *Whack*. "Oh, he's pretty tough, class. Not crying out yet."

I clenched my teeth. I can't cry. Can't cry. Greggie wouldn't cry.

"THREE." *Whack*.

"FOUR." *Whack*.

"FIVE." *Whack*.

"SIX." *Whack*.

She is doing it for my own good, I thought. She likes me. I know she does.

I looked at my stinging hand. The flesh was raw. Blood was starting to ooze.

"SEVEN." *Whack*.

"Stop… Miss Long, please stop! My hand is bleeding. I scraped it yesterday."

"What do you think, class? Says his hand is bleeding, but I don't see any blood. Should we stop, or keep going?"

"Keep going," some shouted. "Other hand, other hand."

Miss Long began to cackle. "Class, you're mean. Didn't you hear him? He's bleeding! We'll do five on the other hand. Do you have a scrape on that hand as well, Darrel Two?"

I DIDN'T GET to run home after school that day to tell Mother what the teacher had done. I had begged her to write me a note so I could take the school bus to Spurfield to spend the weekend with Teddy and my other cousins. It would be my first ride on the big Blue Bird bus—a mustard-coloured shuttle between two worlds. The bus would take my cousins and me as far as the turnoff. From there we would cross a scary swinging footbridge and stroll the remaining few miles.

My hands were still stinging as I stood in line to get on the bus. I was thrilled about the trip, but scared. Debbie and Greggie had warned me that some of the farmers' kids on the bus were mean. I couldn't have imagined the scene that awaited me: the fetor of orange peels, mouldy bread, garlic sausage and aged cheese; tall white boys pushing and shoving each other as they crammed into the front seats; crumpled paper bags flying through the air. The stench of a fart—loud *eeeews*, laughter and shouting back and forth: who done it? He who smelled it dealt it! I pushed my way along the narrow aisle until I got to where my cousins were seated at the back.

After the raucus ride, we shuffled across the swinging bridge and made our way through the forest of white poplars, skipping now and then, until we came to a meadow where the vista opened up. Auntie Margaret and Uncle Pat's whitewashed log cabin stood in a vale above the creek, where they got their drinking water. Smoke was coming out of the chimney, as always. Pleasant aromas filled the small house: moose stew simmering in a giant cauldron on the cookstove, peppermint tea, pipe tobacco, bannock baking in the oven. Auntie Margaret's gentle voice: "*Astum* Lapatak, give me a kiss." I wasn't sure when I would get over to Auntie Agnes's house, or Auntie Rosie's, but I knew I would. I loved hearing the stories about how my aunts had passed me around as a baby, feeding me breast milk that rightfully belonged to some of my cousins.

We ate in shifts at Auntie Margaret's place: five or six younger cousins first, then me and the other five or six kids my age and last, the teenagers and adults. Mother had once told me that besides Auntie Margaret's fifteen kids who lived, she also had had two miscarriages. If a woman birthed twenty-one kids in all, everyone said the church would send her to Rome to be blessed by the Pope.

That evening, ten or so of us kids helped Uncle Pat slaughter chickens in the old woodshed. After he wrung their necks and chopped off their heads, the chickens scurried about in a frenzy, spurting blood everywhere. Our job was to catch them.

I was stunned by the sight of a still-blinking chicken head on the ground beside the chopping block. I wanted to cry, but couldn't be a sissy, so I joined the chase, laughing and yelling with the others. The chickens would be delicious the next day, and I looked forward to making toys out of the feet, the way my cousins did. When we pulled on the tendon, the claw would contract; when you let go, it would go back to normal. We did it over and over again.

I forgot about school until there was a lull in the activity or one of my hands started hurting. Then worrisome thoughts took over: what would next week bring? Another strapping, or just shouting and ridicule? What if Miss Long failed me—kept me for another year, like she had done with Stormy and Teddy? And then there was the bus ride back to Smith on Monday morning—would I get beaten up? Would my cousins defend me? How could I have been so keen to leave Mother for the weekend? Had I hurt her feelings? Was she okay?

The day wrapped up with the kids in bed and the adults sitting around talking a mix of English and Cree. We listened to news on a big wooden radio that was hooked up to a car battery—the only source of electricity at the house. *I have a dream...* I heard. A deep male voice with some kind of accent.

Sometimes our whole family went to stay at Auntie Margaret's. Then Uncle Pat and my stepfather, Ned, would sleep in the living room so Mother could sleep with her sister. We would fall asleep listening to Mother and Auntie Margaret chattering in Cree and giggling: trading stories and making jokes about sex with their husbands, Mother told me years later. At times their voices were hushed and stressed, talking in English about things that happened to them as small girls at residential school.

Once the kerosene lamps were blown out, complete darkness enveloped us. Then it was the usual prank: "Listen. *Muskwa*—a bear," an older cousin whispered.

"*Muskwa?*" The littlest kids gasped and huddled together.

"Shhhh. *Pahagaton*. Listen."

The older kids laughed and made faces to mimic the terror they saw in ours.

WE CHATTERED AND giggled until each of us in turn nodded off. A sea of brown bodies.

In the morning, I was cozy—one cousin's leg thrown over my legs, the warm arm of another over my chest, a torso nestled up against my backside. Raven hair all around, long and flowing on some heads, short and spiky on others. Six slender, tawny bodies lying mostly sideways on the old double army cot. We could fit more of us on it that way. I was the first one awake, but I lay there pretending to sleep, basking in the humid, tangled web—were the others doing the same?

Bannock, lard, peanut butter and wild blueberry jam for breakfast.

"You kids get ready. We're going berry picking," Auntie Margaret announced right after breakfast. "Make sure you wear long pants, in case the mosquitoes are bad."

That day we picked cranberries, highbush and lowbush, to make into a tangy preserve for the winter months. I drooled knowing that when we got home we would eat some of the canned strawberries we had picked in the spring, with fresh cream skimmed from the aluminum milk pail Auntie had traded for moose meat.

EARLY THE NEXT morning, Uncle Charlie and Auntie Rosie came by the house. They had decided to go to church in Smith—something about the bishop being there. They asked if I wanted a ride home.

I was glad to accept. No Blue Bird bus ride, and I wouldn't have to wait until Monday night to see Mother. She would be happy too. Had she baked pies, I wondered, and what would she make for supper—chop suey, cabbage rolls or maybe pan-fried whitefish? I liked that our family could eat together at suppertime. There were only six kids and two adults, three if Mosom or someone else was visiting.

"Tell your mother we don't have time to visit today, but we'll be back next weekend, Lapatak."

I jumped out of Uncle Charlie's Rambler, and there they were perched on the edge of the roof: three black crows. Their *caaaaw caw* louder than ever—how long had they been waiting for me? I ran toward the house but stopped short of the kitchen door, suddenly aware of an eerie silence. The door was ajar. I stepped into a sea of rubble, shards of drinking glasses, sharp chunks of white from our mix-and-match china, and pieces of Mother's favourite brown ceramic teapot. The cupboard doors hung wide open. She must have smashed all of the dishes that Cucuumy, Ned's mother, had left him.

Then the odour—lingering cigarette smoke and stale beer, blended with the fetor of someone who has been up all night burping, vomiting and farting. Mother was leaning over the kitchen table, almost unrecognizable. Dark pools of dried blood under her feet. She was saying something to Ned, who stood in his high-top work boots on the other side of the table. I couldn't understand a word—it wasn't Cree, but it didn't sound like English either.

I stood, willing her to look over at me. The small wooden crucifix with a palm branch tucked behind it that hung above the bedroom doorway was askew. There was one above every doorway in the house, on both sides, to keep evil out. I coughed, but my mother didn't look up.

I stepped back out into the cool fall air, confused and shaking. A crow dive-bombed my head. I ran to the living room door, pushing it open. Deb and Greg were sitting on the couch, facing away from each other and looking grim. I cleared my throat, but they didn't notice me either. Nobody noticed me. No one cared that I was back—that I was there at all. Even Miss Long didn't bother to call me by my right name.

All at once, a solution hit me—a tantrum, just like in the Archie comics. I had been wondering if I'd ever find the right time and place to throw one myself. I knew I'd have to really let go. After all, Archie, Reggie and Jughead had smoke coming out of their ears when they threw theirs. I got down on all fours and crept up to the partition between the kitchen and the living room. With my head and shoulders across the threshold, I peeked around, waiting until the house was completely quiet. What good was a tantrum if it didn't shock them?

When the moment was right, I threw myself face down and yelled, "NO NO NO NOOOO!" I faked loud WAH WAAH WAAH sobs, the way I had seen Archie's girlfriend Veronica do. I pounded my fists and feet rhythmically on the floor. I pictured Miss Long's furious face, then Stormy's, then the mean white kids on the bus and the blinking chicken head on the ground.

Once I'd stopped, I just lay there. I felt better. Numb, but better. I closed my eyes and pictured Auntie Margaret's busy house. I could almost taste the moose stew cooking on her cookstove. Ned looked at me and shook his head. He turned on the radio and cranked the volume. Buck Owens's reassuring voice crooned "Love's Gonna Live Here." He repeated that one line over and over, convincingly, but instead of providing comfort, his words intensified the numbness in my head and chest. I sneaked a glance at Mother to see her reaction to my tantrum, but her eyes were closed and her head had drooped even lower than before. I looked over at Greggie and Debbie. They were staring at me with disbelief.

The next day at school, Miss Long ignored me when I raised my hand to answer questions. She didn't pick me to read the Dick, Jane and Spot stories out loud. She scoffed when I told her my favorite book was *The Little Engine That Could*.

At recess I paced the grounds, trying to come up with a plan. By the time the bell rang, I had it. I would return to school early after lunch to make it all happen. I didn't want to be at home anyway. Ned and Debbie had swept the debris to one side of the kitchen, but there were no dishes left to eat off of. We would probably have to eat the same thing for lunch that we'd had the night before for dinner: toast with sardines and onions. If Mother was up, she would be sick and miserable.

When I opened the door to the kitchen, Debbie was smearing a meat spread onto slices of bread she had set out on the counter. Greggie sat at the table, looking dour. The little kids were in the bedroom chattering away, as if everything were normal.

I got back to the school at twelve thirty. Nobody was around—no kids, no teachers. Perfect.

The flower beds that ran beneath the long row of classroom windows were overgrown with weeds and almost finished for the year, but there were still clusters of tall deep-blue flowers near the back. I took out my pocket knife and carefully moved around to cut stem after stem until I had them all. I bunched them together into a gorgeous bouquet. I snuck into the school and crept up the stairs to the Grade One classroom. I knocked on the door, then stood there clenching my toes. I was on pins and needles, anxious to see Miss Long's glee. Everything would be different between us after this. I waited, afraid to tap the door again. I was about to give up and walk away when Miss Long opened the door.

Fury was the only word to describe the expression that took over her face.

"What have you done, Darrel Two? You are in real trouble this time. Someone else has to see this."

She grabbed me by the arm and dragged me along the hallway to the Grade Two classroom. I had never noticed her perfume before. (Or was the fragrance coming from the flower bunch I was carrying?) She paused, caught her breath, then rapped on the door.

Mrs. Drader, the Grade Two teacher, opened it. She was a distant cousin on my father's side, and Ned's niece. She looked down at me and smiled.

"How sweet. He must have thought they were wildflowers," she said as she bent down to take the bouquet from me. Mrs. Drader was pretty, and her eyes were full of kindness. "Let's put these in a vase, Darrel."

I smiled back at Mrs. Drader, thrilled to have pleased her. For once, Miss Long was speechless.

Be Careful Little Eyes

OUR HOUSE IN Smith was a little brown shack on a large grassy lot along a narrow dirt road that my brother Greg had dubbed Tin Can Alley. It had three bedrooms, a living room and an open space that served as a combined kitchen and dining area. Given the logistics of housing seven kids and two adults, hardly anyone ever slept alone. My sister Debbie was the only one—she got her own room once she became a teen. We lived in the white neighbourhood because our stepdad, Ned, was a fair-skinned Métis and a well-respected World War II vet. Our Indian relatives had moved into prefabricated houses in a new development that would eventually be known as Bannock Flats.

The well-to-do neighbourhood was across the railroad tracks, along the Athabasca River, near the sawmill. That was where the Stelters, the owners of the sawmill, had built a spacious home. Greg had a crush on their daughter Debra, and I liked her sister, my classmate Cindy. Greg used to openly declare that he was going to marry Debra one day. He even became a young entrepreneur to impress her parents. He brought the *Star Weekly* to Smith, picking it up from the Greyhound bus depot at LaFrance's General Store and delivering it religiously every Friday night. The newspaper in turn led him to peddle costume jewelry: *Make Money Fast. Become a distributor*, the ad read. In spite of Greg's determination, I knew nothing could ever come of his interest in Debra, nor of mine in her sister. Cindy put up with my banter, but she never chatted with me or my Indian cousins the way she did with other boys. I assumed Debra was the same way with Greggie.

The fair-haired Stelter sisters were beautiful, but people also raved about our sister Debbie, mentioning her pretty round face, full lips, prominent cheeks, lively brown eyes and thick, shiny black hair. One day I overheard a conversation about Debbie after ducking into LaFrance's to escape two ferocious dogs. A handsome young white guy I had seen putting gas in an Alberta Public Works truck stepped up to the counter to pay.

"I noticed ya checkin' out that McLeod girl yesterday, Rory," Leonard LaFrance, the store owner's son, said with a smirk. "You still boarding with the O'Neils?" The Highways guy picked up a piece of fruit and eyed it as he rotated it in his neatly groomed large hand.

"This peach looks ripe and juicy," he replied, flashing a wide smile and winking.

I glanced at his freckled face—his Brylcreemed hair combed in from the sides to form a rooster crest, his charming smile and intense blue eyes. I had a feeling I would see him again, and it gave me a chill.

Greggie used to say that the population of Smith was two hundred, including cats and dogs. There were many dogs around Smith, and even more in Spurfield. There, every one of our aunts and uncles had dogs to guard their cabins and belongings. Big dogs. German shepherds that had bred with wolves over the years, creating stunning lush coats of silver, brown and black, and a piercing ice-blue gaze. Lethally loyal dogs. And sometimes we got to see them breed. At least once a month there would be a ruckus over a pair of dogs that were stuck together. An older cousin had even figured out how to make this scenario occur: he would kick the alpha dog's butt, forcing it to jerk away, and every time it would get stuck. While waiting for release, and now facing opposite directions, the two dogs would rotate, scratching out anxious spirals in the dirt.

"WHY DOES MOTHER always treat you better? We're only a year apart!" Greg demanded of Debbie one afternoon. "Everyone likes you more— just 'cause you're a girl!"

"Quit whining. You'll get your own room when you're the oldest one home. Be a good thing, too. Then the other kids won't have to put up with your grumpiness, or your stink!"

Even though Debbie was only seven years older than me, from the time I was a baby she had coddled me. She took me everywhere she went, carrying me in her arms or pushing me in the rickety stroller. I never understood why it was me she decided to hold on to. Maybe she was trying to appease her grief from our father's death months before I was born. I knew that Greggie was jealous of how close we were.

As Deb's favourite, I occasionally got to share her bed. I would awaken with her arm tight around my neck. I loved to roll onto my side, cuddle close and admire her delicate features while counting how many deep breaths she took before she woke up.

Most nights, I slept in the other bedroom, on the bottom bunk with three of my siblings. Gaylene and I slept side by side at one end of the bed, Travis and Holly at the other. I would lie staring at Gaylene's pudgy, fair face and golden hair with admiration and love. "My blond and blue-eyed Indian," Ned had gloated from the time she was born. The French–Métis genes had apparently won that particular game of chance.

As a small boy, I was aroused by the dolls with wiry blond hair that Gaylene left lying around. I would pick one up and secretly lift the dress to see what was underneath. There was always just a bump—so disappointing. I was sure there had to be more to it than that. I would rub my penis against the bump anyway, and it sent pulsating jolts from my groin up to my head. I didn't understand why that happened, but I liked it.

One sunny summer afternoon when I was seven I met up with Joanie, the blond six-year-old next door, in the well-equipped play-house behind her home. I convinced her that we should pretend we were Mommy and Daddy, and I manipulated the situation so that bedtime came quickly. Sweet and complacent Joanie played along. She lay down on the little playhouse bed; I pulled down her stretchy pink pants and panties and took a good look. There really was more to the female anatomy than a little bump! I lay on top of her and attempted to insert my penis, as I thought should be done. Joanie just stared at me with her eyes wide open and a bewildered expression on her face.

I pulled up my pants and fumbled with the zipper, feeling I had disappointed both of us. "Well, I gotta go, Joanie!"

Halfway back to the shack my family called home, I had my first taste of guilt. That was wrong! I shouldn't have done that! I would have to avoid Joanie from now on. A song the Catholic Sisters had taught us as preschoolers started playing in my head:

> Be careful little eyes what you see.
> Be careful little eyes what you see.
> There's a Father up above,
> looking down on us with love.
> So be careful little eyes what you see.

BY CHANCE, THE very next day I had an encounter with Stormy O'Neil. He was a year older than me—taller and stronger. We had become friends and playmates. Before I met him, my dark cousins were my only buddies. Stormy spoke differently than we did. I didn't hear the drawn-out singsong syllables I was used to with my family, nor the silent gaps that broke up and slowed down the exchanges.

Another difference was that the O'Neils were rich. They had a large white bowl indoors that they peed into and flushed by pulling on a short metal chain. But they also had a two-seater outhouse, with soft toilet seats over the holes in the wood. And it didn't stink.

I was peeing in their deluxe outhouse when I heard footsteps just outside.

"I'm in here," I called, expecting whoever was there would wait for me to leave.

"Just me. Gotta pee." Stormy's clear voice. I turned to look as he stepped into the outhouse. Wavy blond hair, wide grin. I dropped my gaze to the floor as he stepped up to the other hole and unzipped his pants. His black canvas runners separated into a perfect peeing stance, but then moved—shuffling sideways towards me. I peeped up at him as he began peeing into the same hole.

"Come here," he said as he put his arm over my shoulder.

He leaned in close, whispered something into my left ear and then stuck his tongue right in. I jumped, my penis still streaming urine. He laughed and then did it again. We finished peeing, shook our penises and stood looking at each other. Still holding his penis, he stepped forward and rubbed it against mine. Then he leaned over and kissed my cheek. It tickled intensely, and I laughed out loud.

We stumbled out of the outhouse side by side, struggling to pull up our zippers without pinching anything. Stormy stood there with a grin on his face. With my body still tingling, I turned and sauntered toward home, hands in my pant pockets, hoping nobody would notice the wet blotch.

I sat down on the railroad tie beside my sandbox and tried to make sense of things. That morning, I had gone to catechism class as we did every weekday during summer holidays. At the beginning, middle and end of the session, the Sisters had led us in the singing of that same song: *Be careful little eyes what you see. Be careful little eyes what you see...*

How could you help what you saw? You saw what was in front of you. You couldn't tell what was going to appear next. It didn't make sense. The next verse started, *Be careful little hands what you feel...* Well, there might be some choice involved in that. Whew, at least I hadn't *touched* Stormy's thing. *He* rubbed it against *me*. And I didn't touch it with my hands. But what about Joanie? That was my fault.

Was it all a sin? What kind of sin? I ran through them: *vee-niul, card-nul, mor-tul*. Would there be a permanent black spot on my heart, the way Father Jal had described the long-term impact of sinning? Would I stay in hell forever for this, or would three days in purgatory melt it away so I could go up to heaven afterwards and see Daddy? I was too afraid to ask the Sisters if he had gone to heaven, but he must have. He was my father. The alternative was unthinkable.

The pictures of hell the Sisters showed us were convincing. Voracious flames—crimson, orange and yellow—formed a huge circular pool. A cherry-red devil with pointy curved horns stood beside the pool and pushed people into it. Bodies writhed. Faces twisted in agony. Silent screams emanated from gaping mouths. Unable to save the wicked sinners from their fate, angels hovered above.

One night that week I had dreamt that I was roasting in hell. I had woken up screaming, a thin cotton sheet twisted around my body. I was desperate to learn more, to get some clarification, but there was little or no discussion with the Sisters about hell, just its graphic depiction and a road map of how to get there: lying, cheating, stealing, murdering, going to churches of other faiths, missing mass or confession too many Sundays in a row, having sex (except for married couples, and even then, it had to be to make kids). They stressed that a pregnant woman who placed her own life over the life of her baby would definitely go to hell. I had heard Mother harp on this last point when she was drinking, saying she would die giving birth if she had to. The baby came first.

One Sister had explained the story of Adam and Eve and the reason babies are baptized. I was frantic when she said that anyone who died without being baptized would burn in hell. Their souls would perish.

I put up my hand.

"Yes?" A stern look.

"But I have an older brother who was stillborn. He died before he could get baptized—what happened to him?"

"Unfortunately, his soul would go to *hell*," the Sister replied in her French accent, then moved on to discuss something else.

THE SWIRL OF thoughts and memories made me dizzy—I was shaking. Invisible crows cawed menacingly overhead. With my hands in my pockets to fold my pants over the wet spot, I snuck into the house to find Mother. There she was in the kitchen, ironing. I sat on the floor off to one side and tried to calm myself in her presence.

A firm *knock knock* at the front door brought me out of my daydream. I jumped up to look out the kitchen window.

Holy, it was Mr. Ewaschuk, Greggie and Debbie's math teacher. What did *he* want?

Mother went to the door. I hid behind the full-length curtains that separated the kids' bedroom from the kitchen, so I could peek at him and listen. As always, his wavy blond hair was neatly combed, but instead of a formal suit, he was wearing blue jeans and a red shirt open at the neck, a perfect toothy smile on his clean-shaven face. He stood a full foot taller than Mother.

"Mrs. McLeod? Bertha McLeod? Are you Debbie's mother?"

Oh no. What did Debbie do? Had she failed math?

Mother put on the *sophisticated* accent she used when she spoke to people she thought were important. "Yesssss. I'm Debbie's mother, but my name is Missusss Villeneuve now. I remarried after Debbie's father passed away."

"Well, so pleased to meet you." Mr. Ewaschuk extended his hand. His fingernails were chewed down to stubs, and his right index finger was yellow from cigarette smoke. His voice sounded so different from when I'd heard him scolding kids in the hallway at school. It was gentle now—almost kind.

"Well, I don't know how to say this, really, so I'll just get on with it."

Mother stood motionless, her face slightly red. A strange smile crossed Mr. Ewaschuk's face.

"I really like Debbie, your daughter. You know she's the best basketball player in high school, and she's so popular. She's kinda, well, like the tune says, the 'Leader of the Pack.' I'd, uh, like to take her out on a date. Maybe drive to Athabasca or Slave Lake. Go for supper and see a movie."

Mother stepped back from the door and pivoted away from the teacher, her eyes wide open, her face pale, her plucked eyebrows arched higher than I had ever seen them. Her lips went into a pout for a second, then she coughed, and turned back to face him.

"You want to go out with my *daughter*? She's in Grade Nine. She is about to turn fourteen, for chrissakes."

"Oh, really? But she looks and acts so mature. I would sure like to get to know her better."

Silence, as he gave Mother the eye. "I see where Debbie gets her beauty. Her complexion's a bit lighter, though. Ahh, would *you* like to go out tonight—grab a burger and a beer at the bar?"

"What? You goddamn pig!"

Mother slammed the door and stood there frozen. I wasn't sure if she was laughing or crying.

"*Wuh wah... sosquats!* Wants to take my daughter out! I don't believe it. Then he asks me out! Bastard! *Kohkôs -ss!*"

Before Mother had time to cool down, the phone rang. I slipped out from behind the curtains and sat on the kitchen floor. Mother's voice mellowed as she talked. "Tomorrow—you'll be here tomorrow? Stay for the weekend? *Tapwe. Eh-heh, miyosin!*" By the time she got off the phone her mood had shifted. Uncle Andy was coming.

An hour or so later, Debbie and Greg got home. I was anxious to see if Mother would tell Debbie about Mr. Ewaschuk's visit. She didn't, but she did tell them that Uncle Andy was coming. The three of us skipped around the house chanting, *Hippity hop to the barber shop to buy a stick of candy. Some for me and some for you, and some for Uncle Andy,* knowing he would give us his pocket change to go up the street to Mrs. Freeman's corner store for treats.

THE NEXT MORNING, Mother baked lemon meringue pies, apple pies, fresh bannock, white bread and cinnamon buns. The wonderful blend of aromas filled the house all day.

Uncle Andy, only a few years younger than Mother, was a perpetual bachelor with a reputation for being a heartbreaker. He was always handsome in his clean khaki shirts, dark-green pants and black bomber-style leather jacket. An ultra-masculine version of Mother with an unmistakable fragrance—a musky blend of leather, Brylcreem, shaving soap and Old Spice aftershave. A killer smile.

He showed up Thursday afternoon just before supper.

After dinner, we lingered around the table telling stories and savouring Mother's pie. She served Uncle Andy extra. Then he and I began to poke at each other and wrestle. These times were the only physical contact I had ever had with a grown man. I loved the power of his touch, the feeling of his strong arms lifting me or squeezing me into a tight bear hug. He rubbed his whiskers against my fuzzy cheeks. During those precious moments, when my uncle pressed me against his chest, I inhaled the vapour of his breath and his fragrance, held it in as long as I could.

The first few days of Uncle Andy's visit unfolded as usual. He and my mother and Ned sat around drinking wild peppermint tea and visiting in a blend of Cree and English. They discussed all kinds of things, including doom and gloom scenarios about another war or the world coming to an end altogether.

Saturday unfolded predictably too—except that after supper, instead of tea, Mother, Ned and Uncle Andy each had a few bottles of beer. Mother had put on her Maybelline makeup and red lipstick; Ned had shaved early in the afternoon. We knew they were going to the bar that evening and that Deb would babysit. But as they got up to leave, Uncle Andy announced that he would stay home with us. We were thrilled. We played and laughed with him non-stop for a while. But after he'd had more beer his energy shifted.

Suddenly he got up from his chair. He locked the deadbolt on the back door, then slid a butcher knife high up between the kitchen door and its wooden frame. He secured all the windows by rotating the metal latch at the top of the lower pane.

"You kids get inta yer room now and stay there! Bedtime! Debbie—put the radio to CJCA and make me some tea." A strange, mean gaze. Robotic movements. A heaviness hung over the room, and I noticed a smell that was new to me—Uncle's unique manly scent, but ten times stronger.

I went to Debbie's bedroom off of the living room, as Uncle Andy ordered, but I hid behind the curtains, adjusting them so I could peek through the panels. Greg and the little kids were in their bunk beds in the other bedroom and didn't make a sound. Was everyone as scared as me?

Uncle Andy turned up the radio so that the country music was blaring. I couldn't hear what he was saying to Debbie. Her back was against the wall and he was pressing up against her—forcing his mouth onto hers. Then he covered her mouth with one hand while the other slid down her dress. Debbie's face contorted. I had only seen that kind of terror in the pictures of hell the nuns showed us. My mind kicked into high gear. I became frantic: can't let Uncle hurt Debbie. Have to do something *fast*.

I tiptoed into the living room, climbed onto the windowsill, opened the latch and then pushed up on the window frame as hard as I could, stealing glances in the direction of Uncle Andy and Deb. I saw Uncle's back. Wilf Carter's voice wailing "Blue Canadian Rockies."

I scrambled through, jumped to the ground and ran up the dirt road toward the bar. The malt-laden air from the bar's huge exhaust fan swamped me. I darted up the steps to the hotel lobby, pressed and held the buzzer.

The manager pulled the door open, leaned over and glared at me.

"Whaddaya want? Why you ringin' like that? You can't hang roun' here, boy."

"I want my mother—kin you get her? Need my mother."

"What's her name, boy? Does she have a name?"

"Bertha. Bertha Villeneuve. Kin you get her?"

Finally the manager went to find Mother and she came to meet me at the door, but her smile vanished when she noticed my moist eyes and runny nose.

"*Mah*! What's wrong, my boy?"

"Uncle Andy—he's hurtin' Debbie," I sobbed.

Mother called Ned, and we all jumped into his blue pickup.

"*Kwee ah hu*, hurry," Mother urged over and over as Ned swerved around the larger potholes. As soon as he put on the brakes, Mother sprang out and helped me down. "You stay here. I'll call you in a minute." I had never seen her run before—Ned trailed. She body checked the kitchen door. When it didn't open, she pounded on it and yelled, "Open this goddam door! *Cemak*... NOW! *Sosquats macimanto!*"

I stood in the dim glow of the streetlight, tears blurring my vision. Was Debbie dead, or badly hurt? Why hadn't I run faster?

Uncle Andy swung the door open, flashed his charming smile and rubbed his eyes. Mother pushed past him. I moved closer to the door. I heard Debbie mumbling something, then Mother's wavery voice cooing, "Oh my girl. Did he...? Are you... bleeding?"

"No. No. I'm okay, Mother. I'm okay. He didn't..." Deb choked out, sniffling noisily.

I let the tears roll down my cheeks.

"Your lip is bleeding."

"His teeth. He grabbed me—tried ta' French kiss me. Touched me. I fought back. Let me wash up—go to bed. I'll be okay."

"Oh my girl..."

In the morning, Uncle Andy was gone. From that day on, he and everyone else knew that Mother was fiercely protective of her cubs.

MOTHER ONCE TOLD me that Daddy was the only person other than her own mother ever to see her naked, and only after they were married. "Even then, I still felt ashamed," she said. She didn't have to explain that shame. I knew where it came from, because I carried it too. It went back to the catechism classes where the Sisters had so vividly described the scene in the Garden of Eden. Eve was doubly guilty, first for eating the forbidden fruit and then for becoming a seductress. Her nakedness drove Adam to rebel against God. Once he became aware of his own nakedness, Adam ran and hid. The Sisters were clear that while baptism erased the sin we were all born with, nothing could eliminate the shame of nakedness.

Mother said that her *mosom* and *cucuum* hadn't known that shame. They were proud of their bodies, spoke about sex freely between them, even made funny jokes about it. In books and in movies, I was thrilled to read about or see muscular Indians clad only in loincloths, and hoped that someday I would have a body like that.

In the summer, we ran around the house buck naked until the age of four or five. Inevitably, Mother, an auntie or an uncle would tease: "Look at those chubby little cheeks. Look at that little *tugaloo*." But after that, things changed. Even when we were taking a bath, the boys had to wear swimming trunks. For the girls, Mom and Ned would set up makeshift walls of bedsheets around the three-by-three galvanized steel tub. As the oldest, Debbie always went first. Then came Greggie, and then me. They would change the water after that, and then bathe the younger kids. After the horrific incident with Uncle Andy, Deb insisted on bathing at the O'Neils', in their tub, with the bathroom door locked.

Getting the bath water for our family was always a chore. In the summer, we hauled it by bucket from the well a few feet away from the house. In winter, Greggie and I would haul snow for Mother to melt down. We sighed as each huge vat of snow melted down to a quart or so of water. One afternoon Greg couldn't take it anymore. Every half-hour or so he would stop, jam his chubby frame into the doorway and protest.

"I don't know why we have to haul this stupid snow! The O'Neils have running water—why don't we? I hate doing this! I hate it and I'm not doing this again, ever. I'll run away first!"

Mother looked exasperated. The next morning as we were heading out the door for school, she handed Greggie a bundle of towels and a note. "Greg—you take this to the principal to ask if you and Darrel can shower after school. Make sure yous wash up good. Debbie'll be in her basketball practice. You can all walk home together."

Greg stood speechless, auburn hair slicked back, hazel eyes glaring. His lips parted, revealing the two pointy eye teeth that were an eye-grabbing feature of his smile. But he wasn't smiling now.

"I don't *wanna* shower there. The older boys tease me."

"You just do it! You can fend for yourself. Don't let them push you around!"

After a typical day in Marlene Drader's second-grade class, I went to the locker room and shower area at the high school end of the building for the first time. I was thrilled. Freshly scrubbed beige floor tiles, tiny pale-green tiles on the walls and so much space. Shiny shower heads high above produced an endless hiss of steaming-hot water. Lingering vapours of bleach and Pine-Sol, shampoo and soap.

I basked in the misty flow, rotating often so the hot water would touch every exposed inch of me. I pulled open my swim trunks to wash my *thing*. I held out my hands to feel the spray, stuck my face directly into it, then turned to soak my hair and watch the suds run in channels down my chest and thighs.

"Oh—feels *so* good, Greggie. I *love* it! We're so lucky the principal let us do this!"

"Just hurry and wash up good like Mother said, or I'll be in trouble." Greg was half yelling. "I wanna get outta here! Hurry up—*wash*!"

I was mellow and dopey and had just peeled off my swim trunks when they appeared. My cousin Dwayne led the gang that sauntered into the shower area, fully clothed. Auntie Joyce, Granny McLeod's youngest daughter, was his real mother, but Granny was raising him. She doted on him and our other fair-skinned cousins. His gang was made up of those cousins and a few well-known bullies and snobs.

Oh, it's *them*, I thought. So that was what Greggie was so afraid of. Were they gonna push us around, or just tease us?

"Look at that little *tugaloo*. How tiny! Hope it grows bigger than *that*, Spuds." Dwayne pointed at my penis and laughed, turning back and forth from me to his buddies.

Then he pointed at Greggie. "Hah! And look at you! You're fat and got a small wiener too! Look at those girlie titties and that chubby butt!" Dwayne screwed up his face in disgust. Then he grabbed our clothes and threw them onto a bench at the far end of the locker room.

Greggie pulled his towel tight around himself. I had never seen such fear in his eyes. I had heard these boys were rough, always fighting with our Indian cousins Beaver, Chummy and Wilfred. I watched Greggie closely, ready to take my cue from him about whether to yell, run or whatever else he might come up with.

I was confused. These guys were our *cousins*. Did Granny know they were like this? Or Aunties Dorothy, Joyce or Francis, their mothers? The Thompson and Cook boys were always nice to *me*. Why did they hate Greggie? Was it because he was chubby, or because of his toothy smile?

I stood there holding my towel in front of me, shivering—chicken skin all over, bottom lip jutting out, reddened eyes, but I knew if I let go and howled, Greggie would yell at me for being such a baby.

"Just leave us alone. We didn't do nothin' to you guys," he blurted.

"Leave 'em alone, Dwayne," an older Thompson cousin named Ronnie called out. "They're just havin' a shower."

They did, finally, but that wouldn't be the end of it.

The next day after school, I was sitting on the kitchen counter looking out the window when I saw Greggie wobbling toward the house. His white shirt was hanging loose. Both it and his pants were muddy. As he got closer, I noticed blood smeared on his cheek and his chin. He opened the kitchen door, then stood frozen in the doorway, his face pale. As soon as he saw Mother, he closed his eyes tight and grimaced. A few silent tears ran down his cheeks.

Mother hesitated for a second while she studied his face, then put her hand on his shoulder. She pulled a chair over to the kitchen counter where the basin sat, told him to sit down. He sputtered what had happened as Mother poured water into the kettle and reached for a clean face cloth and towel.

Dwayne and three other boys had waited for Greggie after cate-chism class. They forced him to go to a secluded spot near the big propane tank beside the church. Dwayne punched Greggie in the mouth, and the other boys pushed him to the ground, face down, and kicked him in the legs and butt. They grabbed him by the hair and rubbed his face in the mud. Then they pulled his pants and underwear down and *cornholed* him, one after the other.

"Which boys done this to you? Dwayne and who else?"

"I dunno, Mother. Couldn't see. Dwayne held my head down. Couldn't see who was hurtin' me. White boys. They were callin' me a fatso girlie Indian."

"*Sosquats,* haven't we been through enough? When will it stop?"

Mother looked as if she was going to cry too. "This wouldn't be happening if your dad was alive! Come with me." She took Greg into her bedroom with the basin of hot water, face cloth and towel.

After a while, Mother came out of her bedroom, walked over to the phone, picked up the tulip-shaped black earpiece and turned the metal crank on the right side of the wooden box. She leaned into the receiver.

"Yes—four-nine please." She put on her best English pronuncia-tion, as usual, to speak to the operator.

She was calling Granny McLeod. Dwayne's in big trouble now, I thought as I watched from the doorway. When Granny answered, Mother spoke fervently in Cree. I only understood a few words, "*sosquats,*" "*wuh wah*" and "*macimanito,*" the words Mother spoke when she was enraged. I knew *macimanito* meant *the real evil spirit,* who was even more dangerous and wicked than the red Devil the nuns and priests conjured. Mother was right to use the strongest words she could find in Cree. Only that word, *macimanito,* could convey what she needed to get across to Granny.

Mother's conversation with Granny didn't last long. She sat down at the kitchen table, rolled herself a cigarette and took occasional puffs as she sipped peppermint tea. The little kids sulked in the bedroom. Debbie was in her room too—had been there the whole time. Mother went to find her. I strained to follow their low voices.

Debbie came out of the room with fire in her eyes. Those bastards would pay, she said. She and her pack of girls would make sure of that. She would tell her girls and a group of older boys what Dwayne and the others had done, and in that small town, where people didn't forget or forgive, their reputation would be set. My chest swelled as I watched her brush her hair, put on her makeup and paint her lips bright red. But somehow at that moment I knew that even she wouldn't be able to protect me from what was to come.

Madonna of the Athabasca

SUMMER HOLIDAYS WERE over. Instead of wandering along the turbid Athabasca river, or playing hide-and-go-seek in the spruce forest around Smith with my cheerful brown cousins, I spent my days reading meaningless stories about Dick, Jane and Spot (for the third year in a row) and listening to Miss Litwin's lilting voice repeating the basic concepts of arithmetic. That was bad enough, but this Monday was worse than any normal early-September day. I was afraid to go to school, nervous about seeing the other kids. I was sure the whole school would be buzzing with gossip about what had happened over the weekend.

Neither before classes began nor at morning recess did anyone speak to me. Even the other Indian kids, including Nancy and Evelyn, cousins my age who were usually happy to see me. I guessed Mother had gotten as far as their place yesterday.

Miss Litwin was short, frumpy and kind. She usually doted on me—smiled and came to my desk to chat as the day began, checking to make sure I had my pencil, scribbler and an eraser. But today she was abrupt, barely scanning my homework. Lunchtime came and went, and still nobody spoke to me. How many people knew? How could everything shift from one day to the next? When silent reading time came, after trying to concentrate for a few minutes, I put my book to one side, folded my arms on my desk and nestled my face into darkness.

THE PREVIOUS MONDAY, my mother had been so happy to attend, for the first time, the Catholic Ladies' Altar Society. The "ladies" were all white women, with the exception of Granny McLeod and Mrs. Beaver: Mrs. Neshoshnee, Mrs. McAughnechie, and Mrs. Remple—people who never even said hello to Mother or my aunts. They had let her join, but she came home from the meeting complaining about how snooty everyone was. At supper, she imitated a woman who had given the others a hot tip about cleaning an oven with Coca-Cola. She stood tall, stuck her nose in the air and put on a prissy accent with a slight lisp: "Just apply sssparingly on the sssection of the oven where you have burnt sugar or grease, and in a few hours, you can wipe it clean." Then she laughed, and we joined in.

On Tuesday, Mrs. Barnett, our new neighbour, had complained to Mother about Greg and me. Mrs. Barnett was a high-strung mother of six. Her hair was messy—a northern mockingbird's nest upside down on her head—and she had a shiny red wart on the right side of her nose. Many days, in her flowery blue-and-white sack dress, she stood on her back porch screaming at her husband, John, or at her children. Our conflict with her kids had happened when we were playing Auntie-I-Over. Greggie and I were tossing a red rubber ball over the roof of our shack to cousins on the other side. The Barnett kids yelled at Greggie to get out of their yard, and the fight was on. He and the oldest Barnett boy, John Jr., started pushing and shoving each other. Rocks became ammunition, flying fast in both directions, the bigger the better. I had to do my part to defend our territory, so I threw rocks along with the others, even though I knew it was wrong and that we would get a lickin' if Mother found out.

Sure enough, Mrs. Barnett tattled on us. The minute our neighbour left, Mother shouted, "Darrel—go get a willow. *Sosquats!* Any more rock throwing, I'll use it on your bare asses! You brats!" I went to cut a willow, but took my time at it, knowing she would forget about using it by the time I returned.

On Wednesday, Mrs. Barnett came over again, this time to complain about my stepfather, Ned, who had set fire to the quackgrass in our large backyard. My mother tried to explain that this was what Cree people did every spring and fall—burn the grass and weeds as a way of controlling both them and the mosquitoes. Mrs. Barnett didn't buy it. She just yelled that Ned should put the fire out and never do that again.

Thursday, when we walked to the post office, Mother received two pieces of mail that made her anxious. One was about property taxes being overdue, and the other was a letter from Bill Rempel, the man who had sold Ned the house, saying the payment had not been completed. Mother held the documents in her jittery hand as she paced the kitchen, shaking her head. She lit a cigarette, set it in the ashtray and fumbled through the kitchen drawer where she kept records and receipts. After a few minutes she pulled out a single page. She took a roll of Scotch tape and tore off long strips, using them to cover the paper's entire surface.

When I asked her why she was doing it, she told me that this was the deed to the house, and she wanted to be sure nobody could change it.

She sat down and wrote a letter to the government telling them about giving money to our Jehovah's Witness neighbours, the Landons, to pay the property taxes on our behalf. Then, morose, she went about her usual household chores: scrubbing and waxing the floors, pulling the clothes off the line and folding them, ironing, patching Greggie's jeans and sewing a new crazy quilt for his bed.

On Friday, Mother sent me to deliver a note to the priest, Father Jal, asking him to pray for my great-grandfather, Mosom Powder, who was in the hospital in Edmonton. The doctors were sure he wouldn't live another week. We all dreaded losing Mosom, but nobody uttered a word about it. In fact, Mother barely uttered a word all that day—just went about her chores looking as if she would burst into tears at any moment.

I was relieved on Saturday afternoon when she told us that she and Ned were going off to play shuffleboard at the bar with Artie and Sybil O'Neil. That evening, my sister Debbie was in a cheery mood. After she put the three little ones to bed, she switched the radio station from CJCA Country to CHED Rock and Roll and turned up the volume. A few older cousins came over, and the teenagers showed off their dance moves. Debbie and Greggie taught me to rotate my feet side to side to the rhythm of Chubby Checker's "Twist" and how to jive to Elvis's "Blue Suede Shoes." After the cousins left, Debbie and Greggie stole tobacco from Mother's bedroom, rolled fence post cigarettes and sat on the back porch to smoke. They encouraged me to be brave and take a puff too, so I wouldn't squeal. Often the two of them fought, but that night they got along, talking and laughing until late while I lay in my bed with the room spinning, dizzy from the unfiltered nicotine.

Around eleven o'clock, I heard Ned's truck pull up beside the house. I scooted to the bedroom doorway to see who all was with them. Mother and Ned came in with Sybil and Artie in tow, packing a couple cases of Pilsner beer. Good. Sybil always made Mother laugh. They perched themselves around the yellow Formica table, got out the ashtrays and lit up cigarettes, settling in for a long session of drinking, smoking and visiting. In no time, a cloud of blue smoke wafted above their heads, and my nostrils were irritated. Mother and Sybil talked about the time they had flunkied together in a logging camp and how the men used to rave about their cooking, wink at them, tweak their butts and ask them out.

When Ned and Artie began to reminisce about their experiences fighting in World War II, Mother nudged Ned with her elbow, saying *pahagaton*—shut up. But as usual when he talked about the war, Ned was already in a trance—eyes glazed over, a trace of white foam in the corners of his mouth. Artie was in another world too, nodding and moaning *mmm hmmm*. Mother yelled at Ned to talk about something else. He fidgeted with his tobacco and a rolling paper, squirmed in his chair and began to speak louder. Uh oh, another night of arguing. Sybil tried to intervene, but when Mother's voice got loud too, Sybil and Artie stood up, grabbed a few bottles of beer and left without good-byes. I went back to bed, powerless to do anything to stop what was about to happen.

Once again, as in other fights, Mother threatened to tear the distributor cap out of Ned's blue truck. I lay there trembling, wondering if the other kids were as scared as I was. This wasn't one of the nights we'd be lulled to sleep by the sound of Mother and Ned talking in melodic, slow-paced Cree over a cup of peppermint tea, debating the news of the day, the weather or the latest gossip in Smith. I loved that.

I AWOKE TO Mother hollering:

"Lady Godiva rides again!"

The day was dawning—across the room, hazy yellow light through the single glass pane. Birds chirping and whistling. I jumped out of bed, went to the doorway to peek through the full-length curtains.

Mother was standing in the living room naked. Debbie stood in front of her, holding a housecoat.

"Mother, put this on now. You'll catch a cold!"

"It's still warm out. I don't need no clothes. I'm Lady Godiva."

"No, you're *not*. C'mon, Mother, you need some sleep."

Mother finally pulled the housecoat on and sat down at the kitchen table. She clasped her strong brown hands together on the tabletop and tucked her legs underneath its frame.

"We're going to church this morning, Mom. We'll leave early. The house'll be quiet. You can get some sleep."

Ned stumbled out of the bedroom. Even from where I was, I could taste his bitter hangover breath and heady body funk. Between his mustardy smoke-stained fingers and thumb he held a crisp blue bill. "Debs, here's five bucks for the collection plate. Gaylene and the little ones'll be okay. They're still snoozing."

Debbie ordered Greggie and me to get dressed and threw on her favourite blue shift. As usual, we would arrive at Sunday mass with empty stomachs, so that after confession we could take communion. I forced my feet into my black oxfords, knowing I would have blisters by the time we reached the church. But a few steps away from the house, Deb told us her plan: we would head to the other side of town, cross the bridge, walk along the riverbank and then circle back to the hotel café for ice cream cones. Whew—no church! I pulled off my shoes and socks. But a chill went through me as I thought about crossing the huge bridge with the see-through bottom. Every time someone suggested we go walking there, I refused. Even when crossing the bridge in Ned's blue truck I huddled close to Mother, sure I would somehow be plunged into the river below.

We took a shortcut, turning north toward the railroad tracks. Less of a chance of anyone seeing us, Debbie explained. The dead-end road that led to the tracks was lined with stands of trembling aspens, their leaves no longer green but not yet golden either. Then a swampy area full of cattails ready to burst. The mosquitoes at this time of year could be managed with the occasional swat, so we didn't need the usual willow switches to brush them away. Pesky blackflies were everywhere, but the cool nights had caused their numbers to dwindle.

As we reached the clearing between the swampy area and the railroad tracks, we heard a cacophony of honking and looked up to see Canada geese high overhead in a partial V formation, rehearsing their long migration south.

"I wonder where they go," Greg mused.

"Wherever it is, I wish we could go with them," Debbie answered.

The bridge spanned the wide, turbulent Athabasca at the place where a determined smaller river pushed its way in at a strange angle. Water gushed in one direction, then back—whirlpools and standing waves. The three steel arches looked solid, but the platform for driving and walking was made up of black railroad ties with wide spaces in between.

As we started across, I imagined slipping through the cracks and falling into the swirling river far below. If I fell in, I would be carried downstream—away from the worries at home. I closed my eyes and felt my body plunging feet first into the cool brown waters, flailing and bobbing in the current.

"C'mon, Dades, don't be a scaredy-cat," Greggie goaded me.

I looked down into the glimmering water. With each second that passed, I felt dizzier. Slowly, I lowered myself to my hands and knees, then onto my belly, and slithered across the ties. Greggie and Debbie called to me from the other side, doubled over with laughter. I was too focused on the might of the river below to care what they were saying. It took forever to cross. Once I stood, vibrating, on the other side, I felt drained, but curious. I knew I would have to come back—alone next time—to understand what the river was offering me.

Back at home, we didn't need our hastily conceived alibi. Nobody was concerned about where we had been. Ned had kept the small kids in the bedroom, and we soon understood why. Mother hadn't gone to bed as we had hoped. She was still sitting at the kitchen table, and she had shed the flowery pink housecoat. Her brown backside and legs were completely exposed. Greggie and I looked down at the linoleum floor she had recently painted while Debbie grabbed the housecoat and hurriedly draped it over Mother. I kept my head lowered, trying to follow my mother's movements by watching the shadows cast by the bare light bulb suspended from the ceiling. Mother pushed her chair back. A dramatic flying shadow as she threw the housecoat across the room, then jumped up and stumbled outside through the living room door. We hurried after her into blinding sunlight.

Mother staggered over uneven ground toward Debbie's blue bicycle, where it leaned against the rickety wooden fence. She tugged on the handlebars, placed her bare foot on one pedal and struggled to lift her other foot across the frame. She balanced awkwardly, faltering down the path toward the gravel road that led to downtown Smith.

"Mother, come back here!" Debbie squawked. I stood aghast, watching my mother's bare back glide into the distance. I could feel my adoration dissipating, turning to shame or maybe even hatred. Where was she going? Would she ever come back? What if she ended up in the river? I pictured her, hands clutching the handlebars, floating on her side, partially submerged and still pedalling as the undulating current swept her away.

"Lady Godiva rides again," we could hear Mother calling out each time she passed a different house or business. "Lady Godiva!"

MY HEAD STILL on my school desk, I struggled to understand why my mother would have pulled a stunt like that. I couldn't find a clear explanation, but I knew she hadn't slept for at least two days, and I remembered that in the past few weeks she had played "Harper Valley PTA" over and over on our portable record player and sung along to it. Her full melodic voice got louder and her reddened eyes opened wide as she stressed the word "hypocrites" at the end of the last line.

I couldn't stop my imagination from firing up. I began to envision the reaction of the white townsfolk to Mother's surprise Sunday afternoon bicycle ride, and the images that played through my mind that day would never leave me.

Mrs. Freeman, the lonely British widow who owned the corner store, stood at her window. Her pasty face reddened. She adjusted her wire-rimmed spectacles, ran a wrinkled hand through her fine white locks. Could this be real? She dashed over to crank the phone to call her sister in England, sighed when the daft operator didn't respond.

Alice Bartel, the local operator for Alberta Government Telephones—curly bronze hair, rouged cheeks and luscious bright-red lips—sat sideways on the steps of the old building that was both office and home. She dropped her cup of coffee, and her cigarette fell out of her mouth. "Fred! Fred! Oh my god. It's 5-2 riding naked down the road. It's Bertha McLeod ahhh—Villeneuve now, I guess. We have to call 4-9, Mable McLeod, her mother-in-law, to stop her."

Joe Hugo, the mechanic who owned the gas station and garage, dropped his red tool box on the ground. "Mildred," he gasped. "Come see this. Come here—hurry!"

Brrrinnnnng brrrrinnnnng brrrrrinnnnng—the switchboard reverberated.

Oh—it's the Hugos. Mrs. Freeman. The Guenettes. The O'Neils. The Youngs. Even the Beavers. The switchboard was jammed. "Fred, come help me *please*."

Father Jal was walking from the rectory to St. James Catholic Church when he saw her. He stopped in his tracks and gawked at her. After getting an eyeful, he made the sign of the cross and mumbled to himself, "She's really lost it now... gone downhill since her husband Sonny died. I tried to comfort her like any man would. She pushed me away. Called me a pig! Look at her now. Married to that old guy, Villeneuve, twenty years older."

Jack Mah, the owner of the Smith Hotel Café, was out in his yard playing with his son Perry, my classmate, when he spotted Mother riding by. He muttered something to himself in Cantonese, then said aloud, "Son, go into the house!" He had heard things weren't good with Mother. As he and Perry brushed past Mrs. Mah, who was now standing in the doorway, he leaned over and whispered, "Too bad. She smart, funny, hard worker. Very nice person. And she look Chinese!" He ran inside to the telephone, lifted up the earpiece and cranked.

"5-2 please, get me Ned Villeneuve, his wife in trouble. Big trouble."

"Lady Godiva! Lady Godiva rides again!" Mother yelled as she pedalled the final stretch, heading back to our house. "Harper Valley hypocrites—every last one of you!

"Whheeeeee-heee, this feels good! Shoulda done it years ago. Let 'em come 'n see me—stare at my heavy, bare *chochos* so many of 'em tried to feel right after Sonny died. Hope the women catch their husbands gawking at the bare ass they grabbed when they thought no one was lookin'. Hope that bastard of a priest jizzes himself—he's goin' ta hell for sure. There are the kids waiting for me. Debbie's gonna be mad. Darrel will be so ashamed. Greggie couldn't care less. Hope they don't discard me. Lady Godiva rides again," she called, laughing maniacally.

WHEN MISS LITWIN announced that we were going to do to a printing exercise, I kept my head down, sure that if I sat up rage would fly out of me. Would I throw something? Bang my head on my desk or scream the thoughts thundering in my head? I looked just like Mother, could never deny I was her son. I didn't like my round, brown face and squinty eyes. I didn't want to talk like Mother or carry her scent. Why couldn't she be normal, like other kids' mothers? I hated my thick black hair, my patched-up clothes and floppy runners. Was this what it meant to be Indian? Why was even our *river* brown? Why couldn't it be a welcoming blue, like in the comics?

THUNK   THUNK THUNK   THUMP

I bolted upright. My cousin Evelyn had catapulted herself out of her desk and was writhing on the floor, her eyes rolled back in their sockets. Miss Litwin darted over and pushed desks away, clearing a space for my cousin to thrash around. I crept over to where Miss Litwin was crouched on the floor, cradling Evelyn's head in her hands. I whispered into her ear, "It's just a fit. She's an *e-pa-lep-tic*. She'll come out of it." Then I slipped out of the classroom, down the hallway and out through the wide double doors.

Flying around the Maypole

1

I AWAKE WITH an aching hollow in my chest. It's not a dream—it's just weeks before my tenth birthday, and Mother is gone. Should I go looking for her like I had the winter before, struggling through thigh-deep snow for hours, knocking on the doors of all the known party houses, including that of Mr. Robertson, the high school teacher, imploring, "Is my mother here? Have you seen her?" Across the railroad tracks to Uncle Leo and Auntie Rachel's plywood shack, checking each barren room, then trudging through the wintry forest to Auntie Margaret's house, though I doubted Mother would go there to drink; Auntie Margaret hadn't partied for years. I arrived shivering, with wet pants and soaked feet.

"You should have brushed off the snow before it melted," Auntie scolded affectionately. "Give him an aspirin for his toothache and fever," she directed my cousin Luh-pi.

"Do you know where my mother is?"

"No, my boy."

Caaaaaw   Caaaw

        CAAAW   CAAW   CAAAW

They call me out of my morning haze; they're waiting. I feel fear coming on, but talk myself out of it. There's no one to protect me now anyway. Ten o'clock. When I wander into the kitchen, my stepfather, Ned, hustles me into his 1957 Chevy.

"T'airl, we're goin' shoppin' fer clothes at LaFrance's. Yer gointa Edmonton."

As usual, his pale hands grasp the steering wheel at ten and two, and his eyes are glued to the road. He raises his left index finger to greet passersby. The sun blasts through the windshield, scorching my thighs.

"Me? Edmonton? Why? Alone? On the Greyhound?"

A grunt and a nod, no eye contact. "Yup—one day this week. Ta see Debs and Rory. Midnight bus from Hondo junction."

A pang of excitement. I haven't seen Debbie and Rory since their wedding a year ago. Mother worked for months to make it special—even though she had grumbled that Debbie was too young; she even had to sign for her. I miss Debbie; thinking about her brings tears to my eyes.

My mind fills with questions that I don't dare ask: Will I see Mother in Edmonton, or Greggie, who ran away to the city and is staying with Auntie Mable now? Where will *I* stay? How long will I be there? Will I come home afterward? Is this still my home?

New Levis, black Converse canvas runners, plain white T-shirts, underwear and socks.

That night I lie restless in the bottom bunk, thinking about the day Mother left. She stepped in front of me the moment I entered the kitchen. I had run home for lunch, but there was no food prepared. I knew something was up.

"Darrel—I'm leaving," she announced.

"Why, Mother?" I asked, keeping my face expressionless. "Where are you going?"

"Gointa live in the city with Swede, a *moniyaw* truck driver—met 'im at the bar. You'll stay home this afternoon, my boy. Needja to babysit."

"I'm not babysitting while you go to the damn bar!" My reaction surprised me. I had never spoken to her or any adult like that.

I hoped she was simply trying to make me cry, like she had done many times with her dramatic stories and threats that never came to pass. Maybe she would disappear for a few days again—that would upset me, but at least it wouldn't be so final. Well, somebody else would have to babysit, not me. I stomped my way back to school in a rage. How could she ask me to miss school? I was goin' to university someday, gonna be a doctor. Didn't she know?

2

I RUB MY eyes. Is this real? This is what the city looks like? Wide sidewalks on both sides of the smooth paved street; swarms of people bustling by, looking straight ahead with expressions ranging from serious to glum. Tall white people, men wearing suits, ladies in tight knee-length skirts with tan or black nylons, dressy blouses—some frilly and others plain; faces made up and hair done as if they were going to a wedding, or maybe a funeral. Waves of fragrance, one second roses, the next a blend of green apples, peaches and moss. A handsome blond man with pale-blue eyes strides by in an invisible cloud of sage and mandarin orange peel. I catch a glimpse of his perfectly manicured hand.

In the gutter, a crow is ripping apart a crumpled A&W hamburger wrapper—doesn't even notice me.

"Hello.

"Hello.

"Helloooo?"

I greet every passing stranger. No response, not even a nod.

Am I invisible?

Curvy red letters read Lido Café, long angular blue letters spell Paramount Theatre, a white sign for Teddy's Diner and flashing red for the Black Hat Café. Tall buildings, including the CN Tower—the new skyscraper we had seen pictures of in school. I read each sign aloud, my voice warbling. Then I stop—turn around and turn again. I don't recognize one landmark. I start to wail.

Minutes later, I'm standing in the same spot holding a strawberry ice cream cone an old man bought for me. He looks on as I lick. What I am doing here? Why didn't anyone meet me? Where will I sleep tonight—at this old man's house? Why did Ned want to get rid of me? I could have stayed with Auntie Margaret—she wouldn't have minded one more kid. Where is Mother?

The old man stays with me until Greggie and a few of Auntie Mable's kids show up and take me home with them. Boiled wieners and macaroni for lunch. Tigertail ice cream in the evening.

3

WHISTLES, BELLS, METAL grinding against metal, tinny music, booming explosions, amplified voices commanding us to go watch the midget toss or thump miniature clowns into little holes. A machine blows threads of sugar into elongated pink and blue beehives. The unfamiliar aromas make me drool: corn dogs, miniature donuts, french fries, caramel apples.

A giant sign flashes: WELCOME TO KLONDIKE DAYS AT THE EDMONTON EXHIBITION. POT OF GOLD TICKETS HERE. An enormous wheel strung with hundreds of bright bulbs and dangling bench seats rotates upward into the darkening sky. Beside it, a gigantic machine with two similar wheels, but half the size, begins to flip end over end. A chorus of screams and laughter. I try to calm the quivering of my stomach.

My brother-in-law, Rory, leads Debbie and me toward another huge metal structure. Multicoloured cars move along parallel tracks, climb slowly to a high point, then dive over the other side. They swirl around a tangled mess of steel, climb even higher and then swoop down in a near freefall. At ground level, harried riders stumble out and wobble away.

"We're goin' on that one, Darrel!" Rory says.

"Are Mother and Swede coming? Mom said they would."

"C'mon. You'll be in the same car with me and your sister. We'll hang on to you."

Our car inches up the rails, jerking slightly every few feet. Maybe I'll be able to spot Mother from up here. Seconds later we are at the top. In front of us, a void of dark sky.

"Oh my God! We're gonna fall. We're gonna die!" My hand clutches Debbie's thigh.

The car dives. I scream, squirm and duck under the metal frame. Rory and Debbie holler something I can't make out. I pull myself back onto the seat. A breeze cools our faces as the car swoops, then slows and rolls smoothly onto a level stretch of track before it starts climbing again.

"No… No—oh my God, let me off o' here! Can they stop it?"

Rory and Deb laugh loudly, their voices blending into the din around us.

4

MY SECOND NIGHT in the city. This bed is so comfy. A fuzzy brown bedspread with cozy blankets in a basement bedroom that I have all to myself, in Rory's father's house. It's like in the Dick and Jane books: a white picket fence, tidy lawn and cement walkway. What if we got to stay here? I think about Gaylene, Travis and Holly—cramped together in the bottom bunk in our tiny room—or has Gaylene moved to the top bunk now that Greggie and I are both here in the city? I tear up as I picture the pudgy, berry-stained cheeks I kissed goodbye. Cousin Luh-pi, our babysitter, had baked a blueberry pie that day— in my honour, I thought, since she knew I was leaving. I was baffled when she didn't give us any for dessert. After she left, I took the pie and four forks into the bedroom. I woke the kids. We sat in a circle on the floor and devoured the whole thing while giggling triumphantly.

I replay my day in my mind—the morning at Auntie Mable's, then the afternoon and evening at the fair. I begin to squirm in the bed. Mother and Swede came by Auntie Mable's house to see me, but only stayed for a few minutes. Debbie and Rory showed up unexpectedly, and now I was spending the night with them. Questions fly through my head: Where will we go tomorrow? Debbie said they might take me home with them, to Two Hills, on the prairies. For the day? For the week? Forever? Why are *they* taking me? Why doesn't Mother want me?

5

THE ROAD IS arrow straight. A rolling sea of tiny yellow flowers on lime-green stems contrasts with the Crayola-blue sky that spans the flat horizon.

Now and then trampled fields interrupt the waves of yellow. Inside barbed wire fences, cattle stand alone and in clusters, munching patches of grass and mounds of hay. Close to the road, a protective chocolate bull shifts his head to look over at us—milky white face and curved horns pointing downward. A large, diamond-black crow perches on the head of a standing calf. Where is this place, Two Hills? No trees, no shrubs, no rivers or streams. And I don't see *any* hills.

6

IN THE HALLWAYS and on the playground the teachers speak Ukrainian. Odd names at roll call every day: Boida, Chorney, Karbashewski, Paziuk, Verenak. After six weeks, Mr. Pawliuk still doesn't call my name in the morning; he looks to see if I'm present, makes a check mark in the class register and calls the next name. Thirty percent on my math test. The other subjects aren't any better. I seethe as I look at my results. After dinner I take Rory's cheery Samoyed, Mickey, for a long walk, on the verge of tears the whole time. Debbie notices my reddened eyes as I step in the door. She asks me what is wrong, but I can't speak, so instead I brush past her to go my tiny room at the back of their rusted trailer. What is happening to me?

Saturday afternoon, I lie resting in bed. The afternoon sun filters through a square skylight with brown stains around it. Just as I begin to doze, Rory comes in. Without a word, he pulls my pants down, squeezes my thing between his index finger and thumb and pokes at my hairless balls. "Just growing pains," he calls to Debbie. "No need to go to the doctor." I had complained to Debbie that my thing hurt. Next time I'll keep it to myself, I decide. I don't come out until the next morning.

7

"DARREL. WE'RE HERE—Canmore, our new home," Debbie says as she removes her arm from my shoulder. The headlight beams of the big truck Rory has hired to tow their brand new twelve-by-sixty mobile home shines on a row of log cabins and a few holiday trailers. "One of those cabins is ours," Rory says as he helps me down from the cab. "Just for a couple of days, till we get set up." He opens the door of our new mobile home to let Mickey out to pee. She's panting and wagging her bushy white tail. Fresh cool air gives me goosebumps.

My jaw drops. If there is such a thing as love at first sight, this is it. Silhouettes of gigantic mountains everywhere I look. What a change from the prairie horizon. Puffy pillows of clouds illuminated by a waxing half moon. Shimmering reflections of the same light in a stream a few feet away from where we stand. I dash toward the water—Mickey at my heels, squealing and yipping.

"Wowie! WOW! Holeee cow," I yell. "Deb. Look—look at them mountains. Come here, come see the creek. Listen."

"You'll be able to see it better in the morning. C'mon, we gotta get some sleep. Lotsa work to do tomorrow."

"We all gotta sleep together in this tiny space, Darrel—one bed. Your sister had better sleep in the middle, in case I get a hard-on—have sexy dreams. Been known to happen," Rory says as he laughs and slaps Debbie's bum.

Debbie butts out her cigarette. I don't know what to say. Rory's comment sends me into a tailspin. My eyes want to twitch. I can't believe the images his words conjure in my mind. Surely talking like that is some kind of sin. I climb into bed and mouth the Lord's prayer. I think about Mother, Ned, Greggie, Gaylene, my younger brother Travis, my little sister Holly and baby Crystal, who is now two. When we were still a family, we would take turns shouting out, "Good night, Mom, good night, Ned," until they yelled, "Enough now, get to sleep."

I snuggle close to Debbie.

8

6:00: RED NUMBERS on the bedside clock radio. I pull on my jeans and T-shirt, and sneak to the door. "C'mon, girl." Mickey dashes past me. The crisp air stuns me. For a moment I stand still, fascinated by the mountain in front of me. Three striking snow-capped peaks share a common base. An avocado-green blanket with splotches of gold covers their lower slope.

Mickey and I run along the bank of the stream. I yank off my runners and socks and wade in up to my knees. Glacial water over smooth, slippery stones. I fall over backwards, land on my hands and butt, and the force of the water pushes me farther down. Flat on my back, I feel the icy creek gush over me. Mickey bounds towards me, yelping. I rise and sputter, shaking with cold. A flock of crows, observing from their perch in the scrubby pines, takes flight as I emerge.

I don't care, though. Something is different here. I feel a new lightness in my chest.

"You're soaked! Better get changed," Rory says as he gets up from the bed. The word *Jockey* is repeated in black letters around the elastic waistband of his white underwear. I'm embarrassed that he isn't wearing more clothes; I avoid looking his way. The red digits on the clock radio read *8:01* as he turns it on. A serious bass voice—British accent:

> *And now the CBC news. Anti-Vietnam war protests continue to build across the United States, with thousands of draft dodgers taking refuge in Canada… A defiant Che Guevera was executed in Bolivia yesterday.*

"Damn communists!" Rory sounds like he's about to begin one of his rants.

9

WHEN WE EXPLORE the village, Rory insists on poking his head into the whitewashed log building that is the hundred-year-old Anglican church. "I only became a Catholic to marry your sister," he sneers. "My family is Protestant." He complains about the main street—such a dull town, he says, as we pass the run-down Triple A grocery store, an apothecary and a few wind-worn bungalows. "Geezus, look at that old fire-trap." He points to a pale-green two-storey building with an A-frame facade and a large sign that says CANMORE HOTEL.

On the hotel veranda three men sit on a glossy grey bench. Their legs are crossed, blackened hands in their laps. All three are dressed in green brushed cotton work clothes, like Ned and Swede wear. Oh my God, are they wearing black eyeliner and purple eye shadow? Their eyeballs are the whitest I've ever seen.

"Darrel! Don't stare," Rory snaps. "They're coal miners. It's a mining town."

"Are yous new in town?" the first man calls out in a lilting tone.

"Yeah, we just moved here." Rory's smoky voice is deeper than usual. "I'm the new office clerk for Alberta Highways. We're building the twin highway from the Banff gates to Calgary." He smiles at the men, his freckled hands hanging by his sides. Debbie waves to them and smiles. Their eyes linger on her for a minute.

I'm fixated by the enormous jagged, flat-faced peak straight across from us, and one of the men notices.

"That there's Mount Rundle," he says. "And yonder—that's Chinaman's Peak. True story 'bout a little Chinaman who lived here, made a bet he could walk from the hotel here, climb that mountain 'n come back the same day. 'N he done it! His name was Ha Ling."

We smile, nod again, say goodbye and shuffle along.

"Such bullshit," Rory barks. "Probably queers."

10

SWARMS OF KIDS in the playground—yelling, playing hopscotch, skipping with a long rubber rope in groups—*pease porridge hot, pease porridge cold, pease porridge in the pot, nine days old.* Some kids fly in a circle, hands grasping triangular bars attached to chains suspended from a high metal pole.

"Where's the Grade Five room?" I ask nobody in particular.

A delicate-looking boy flits over. "I'm in Grade Five—I'll show you. I'm Brian Wilson."

Mr. Plumeck, our teacher, sits on a bench at the front of the classroom glaring straight ahead through thick lenses with wire rims.

"Mr. McLeod, velcome to our claussss. You'll sit in the empty desk at the end of row four. We have anot-er Darrel, so you'll be Darrel Two."

Oh no. Not Darrel Two again! I feel my face redden. I'm already scared of this man. Many other sets of eyes scrutinize me. The gaze from a tall blond boy sears the back of my scalp. The buzzer: morning recess. I can't wait to get outside. As we flow through the open doors, Brian, the boy I met earlier, presses up against my side, chattering. "My dad is a cop, RCMP; we live by the golf course. I have one little brother. A sasquatch lives in the forest by our house. Have you seen the hoodoos yet?"

Harry Helmuth, the blond boy with the laser gaze, darts up behind Brian and rams into him. "Outta my way, Twinkle Toes. How did a cop's son get to be such a fairy anyway? And now you're friends with the new *chink*. Or is he a chimp, as in chim-pan-zee?"

Brian turns towards me. He keeps talking and gives me a knowing look. Gee, does he think *I'm* a fairy? Just what I need. Harry is already calling me names. *Chimp?* That's a new one. *Chink* isn't so bad. Maybe he thinks we own a restaurant.

11

IN THE CLASSROOM, Mr. Plumeck rules supreme. Each time he catches a kid doing something, he roars out their last name, writes it on a list attached to a wooden clipboard and demands, "Will that be *cash* or *carry*? For your benefit, Mr. McLeod, that means ten straps or twenty minutes' detention."

He barks out our test results, starting with the highest score and ending with the lowest. He always ends the drama by slamming the last test down in front of Bobby Jones's pimple-covered scarlet face. "You're going to have to try much harder, Bobby!"

By my third week in Canmore, I'm back at the top: Spelling, 100 percent. Math, 100 percent. Social Studies, 95 percent. The other kids glare at me each time I get my exam back first. I try not to gloat.

Everyone knows that Ricky Matthews has a crush on Gail Pasemko. He is so confident—hair slicked back into a high golden wave, intense blue eyes and a compelling alpha-wolf smile. She doesn't spurn his attention, always accepts the love notes he passes down the row. I am sure Mr. Plumeck will eventually intercept one, read it aloud and then give Ricky the strap. Instead, the next dramatic scene, at two o'clock on a Friday, involves me.

WHACK

The yardstick strikes the wooden bench under the chalkboard.

"McLeod—*sit down*. You're on the list! Will that be *cash* or *carry*?"

I freeze in my tracks beside Brian's desk, then look to see Brian's reaction. The two of us had been talking. Blood gushes to my head. Across the room, Mr. Plumeck's eyes are spewing darts in my direction.

"What? *Me*? But Brian and I were just discussing the math problem."

"*Cash* or *carry*, McLeod? Your choice. If it's cash we do it right now, right here—in front of the class."

My cheeks are tingling; my mouth is parched.

I cough. Then I hear myself stammer.

"*Neither*, Mr. Plumeck—I can't stay after school. My parents—uh, my sister and brother-in-law—are picking me up to go to somewhere. And there is no way I'm taking the strap. Not now and not ever."

I can hardly believe I have uttered these words, and neither can the other kids.

As for Mr. Plumeck, he is apoplectic. I feel the heat as he strides past my desk, heading for the front of the room. His thigh collides with my elbow. I catch a glimpse of his hands—as big as Rory's or bigger, but not as neat. Suddenly, I need to pee. All eyes are on me.

"Come up to zee front please, Mr. McLeod. It sounds like you have something to say." He sits down on the bench, in his usual position.

You could hear a snowflake twirl.

I shuffle up to the front of the class until I am standing in front of him. I turn sideways, my face on fire. I draw in a deep breath, smell the sweaty wet spots under his armpits. The top of his head is carnation red, as are his cheeks. He clasps the yardstick tighter. White knuckles. I look out the window at Grotto Mountain, picture the neighbouring Three Sisters. Another breath. Be brave, Darrel. He can only hurt you once.

I feel a flash of anger—decide I don't care. I take a step forward and stand as tall as I can.

"Who do you think you are?" I say. "You stroll around here like a dictator, jotting down names for any little thing and dishing out punishment. We're not prisoners or peasants. I'm not staying after school, and you're not giving me the strap!"

There is a pause. Then, to my astonishment, he laughs loudly.

"Well, Mr. McLeod. You're a brave man. What about the rest of you, Grade Five? Do you agree with him?"

Mr. Plumeck scans from left to right and back again, his spectacles askew. A thought leaps into my head: he's just like Colonel Klink from *Hogan's Heroes*. A flash of comic relief.

Silence.

"I didn't think so. Well, McLeod, I will let you off this time for being brave and because you are new here. Take your seat, and do not let this happen again."

Jawohl, I think but don't say as I force my wobbly legs to carry me back to my desk.

We stream like a school of fish through the hallway and into the cloakroom. I enter last, and the whooping and hollering begins.

Ricky Matthews flashes me a smile. "Way to go, McLeod. You told 'im."

Harry Helmuth pats my back. "Crazy! Wild. Way to go, *Chimp*."

"You're insane, but that was awesome." Gail Pasemko's melodic voice, sweet smile—her hand singes my shoulder.

12

HAVING A BIKE means that I can get home for lunch fast—slurp my soup, savour my toasted bologna and Cheez Whiz sandwich, ride back to school and still have time to play baseball or swing on the maypole.

Flying around the maypole is exhilarating, especially when it's Ricky who grasps my legs and runs the circle to get me airborne. He lofts me higher than anyone else can. I squint my eyes to see the Three Sisters, Mount Rundle, Pigeon Mountain, the Squaw's Tit and Grotto Mountain whirl past. They are magical. At times, the fluttering in my chest is so strong I worry that I'll either float away or faint.

13

RORY COMES HOME for lunch most days, driving the vintage Studebaker he recently inherited from an aunt. Today I get home first—the wall clock reads 12:10. I put the Campbell's tomato soup on, like Rory and Deb have shown me: add two cups of milk and stir over medium heat. Everything has to be just right—there can be no lumps or burnt flavour.

12:15. "Hello," Rory calls from the doorway.

His voice puts me on edge. What will I do wrong this time? I've learned he can fly into a rage at the slightest thing. I am discovering his version of table etiquette by trial and error. *Hold your spoon right; for God's sake, Darrel, it's not a shovel. Your thumb goes over the handle of the fork. Put the handle between your bent index finger and thumb. Smarten up. Get it right.*

Mickey skulks beneath the kitchen table to rest her chin on my feet. Rory and I eat with no eye contact. I decide to make conversation.

"I seen a deer today grazing alongside the creek."

"You mean you *saw* a deer today."

"That's what I said, I seen a deer."

"Oh, for chrissakes, Darrel, I told you before. The past tense of *to see* is *saw*. So if you are talking about the past you have to say *saw*—not *seen*."

He pushes up from the table and shuffles to the master bedroom at the end of the hallway. Oh good, he is going to lie down and relax.

12:20.

As usual, I gulp down my food and clean up the kitchen.

12:25.

I'm shuffling down the hallway to use the bathroom when a fluttering movement off to the side catches my attention. What is that mirror doing there? I see the reflection of Rory lying on his and Debbie's bed, stark naked. What is he doing? I peep at the clock on their dresser: the 5 is rolling over to a 6.

I freeze. I want to flee but can't.

The 6 rolls over to a 7.

In his reflection—smooth chest, muscular freckled arms and shoulders, flat belly, his confounding *thing* standing straight up in the grasp of his right hand. It looks so strange: milky-white skin with a road map of blue veins, the shiny purplish-red cap a miniature French beret. Hairy, muscular thighs—baby oil, cigarette smoke and a strange new odour. From that angle, reflected in the mirror, every part of his body seems odd. My eyes gravitate to his slick thing. His big thumb, with its perfectly filed nail with a perfect half moon, traces small circles at the very top of it.

12:28.

In the other hand he holds a magazine. Pensively, he eyes a glossy photo of a naked woman with big breasts.

If I move, I'll draw his attention—he'll know that I seen him.

The *8* rolls over to a *9*.

I have to get out of there—fast. I step sideways into the bathroom but don't close the door. I aim my nervous stream of pee into the inside edge of the toilet bowl, then tiptoe out with my back against the wood panelling of the endless hallway. Whew, he can't see me. Thank God, he won't know. He won't tell Debbie that I seen—oops, that I *saw* him.

The hands of the dining room clock are now straight up and down.

I shoo Mickey outside and chain her up. I give her a hug, then jump on my bike and pedal as fast as I can down the road and into the forest. I'll be late for PE class, but I don't care. Frantic thoughts. Then the song, the torturous chant, reverberates in my head. This time it's a chorus of high-pitched kids' voices, like in catechism class:

> *Be careful little eyes what you see,*
> *Be careful little eyes what you see,*
> *There's a Father up above,*
> *Looking down on us with love,*
> *So be careful little eyes what you see.*

After a few minutes, I start yelling. "It wasn't my fault! I didn't want to see him. I escaped as fast as I could. It can't be a sin—can't be!"

From a clearing in the bush, I feel the gaze of the Three Sisters. They're towering over me. Did they see what had just happened? Then I notice the cluster of crows.

wekekekek   *wekekekek*

caaaaw caaaaw caaaaw

caaaaw   caaaaw
caaaaw

Prince Charming

RORY LIKED TO organize house parties for his Alberta Highways coworkers. We were living in an industrial part of Calgary by now, in a nondescript trailer park far away from the reassuring Three Sisters, miles from my Canmore friends and, worst of all, from Mickey, the attentive Samoyed I loved, with her pure-white coat, constant smile and furtive tail. We had left her behind—no dogs allowed in the new place. Rory had planned this particular evening carefully. "That Old Black Magic" would come on right after the last couple arrived, followed by snacks and drinks. Everyone was going to learn the cha-cha-cha from an instruction book and record set, and finally they would play Twister.

The guests included Alan and Margie Tadich and three couples I didn't know. Alan and Margie were a well-matched nerdy couple: his complexion olive, hers a pasty white, his eyes brown and beady, hers round and framed by black cat's eye glasses. The other couples were good-looking and stylish in comparison: hair slicked or back-combed and sprayed; shirts and blouses open to the second or third button to reveal hairy chests or well-formed cleavage; tight, casual slacks or skirts to showcase muscular legs and shapely derrières. Spicy aftershave and provocative perfumes. Smiles, handshakes and backslaps.

As usual, Rory had asked me to pour drinks, to replenish the bowls with pretzels, chips and dip, and spicy nuts and bolts, and to empty the ashtrays. Even though I was only twelve, he gave me rye whisky watered down with 7 Up on the rocks. At times like this, I felt close to him, like I would with an older brother, uncle or father. He was smart, organized and popular. I felt a pride I didn't understand well up in me as I watched him work the room: his handsome freckled face and winsome smile, raspy voice and piercing gaze. I loved that he treated me like a grown-up, introduced me to his co-workers as his little brother. He didn't ever mention the differences between us—that his Scottish father was well off, and that Debbie and I were from a poor Indian family.

I went to bed around nine o'clock. In the living room, people were chattering loudly, munching snacks, telling dirty jokes and occasionally laughing so hard I was sure they were doubled over. As I lay in bed listening, I wondered how Gaylene, Travis, Holly and Crystal were coping in the foster home. Granny McLeod had urged Ned to give them up. I felt guilty about having my own room and bed, and about living with Debbie while they had been sent to live with white strangers. "At least they are together," Debbie said when she saw the look of horror on my face upon hearing the news.

Twister time. Rory's voice sounded authoritative as he read out the instructions. I sneaked into the hallway and watched as they squeezed themselves, one after the other, into various contortions. Al draped his arm over one woman's waist to reach a red dot on the other side of the large vinyl mat. Margie positioned herself on all fours, while another man nearly mounted her to reach a blue dot. I returned to bed with my thoughts churning. Why would Rory buy a game like that? It couldn't lead to anything good. This party was different from the ones Mother had hosted in our little house in Smith. If some guy had touched another man's wife, there would have been fights within seconds. Even an exchange of glances could lead to a brawl. I worried I wouldn't be able to fall asleep, between the party noise and the trucks flying by on the freeway.

I woke to the sound of heavy thumping, and then heard Debbie grunt and begin to sob.

Silence.

In my briefs, I scrambled down the narrow hallway. My sweet eighteen-year-old sister was on her knees in the middle of the living room, crouched over, holding her stomach with both hands as if she had been punched. Smeared mascara.

"Oh… Oh my God!" Her face was contorted with terror and disbelief. "What are you doing? What's wrong with you?"

When I saw Rory behind her, the rage in his eyes shocked me. I had never seen him so drunk. He strode towards Debbie, cocking his clenched fist up behind his ear. Al seemed paralyzed with shock at how his best buddy was acting. Margie elbowed her husband, as if to prompt him into action, but Al was probably thinking he shouldn't interfere in Rory's business—that's how men were.

Nobody budged. Once, in Canmore, Rory had thrown Debbie around in their bedroom behind a locked door, and now here he was doing it in front of everyone. I had witnessed a couple of incidents where co-workers of his hit their wives, hard, when I was babysitting in their homes and stayed the night. There was no way I could let Rory hurt my sister again, and I didn't expect the other men to intervene. I knew it was up to me. In spite of my puniness, I would have to act to protect Debbie.

I lunged toward Rory, yelling as I advanced. "You're not hitting her again, you bastard!"

He sidestepped me and moved into striking position in front of Debbie, who was now on her feet but unsteady. I stepped between them, turned to face Rory, then wrapped my arms around his waist and clasped my hands behind his back. He forced my arms down and shoved his hands under my armpits. Effortlessly, he lifted me and flung me to the floor like a rag doll. I moaned, winded and hurting.

Three men jumped to their feet, while Margie went to Debbie's side and put an arm around her shoulder.

"Rory," Alan yelled. "What the fuck, man? You can't hit a *kid*."

ALAN AND MARGIE took Debbie and me to stay with them for a week or so, until Debbie decided it was safe for us to return home. A few mornings after we got back, Rory stayed home with a head cold. Debbie had left early, as usual, to go to her waitressing job in a small truck stop in Ogden. It was silent inside the trailer except for the occasional *whoosh* of an eighteen-wheeler speeding along Blackfoot Trail.

As I went to wash up and get ready for school, I stepped into the hallway and froze. There it was again—as it had been almost daily since the move to Calgary—the full-length mirror, sitting on the floor, angled between the dresser and the wall so that I could see into the bedroom. Rory lay in bed with his left elbow crooked over his forehead. I knew exactly what his right hand was doing. I stood there in my briefs. I had wished and prayed that this would be over—that it wouldn't happen anymore. I thought maybe Rory had ended it by slamming me around like that and striking Debbie.

What if I didn't go to him? What would happen if I simply went on with my normal routine of getting ready and then gathered up my scribblers and homework—completely ignored him this time? Would he tell Debbie our secret, saying that it was my fault? Would he hit her again? Would he hit me? I recalled the rage in his eyes and his rock-hard fist hovering in the air above his head. I didn't understand why, but his physical strength, and the wrath I knew he was capable of, both terrified and thrilled me.

I stood still for a few minutes, watching as Rory coolly caressed and fondled himself. Then I entered the bedroom and shuffled toward the bed. He reached over and squeezed my butt cheek, then I felt his middle finger probing beneath my underwear. He drew me in close, placed his hands on my hips and lifted me right over him to set me down on the bed, my pint-sized body lying parallel to his. He took his dentures out and set them on the bedside table. Every time he did this it astonished me—Rory never explained why, at his age, he had already lost all of his teeth.

When his warm lips touched down, I winced. The tingling was hundreds of times stronger than any tickle or itch, first on my abdomen, then my thing. I closed my eyes and zoned out. It felt so good, but I knew it was so wrong.

I would burn in the flames of hell along with thousands of other sinners.

I opened my eyes and saw the red numbers on the clock radio.
9:15.

I was late for school. I jumped up, stumbled around the bed, naked and barefoot, and hustled to the bathroom.

"Do you want a ride to school, Darrel?"

I saw my astonished expression in the bathroom mirror. I looked into my distressed brown eyes for a second, then hurried to get dressed.

"It's okay. I'll ride my bike."

If anyone saw him dropping me off, I was horrified they might guess what we had just done.

THE EXCRUCIATING ENCOUNTERS with Rory became even more frequent. In the evening I lay on the orange shag carpet in the living room reading the comics in the *Calgary Herald*. When I glanced up, there he was—sprawled at the dining room table wearing the striped terry cloth housecoat Debbie had given him for Christmas. It hung open, no underwear, hairy legs wide apart, relaxed thighs leading up to the enormous erection in his right hand. It beckoned me—and that was his plan. I knew he wanted me to sneak over to touch him right there under the table, while Debbie was in the kitchen, cleaning up after supper.

Football and hockey games were always stimulating for Rory. He would stretch out on the sectional couch or sit in the matching corner armchair wearing his housecoat. As soon as Debbie got into the car to go to the laundromat or left the room for a moment, the housecoat fell open, and his hand started the familiar stroking—flaccid to erect in seconds. The reckless bouquet of clean sweat, pulsating manhood and cigarette smoke hypnotized me.

I did simple math problems to avoid getting aroused: the square root of sixty-four is eight, one hundred twenty-one—eleven. One hundred twenty-one is a palindrome. I felt pressure between my temples; my head was fuzzy. But there was no way I would do something *that* risky. To get caught would mean the end. There could be no life or future if Debbie found out.

ONE DAY AFTER school, I spotted a paperback with a tattered red cover on the edge of my bed. It sat open, overturned. Oddly, two shiny quarters sat next to it. What were they doing there? I flipped the book over and scanned the first couple of paragraphs. It was about Annie, a ten-year-old, and her uncle who was her guardian. The chapter was entitled "Annie Kisses the King." The uncle taught Annie to do certain acts that were described in detail. I frenetically scanned two pages, and I got it. I understood exactly what Rory had wanted me to do all along. Annie's uncle left her a reward of fifty cents.

I opened my eyes wide and held my breath. I would never have thought of doing *that*. He wanted me to do to him what he had done to me, toothless. How could it possibly work? He was so big and my mouth was so small, and I had teeth. I couldn't believe he had left me money. I wondered what my new friend Guy would think about all this if he knew.

I was playing one of the wicked stepsisters in *Operetta Cinderella*, and Guy was in the chorus. We clowned around a lot during rehearsals and afterward. He was odd looking—short and scrawny like me, but much more confident and tough. He loved to tell dirty jokes to test the reaction of the various girls he liked to flirt with. We lived in a trailer, but Guy's family lived in a house on a regular city street close to the school.

Guy asked me over to play pool almost every day, while his parents were at work. As he showed me how to position myself to take a shot, he would touch me and even put his arms around me. I was sure that one day he would make a bold move to initiate sex. I probably would have gone along with it, to stay friends and become even closer, but to my surprise, one day he invited our classmates Amanda and Rebecca over. I was thankful at first when Guy took Amanda over to the sofa and started making out with her. But as I sat patiently making small talk with Rebecca, waiting for him and Amanda to get it over with, I began to get upset. Why didn't I want to do what Guy was doing? In Canmore I had consistently had crushes on girls, getting a tingling sensation from our kisses of puppy love. I rode my bike home from Guy's place feeling empty and hopeless.

That night, I wondered what it would be like to be normal— happy-go-lucky and cheerful, raised by both a mother and a father, bringing girls home to experiment. Many other evenings, alone in my room, I lay on my bed daydreaming about Guy's life, imagining I had parents like his, even though I had never met them.

ONE EVENING AFTER supper, while Deb and I were doing the dishes, I noticed some papers in the drawer underneath the silverware tray.

PAY TO THE ORDER OF *Deborah Simpson.* Three cheques for different amounts.

"Deb. What's this? Look what I found."

"Shhhhh. Don't tell." She grabbed the cheques and put them back in the drawer. Her brown eyes were stern, and we both glanced over our shoulders to make sure Rory hadn't seen the exchange. I felt a wave of panic. What did this mean? What was Debbie planning, and why wasn't she talking to me about it? Did her plans include me?

Back in the kitchen, I couldn't cope with the mounting pressure in my chest. As I hurriedly dried dishes I launched into an Elvis song, like I often did in front of the bathroom mirror at the top of my lungs when I was home alone.

"Are you lonesome tonight? Do you miss me tonight? Are you sorry we drifted apart?"

Debbie smiled as she began to sing along.

I copied Elvis's monologue as best I could, trying to make my voice deep like his:

> *Honey—you lied when you said you loved me.*
> *And I had no cause to doubt you.*
> *But I'd rather go on hearing your lies*
> *Than go on living without you.*

Debbie laughed. "You're crazy! Keep going!"

We sang together for a few moments, looking into each other's eyes. I could see that there was something she wanted to tell me but didn't dare. It was the same with me—I had something I desperately wanted to *tell* her. But I recognized the anguish in her eyes, too, and it disturbed me. When she started to tear up, and I did as well, I turned on my heel and went to my room.

I sat on my bed, my eyes moist. Why couldn't I stop doing that with him? Debbie was going to see someday. Maybe she already knew. The night before, he had been playing with himself at the dining room table while I was lying on the floor watching *Star Trek.* He was looking down, pretending to be reading, but he wanted me to see—wanted me to be daring. Part of me wanted to respond. The urge to touch him troubled me. Where would it all lead?

I thought about the three cheques and the determined look on Debbie's face when she realized that I had found them. Was my dream going to come true? Would she and I move into one of the new highrises in downtown Calgary, just the two of us?

I fumbled in my desk drawer for the pocket Bible the Gideons had given us in Grade Five. Most of it held no meaning for me, but I liked the proverbs section that I had discovered by chance one day. I flipped the Bible open to Proverbs 5:22: *The iniquities of the wicked ensnare him, and he is held fast in the cords of his sin.*

Oh no. That must be what was happening—I had become trapped in my own evil.

TWENTY OR SO junior high students clustered in the middle of the stage sang the chorus of "Some Day My Prince Will Come" from *Snow White* in unison. As Hortense, one of the stepsisters, I got to do a solo version of the theme song. I was striking in a scraggly black wig and pancake makeup with bright-red lips. Parent volunteers had applied the makeup, and before they added some warts and blacked out a few teeth, I blushed, realizing I could actually pass for a girl—a pretty girl.

In rehearsal I felt awkward strutting about the stage in a ball gown and a nightie, and I got shivers when I realized I would soon be doing this in front of the whole school. Even though it was a farcical comedy, would people wonder if I really was like that—if I secretly longed to dress as a girl, like Uncle Danny and Greggie did? Would they see through me, guess what I had been up to with Rory over the last couple of years? See what a bad person I was?

The prince was a good-looking Grade Nine Japanese-Canadian kid, Pete Seto. I admired him, thinking him smart, talented and kind. No way would he have been involved in anything weird with a grown-up family member, like I was. The rehearsals were a welcome break. It was restoring to be around normal people. I loved the camaraderie, the escape; for an hour or two, I could forget the stress of the situation at home and the worry of what it all meant for me. The music teacher and the other kids treated me as if I belonged there with them. Maybe I would make some close friends like I had in Canmore, and someone's parents would offer to take me in to live with them.

The morning of the first performance, I bounced out of bed and bounded into the combined living–dining room. The air was already blue with cigarette smoke. Rory and Deb sat opposite each other at the table, not speaking. I tried to melt the tension with a cheery reminder that this was the opening night of my play. I went over to where I had put their tickets a few days earlier, picked them up and waved them in the air. Rory answered for both of them. "We'll see, Darrel. We might make it tonight."

Mr. Sawatsky strode on stage that evening to open the play. He was young with chestnut-red hair and a matching bushy beard. "Ladies and gentlemen," he called out. "Welcome to *Operetta Cinderella*. Find out how the fairy tale really happened. We'll tell the story of Cinderella like it has never been told!"

Unlike in my nightmares, I didn't forget my lines or go out on stage at the wrong time. The audience laughed and clapped at all the right places. My moment in the spotlight came when Prince Charming appeared, looking for Cinderella. I was wearing a tight, flowery flannel nightie that fell slightly below my knees. At centre stage, I decided to ham it up more than I had in rehearsals. I was sure Debbie was in the audience, and I wanted to be hilarious so we could talk about it later and laugh some more—and it seemed that the crazier I got, the more I escaped into a world where I was comical, happy, safe and normal.

When the prince leaned over with the glass slipper, I was supposed to put my right foot up onto a stool to try the slipper on. We were facing each other, with my back to the audience. Instead, I put my left foot up, forcing Pete to bend over more. In the process of clowning around, I decided I would put my hands over his, stooping over with him, but even lower. My plan was to make a funny scene by straining to force my foot into the slipper.

I bent over deeply. I didn't hear it, but I felt it. Suddenly my shoulders and back were bare.

The nightie had ripped up the back, from the bottom to the top. Or was it from top to bottom? I jerked upright and jumped around to face the audience. The nightie fell to the floor. I shrieked.

Every kid's worst recurring nightmare had just come true. There I was, standing in the spotlight in front of the whole school—parents, classmates and all the teachers—in my skimpy white underwear. Oh my God—no. My thing started to rise. Instinctively, I covered my crotch with my hands. The audience was roaring. The other kids on stage were laughing so hard they were doubled over. I grabbed the torn nightie, pulled it around me to cover up and started to hobble off stage. I tripped and ended up scrambling on all fours, to thundering applause and resounding laughter.

In the wings, Mr. Sawatsky scooted over with the wicked stepmother's housecoat.

"Good job, Darrel!" He laughed. "How did you pull that off?"

"It was an accident… Honest!"

I was flying high. My body was reverberating as I got dressed and romped down to the gym entrance to find Rory and Debbie. Maybe we would stop at A&W on the way home, for a root beer, onion rings and soft serve ice cream. People in the hallways were chuckling. Kids I had never seen before came up to me, patted my shoulder and told me how funny I was.

After waiting fifteen minutes at the door of the gym, I gave up. I found my bike, jumped on it and rode home. I was sad they'd missed it, but still I was aglow. The dark streets flew by. I spotted the occasional bat swooping down from a lamp post and pedalled faster. I spotted Rory's brown Pontiac Parisienne in the driveway. I couldn't believe they hadn't come to opening night. Maybe they planned to go tomorrow, but it wouldn't be the same.

I flung open the trailer door. Debbie was sitting on the orange sofa, crying. Rory was beside her, his eyes swollen and red. I had never seen Rory cry before, and it choked me up. Seeing Debbie cry usually triggered my tears, too, but it seemed that the adrenaline-charged experience of the evening had both insulated and emboldened me. I didn't say a word, but as I walked past them to go to my bedroom, Rory blurted out an explanation: "Your sister is leaving us, Darrel—tomorrow."

I froze for a moment and gawked at him. I decided to ignore what he was saying and block the panic that was trying to take hold of me, telling myself Debbie would change her mind by morning. I continued on to my room and went right to bed, hoping to escape quickly into the world of sleep and dreams. It worked.

The next morning, as I stepped into the living room, I was astonished to see that Rory's eyes were still puffy, and tears were streaming down his cheeks. Part of me wanted to say something to calm him, but I also wanted to yell at him: what the hell did you expect, you idiot?

Debbie came down the hallway with a small blue suitcase in her hand and went to stand by the door. A car horn honked. Rory kissed her lightly on the lips and said a curt goodbye. When she opened the trailer door, I saw the Yellow Cab in the driveway. "I'll pick you up for a visit this weekend, Darrel," she said as she turned, stepped down and closed the door.

I couldn't sort out my feelings and thoughts; they were coming on so fast. She was really going through with it, leaving Rory, and leaving me, too, in the process. Surely it was out of desperation—she was saving herself first, and she would be back for me. Or did she think Rory and I had bonded, like father and son? If she knew what was *really* going on, she would have taken me with her, I was certain. But there was no way I could tell her.

Rory explained that Debbie had gone to stay with her co-worker Darlene, who lived in a small townhouse in Calgary's rundown eastside with three kids. I looked him over, hoping to find some sign of warmth or closeness, but it was as if I were gazing at a stranger. I wondered if he felt the same way.

That evening we sat glum-faced at the dinner table and choked down toasted bologna and Cheez Whiz sandwiches as we watched the evening news. Conversation was awkward, and there was no touching, barely even any eye contact. It was like the spell had been broken; Rory's compulsion was gone. Was it the risk of being caught by Debbie that had been the big turn-on for him?

The next evening was similar, and we both went to bed early, right after *The Avengers*. I was convinced it was over. Maybe we could get to know each other all over again, in whatever time we had left together?

Our first Friday alone, Rory came home from work drunk. He had brought home fish and chips from Haliburton's—the usual Friday routine. After eating, he went directly to bed, but after half an hour he stumbled into the living room, still wearing his clothes from work. His shrivelled penis was hanging out of his grey dress pants. He lay on the sectional couch next to where I was watching TV, and pulled me over so that I was lying on top of him.

I inhaled his smoky, alcohol-infused breath, and then suddenly his tongue was inside my mouth. He pulled my clothes off first, and then his. This session felt very different. There was no worry about Debbie walking in on us, and he wanted me to stay with him after the intensity had settled. I lay there beside him until I heard his faint snore, then got up and went to my bedroom. I felt guilty and afraid. What did it all mean? Was Rory expecting we would now act like a couple?

A WEEK OR so later, Rory asked me to go for a drive.

I glanced out the window as an eighteen-wheeler truck screamed alongside of us. Its wake rocked the car. Bursts of yellow, orange and red tulips dotted the grass along my side of the road. In the rear-view mirror I saw three crows taking flight. I wished I could be out there with them.

By now I knew that Debbie was gone for good. She had made that clear when I visited her at Darlene's townhouse the previous weekend. She intended to move in with John, a divorced truck driver she had met at work. He had a small one-bedroom apartment downtown. She asked what I planned to do: would I go back to live with Mother and Swede or stay with Rory? I was devastated but tried not to show it. I worried again that she might know what Rory and I had been doing and feel I had betrayed her. If that was the case, who could blame her for leaving me there with him? Is that what I had to do now, run back to Mother to escape life with Rory? Mother had to take me—surely she would.

Rory took an exit off the freeway and parked on a quiet side street. Why was he stopping?

"Darrel... *Darrel*—you're off in wonderland again. Listen to me."

He shifted in his bucket seat to face me.

I couldn't help but look at the full lips that had kissed me so intensely. They were now tightly pursed. Rory reached over and put his large hand on my shoulder. I winced, then felt a flash of guilt. He was trying to be nice to me. Was he hoping things could be normal between us again? Could they be?

"Darrel—I feel bad about how it's turned out with your sister and me. I love her, but we don't agree on one issue." The furrows on his forehead deepened as he pressed the bright red coil of the car lighter up to his cigarette. His fingernails were chipped, and there was dirt under the nail of his index finger. He inhaled deeply, then blew smoke out of his nose and mouth at the same time.

"She wants kids, but I've told her that I could never have kids with Indian blood. She knew that before we got married."

He spoke in a matter of fact tone, as if expecting I would understand.

"I was sure she was pregnant. That's why I punched her in the stomach that night. I overheard her telling Margie she hadn't had her period, and I thought she'd stopped taking her birth control pills. She wouldn't show me the container."

I broke from his gaze and looked straight ahead—tried to keep a poker face in spite of the acid that filled my throat. He had punched my sister to make her lose the baby he thought she was carrying—*his* baby—*our* baby! Why had he married her if he couldn't stand Indians? What did he think of *me*?

Never again, I resolved. I would never again touch him that way or let him touch me. What I realized next was upsetting: what he did with me, or to me, had nothing to do with love. The same with Debbie. He felt he could own and control us, as if it were his natural right to have his way with us. He didn't care if Debbie caught us in the act; if she had, and made a fuss, who would believe her, a poorly educated Indian woman accusing a white guy—a government worker at that?

I remembered the words Mother used to say with such force when I was little, wagging her finger in the air: "Be proud to be Indian. Don't ever let anyone make you feel like you're less. You're Indian, always remember that and be proud."

Rory was still talking. "Darrel. *Darrel.* Hey, listen. I don't know what you want to do now that your sister is gone, but know what? I want to adopt you—if you want me to. You're a good kid. You do well in school. You work hard. We can have a lot of fun, can even smoke pot together sometimes. Would you like that?"

His tone was kind. He put his hand back on my shoulder and pulled me towards him, but I resisted. He looked desperate—afraid. I knew there would be more sex with him if I stayed, in spite of my determination to avoid it. The last few sessions he had tried to get me to make out a different way, doggie style, he said, and he had started calling me *Honey*.

"Uhhh... no. I have to go back to Mom. I phoned her a couple of days ago, and she wants me to go live with her and Swede," I lied. I stared at the floorboard. "But thanks, Rory. Thanks so much. That's really nice of you to offer."

THE FOLLOWING SATURDAY morning Rory and I took our places at the dining room table. One cup of Maxwell House instant coffee for me and two for him, along with three Rothmans cigarettes. He lit up another just before he turned the key in the ignition of the brown Parisienne. I opened the small triangular window halfway so there would be a breeze on my face during the long trip to Edmonton.

The ditches on both sides of the freeway were covered with flat dead grass with hints of green poking through. The sky was an airy blue, with bulky clouds in the distance. Rory was overdue for a haircut, as was I. He had let his sideburns grow long and shaved them into mutton chops, the way Elvis did. I liked that look on him, and the auburn tinge to the new growth, but since Debbie left he only shaved every second day, and when he threw on clean clothes, they were wrinkled.

Rory turned the radio up loud. Johnny Cash came on singing "A Boy Named Sue." I prayed Rory would open his small window too, to create a cross breeze, but he didn't. What if he had asked me one more time to stay? What would I have answered?

"We'll keep in touch, Darrel. I can drive up to Edmonton once in a while to visit. My dad still lives there."

"That would be great, Rory. I hope you do," I said, trying to sound like I meant it.

In the lengthy cluster of gas stations just south of Red Deer, we stopped for a burger and Coke at an Esso restaurant with a huge red waitress's cap on it, just like the one Debbie had worked at in Canmore.

As we drove down the dramatic hill into the Edmonton River Valley, and over the North Saskatchewan, I was shaking with excitement. In minutes, I would be at Mother's place. We would be reunited after these years we had spent apart. Was she as excited as I was? Greggie was living with her again, and we could get the kids out of the foster home and back with us where they belonged. I couldn't wait.

"Okay, this is it," Rory said. "We're here."

We had pulled up to a beautiful wooden apartment building similar to a house I used to draw in school in Canmore and tell my buddies I would live in one day. Mother was sitting on the front steps waiting for us. She shook Rory's hand and gave me a kiss on the lips before leading us downstairs, through a dingy basement filled with cobwebs and piles of dirt.

"The landlord gave us a temporary suite here in the basement till we get an apartment upstairs," she explained.

Rory asked me to help him get the four boxes of my belongings and my bike from the trunk. I didn't know what to make of the expression on his face. Was he about to cry? Was he angry? After he had set the cardboard boxes on the porch, he leaned my bike against the bottom step, then pulled me into a hug. "Good luck, Darrel. Call me if you ever need anything. You know where to find me."

When Greggie got home a half-hour later, he showed me the room he had cleaned and painted on the other side of the basement. Then he took me to the Chinese corner store, where we bought a large bottle of Coca-Cola and a few Revels.

"I work at a car dealership, Dades, detailing cars, getting them ready for sale," he explained. "Got a really nice boss. Sometimes he lets me hang out with him at night when he does security detail... I'm goin' there tonight." He handed me a five-dollar bill. "So glad you're here, Dades."

Swede came out of the bedroom on crutches, with a full-length plaster cast on his leg. I asked him what had happened, and he began to sputter something about an incident with Mother. "It was an accident," Mother interrupted. Swede ordered Kentucky Fried Chicken for us for supper. His big goofy smile melted my reticence.

"Do you want a beer, Darrel?" he asked as he looked at Mother to check her reaction. She nodded.

"Sure. I'll just have half. Rory and Debbie gave me weak drinks when they had parties."

The three of us sat for hours, chatting and laughing in the stench of smoke, until Swede announced he was going to bed. Mother went silent for a few moments, studying me before speaking. "You've changed so much. Look at those hairy arms. Your hands are big for your age. So, you missed Mom, eh?"

"Yes, I did. But you chose your life. Rory and Debbie took good care of me."

I stood and turned to go to the bathroom, but before I reached the doorway, a brown beer bottle flew past my face, spinning end over end and smashing loudly on the door. Glass flew everywhere.

"What in the hell? Whatcha do that for, Mom? You coulda really hurt me."

I went to Greg's room and lay down on his bed. His smell calmed me. What had I just done? Why had I come here?

Long as I Can See the Light

MOTHER HUNG UP the phone and stepped into the living room to announce that Debbie was coming for Christmas. I wanted to jump up and down with glee, but I suppressed my feelings, worried that Mother might get jealous.

"If everyone is gonna be here, we have a lot of work to do to get ready, Son—shopping, baking and cleaning."

Mother's voice was more animated and high-strung than usual. I tried to read her mood. Was she happy that Debbie was coming, and what did she mean "everyone"? Who else would join us—her boyfriend, Swede, from Edmonton? My stepfather, Ned, from Fort McMurray, where he worked now? Greggie from the city? She hadn't told me yet—and there was only a week to go.

What I hadn't told *her* was that I had been calling both Debbie and Greggie from a pay phone regularly since early November and pleading with them, "Come home for Christmas. C'mon. We can all be together again—like a family."

We had been living in Athabasca, in the house behind the pool hall, for about a year, and I had just begun Grade Nine. I liked to think that the house we rented had been a respectable home twenty-five years earlier, when a Ukrainian family owned the pool hall. I pictured a lawn with flowerbeds in the small backyard. But now, in 1971, the front porch had become a TV repair shop, a sketchy dirt path led from the back alley to the only entry, the archway to the pool hall was sealed and the house cried out for paint and repair.

I wasn't sure why Mother had chosen to move here from Edmonton, instead of back to Smith, but I was glad she had. The schools were bigger in Athabasca, and there was a movie theatre. Best of all, it was a fresh start for our family.

Gaylene and Travis stood side by side in the partition between the kitchen and the living room, looking anxious. "So great, eh, Debbie's coming?" I said to them.

"Yeah, yeah—can't wait to see her!" they answered in unison.

Holly and Crystal, sitting together in the turquoise vinyl armchair, looked uneasy. They knew who Debbie was, but she had left to marry Rory when they were toddlers, and during the three years the four of them had been in the foster home, they probably hadn't heard anything about Debbie, or about me for that matter. Ned, their father, had been the only one to visit and send money.

Mother and I had had our first supervised visit with the kids six months earlier. When she extended her hand to the foster mother, Mrs. Milot took it with a strained smile. They were opposites in appearance: standing beside the dowdy Mrs. Milot, Mother looked dark, slender and fashionable with her carefully applied makeup, permed hair and new cat's eye glasses. The social worker sat behind the two mothers. I glanced back and forth between them, trying to gauge the mood.

From youngest to oldest, the four kids took turns sitting on Mother's knee—awkward at first, then snuggling in once they recognized her familiar fragrance and touch.

"Is it okay, Mom?" Holly had asked Mrs. Milot before she climbed into Mother's lap.

In the middle of the night, I awoke troubled. How would Mother and Debbie get along? Would they drink and then fight? A few years earlier, when Mother and Swede came to visit us in Canmore, they had spent eight hours straight in the bar with Rory and Debbie, arguing the whole time. Mother had ended up pounding on our trailer door at midnight, begging to come in. Debbie yelled that she and Swede should leave and never come back.

Then there was Deb and Greg. I had always been in the middle of it when they had their hellish fights over nothing, trying to quell their anger and not take anyone's side. How would they behave as grown-ups?

I tossed and turned every night that week, but each morning I scampered down to the living room to plug in the lights on the towering Christmas tree. Its fresh spruce aroma calmed me. The majestic white angel with her golden locks and wand had miraculously survived the family collapse and stayed with us. I sat on the floor admiring her atop the twinkling tree until I heard someone else stir.

Thanks to Ned, the fridge and cupboards were full. He always sent more money than he had to. I looked on happily as Mother baked and prepared food to freeze. I helped her decorate the house even more. She hummed Christmas carols and smiled a lot, but her joy seemed forced. Every now and then she would stop what she was doing, stand still and look at me without a word.

DEBBIE AND HER truck-driver boyfriend, John, surprised us with a knock at the door around eight o'clock at night on the twenty-second. We kids hustled to the door with Mother on our heels. I flung the door open, and there they stood, snowflakes on their hair and eyebrows and dusting the shoulders of their parkas.

John looked drained. Or was it just that he was so much older than Debbie and Mother? Debbie hugged each of us kids in turn.

"Darrel, look at you—so big, and your hair's getting wavy! A teenager now, eh? Peach-fuzz moustache... So cute!

"My blue-eyed Gaylene, Momma girl. So pretty! Nine now, eh?

"Buddy bear, Travis—handsome like your dad." She rubbed his brush cut.

The three girls clustered around her.

"Cucuumy, Holly. Look at your long curly hair—just like when you were little. And baby Crystal. Look at you. The sweetest smile of all!"

Mother stood behind me, taking it all in. "Well, so glad yous made it. Been snowing all day," she said as she extended her hand, first to Debbie, then to John.

"Yes, a couple of times we got stuck behind snowplows," John answered. "And I'm heading right back into it. Gotta get home to spend Christmas with my kids."

I glanced at John's face as he sat at the kitchen table with us, sipping hot coffee. My reading was that he didn't love Debbie but was kind to her, like a father. Of course, I could have been wrong. I just couldn't imagine them kissing like she and Rory used to. After he finished his coffee, John and Debbie stepped into the porch to say goodbye.

Debbie's blue suitcase sat beside three large cardboard boxes near the door. She asked me to help carry them to Mother's bedroom, just off the porch. The biggest one was a shape that I was sure my math teacher, Mrs. Pilipiuk, would have identified as an isosceles trapezoid.

I DELIVERED THE *Edmonton Journal* as usual the next afternoon, trudging through the snow in my heavy parka and wool-lined boots from Saint Vincent de Paul. The headlines were still about the FLQ crisis: PRIME MINISTER TRUDEAU ORDERS TROOPS TO WITHDRAW FROM QUEBEC. Would that mean the end of martial law and the nightly curfew in Athabasca— across the country? I hoped so; the curfew alarm every night at eight scared me. I did my route as quickly as I could, but I was collecting for the month, and people were generous with their tips, inviting me inside to warm up with cocoa or mulled apple cider.

It was a rare chance to see how the better-off people in Athabasca lived. Their houses had real entrances off the street, wooden dining tables with matching china cabinets and inviting plush sofas placed at angles on thick shag carpets. Some folks explained why they hadn't even begun their seasonal preparations: Ukrainian Christmas came two weeks later.

We were all smiles and laughter through supper, but as we savoured the butter tarts, I noticed that Mother was starting to slur her words, and her eyes were dull; the syrupy Prince of Denmark wine, which Mother had tasted at Debbie and Rory's wedding, and liked, had come out. I hadn't realized we had any. Mother and Deb were both sipping, and they seemed to be avoiding eye contact with one another.

THAT NIGHT, WITH Travis sleeping serenely by my side in my upstairs bedroom, I strained to hear their voices. I drifted off to snippets of their conversation:

"...kids deserve a good home..."

"...see how *you* do when *you* have kids, *if* you ever do..."

"...won't hit 'em if I do... they won't ever see *me* drunk... How's Darrel doin'? Why does he call me from a *pay phone*, upset?"

"He acts *white* now, talks like a *moniyaw*. Whatcha guys do ta him? Doesn't even *fart* anymore."

GLITZY PAPER WITH scenes of reindeer pulling sleighs, giant snowflakes or Santa and his elves adorned the various boxes that were piled up under the Christmas tree, including the mysterious trapezoidal box. The lights, the tinsel icicles and the silver garlands all shone a bit brighter, as if to say, my time has come, admire me. Mother was giddy. Nat King Cole's nasal voice crooned "The Happiest Christmas Tree," and she sang along. Her eyes widened and she smiled with each repetition of the *ho ho ho, hee hee hee* line. At moments like this, her glee was infectious. Debbie smiled as she sat down to join us with a fresh cup of coffee and a cigarette.

The ice crystals on the window glimmered in the early morning sun. Columns of vapour and smoke rose from the houses nearby. I loved the spiky coleus plant on our windowsill. Its fiery purple leaves with their jagged green edges brought colour and a touch of the exotic to our little house year-round, though in December it had to share the spotlight. Our turquoise couch and armchair looked like new, and there wasn't a speck of dust on the wood-veneer coffee tables. Everyone had helped clean—even Crystal. She'd sat on an old wool blanket so that Travis and I could swing her around to buff the floors Mother had waxed by hand.

GREGGIE WORE A plain oversized parka and floppy boots that I guessed he had borrowed. As we walked through the back alley to get to our house, the constant crunch of powdery snow underfoot made it hard to hear what he was saying. In the half block from the Greyhound depot to our house, he gushed on about life in the city: house parties, clubs and cabarets.

"But you aren't twenty-one yet, Greg."

"Oh, the clubs let me in, Dades. It's good for business. And I still work at the car dealership—they treat me really good there."

Greg kicked off his boots in the porch and swaggered over to where Mother and Debbie sat at the kitchen table. He pecked Mother on the lips, and he and Debbie exchanged brisk hellos. Greg had matured, it seemed to me, not so much in his looks as in his behaviour. He wasn't sulky like he had sometimes been, and he looked like an adult now—smoking, drinking coffee and drumming his fingers on the table. His pockmarked complexion was smoother than it had been, and he was chubbier. Moving awkwardly in his baggy plaid shirt and loose-fitting jeans, he sat on the floor to play with the kids for a while, then looked over at me.

"Let's go for a walk, Dades—find a record store. I wanna play you the tunes I been listening to lately."

Usually the sidewalks of Athabasca were quiet, but not that day; last-minute shoppers were darting from one store to the other, carrying overstuffed shopping bags with rolls of flashy wrapping paper sticking out. Christmas carols everywhere. Scowling shoppers forced smiles and uttered "Merry Christmas" as they brushed past each other.

We hurried home to play the LPs and 45 singles he had bought. I loved the beats and melodies of "Get Back," "Let It Be" and "House of the Rising Sun." We all sang along with "Knock Three Times." I vowed to memorize the lyrics to CCR's "Who'll Stop the Rain." Other songs, like "ABC" by the Jackson 5 and "Lola" by the Kinks, made me uneasy. I didn't understand what people liked about Michael Jackson's tinny voice. A little kid singing about love and seduction made me squirm. I mean, I did it too, but only with the bathroom door closed when nobody was home. I made my voice sultry to sing Elvis songs and practised moving my hips like he did, trying to convince myself I would really sing like him one day.

With just the two of us in the living room, Greg played "Get Back" and "Lola" over and over. He sang along, moving to the beat. "C'mon, Dades—dance."

When I was in Grade One, Greggie had phoned my teacher, Miss Long, to ask her why I hadn't received the academic merit award for getting straight "honours" on my final report card. When I slipped into the murky Athabasca River one afternoon, chasing a jackfish that had flapped back in, he grabbed my arm and pulled me ashore. But my strongest memory was of the time Mother had sent Greggie and me to chop down a Christmas tree back when we were still living in Smith. I was sure we were going in circles in the dark forest, and the howls of wolves and coyotes gave me chills. But in the light of a half moon, Greggie had calmly chopped down a shapely spruce tree, and we carried it home on our shoulders, singing a new carol we had learned at school: *Now the holly bears a berry, as blood is it red. And Mary bore Jesus who rose from the dead.*

MOTHER SET OUT all kinds of snacks for us to nibble as we visited: mixed nuts, potato chips with dip, dill pickles, candy canes, more of her butter tarts and dark fruitcake. The only thing missing, because we didn't have any hunters around anymore, was the *kakiwak,* dried moose meat with butter that we'd usually had for special days. But no one complained.

That evening everyone except Mother sat down to watch *How the Grinch Stole Christmas!* on TV. I heard her dialling the rotary phone in the kitchen, making her usual evening call to Swede. After about ten minutes I sauntered into the kitchen, got a glass of orange Tang and sat down at the table across from her. She hung up and glared at me.

"Look at this. Ned never made this happen."

I glanced to where her hands directed my eyes—to her protruding nipples and engorged *chochos* beneath her thin green blouse.

"Swede's a better lover, but not as good as your dad was. Your dad liked to see me naked, Son, but I was shy. It only happened once, when I was bathing."

Queasy stomach, parched mouth. Her words had the desired effect—I would never again interrupt her when she was on a call with Swede.

Loud enough for everyone to hear, I stammered, "Ah... we're watching TV, Mother. You wanna join us? That Cree girl, Buffy Sainte-Marie, is supposed to be on later! You love her singing, remember?"

CHRISTMAS MORNING. I was the first one up, excited and grateful. Things were working out. I bustled into the living room and saw the expanded pile of gifts under the tree. Santa had come. I put a pot of coffee on. Once it was made, Mother, Debbie and Greggie sauntered into the living room with full mugs, sat down close to an ashtray. I perched beside Debbie on the turquoise armchair. A drum roll of kids' feet on the stairs; we looked at each other and smiled.

Gaylene's eyes lit up when she saw her Easy-Bake Oven. Holly and Crystal giggled as they unwrapped their talking Crissy dolls. Travis turned the knobs on his Etch A Sketch. I was fixated on the mysterious box; what could be in it? When Debbie handed it to me, I could hardly breathe.

"Well, open it, Dades. Everyone will enjoy it eventually," she laughed.

"Oh, Debbie, a guitar!"

"There's a few books in there so you can learn how to play on your own. I wanna hear some tunes soon, okay?"

I held the shiny new guitar in my lap, filled with excitement and worry. Finally, someone had heeded my pleas. From the time I was small, I had begged Mother, Mosom and Uncle Andy to teach me to play the guitar or the fiddle. In Grade Four I had pleaded with my teacher, Mrs. Earl, to teach me piano. Each time the answer had been, "You're too little yet. Wait a while." Many days after school I had sung while Mrs. Earl chorded on the piano, but now I could learn to accompany myself, like Mother did. Would I succeed?

Mother was wearing her pink flannel housecoat with its matching fluffy slippers. Her glasses were slightly crooked, and her permed black hair was dishevelled. Her cigarette sat burning in the large black ashtray. She got up and slid a huge unwrapped box from behind the tree. "This gift is for all of yous."

We clambered over each other to tear it open—a miniature pool table.

As soon as the excitement had died down, Mother and Debbie got to work in the kitchen. As usual on a special day, we planned to eat in the middle of the afternoon.

The rest of us picked out some records to play. Mother requested *Johnny Horton's Greatest Hits*.

Before long, the aroma of roasting turkey filled the house. Along with it and Mother's special stuffing there would be mashed potatoes with gravy, Brussels sprouts, wrinkled peas, boiled carrots and turnips, a salad with iceberg lettuce and tomato wedges, more of Mother's Ukrainian-style cabbage rolls, pickles and canned wild strawberries with whipped cream for dessert.

The younger kids had crammed their chairs close to Debbie's. I got out the camera and snapped a picture of them all huddled together. Greg didn't want to be in any pictures, but I snuck a few shots when he wasn't looking.

By the time we had gathered around the table, the Prince of Denmark wine had reappeared. The sullen look on Mother's face was familiar, but Debbie's dimmed gaze and slight nervous tic, a twitch at the corner of her mouth, were new to me. I didn't like either. I willed myself to get lost in the luscious flavours of the food piled on my plate, but the kids were starting to fidget and fuss. I knew that soon they would be elbowing or kicking each other under the table. I felt an increasing tightness in my stomach.

"I'm catching the eight o'clock bus to Edmonton. I promised my friends I would be back tonight," Greg announced.

"Aw, so fast," I protested.

Debbie and Mother didn't look up from their plates.

"May I be excused from the table?" each of the kids asked in turn. Rory had insisted I do this after every meal, and I had suggested Mother do the same with us.

"*Eh-heh*, you're excused," Mother said and laughed.

I went up to my room, closed the door and started practising chords on the guitar: C, A minor, F and G. With those four chords, I could play so many songs I knew the words to. I started working on "Long as I Can See the Light." Now and then tears came to my eyes, which surprised me, but the poetry of the song moved me—the image of a single candle flickering in the dark to guide me home, even though I wasn't sure where home was anymore.

This would be more fun than learning the trumpet had been. For the first couple of weeks I was in Miss Emmons's band class, I had felt self-conscious about the uncontrolled squawks and shrieks of my instrument, so I practised in the ramshackle basement of our house.

"Greg's gotta go. Darrel, come and walk him to the bus depot," Mother called.

CIGARETTE SMOKE WAFTED over me as I stepped back into the house. Auntie Helen, Uncle Andy and our cousins Joe and Babe Lennie were sitting around the kitchen table drinking beer from stubby bottles or sipping whiskey and 7 Up from clear glasses. Mother and Auntie Helen were chatting in Cree. Uncle Andy and our cousins took turns raving about Debbie. "So pretty!" "Beautiful smile—still got your own teeth!" "Gorgeous. You look like your ma when she was your age."

"*Astum,* Tairl—giff me a Christmas kiss," Auntie Helen called.

She held me by her side for a few minutes, saying how fast I was growing, how nice I looked in my new crimson shirt, what a good kid I was. Her fingers were thick and strong like Mother's.

I went into the living room to play with the others. Auntie Helen's youngest boy, Clifford, and his older brother Vern followed me. Vern was home from the city, where he attended the Alberta School for the Deaf. I tried to communicate with him by mouthing words and inventing hand gestures. He smiled and laughed. The two of us went upstairs to play pool in the extra room.

After a while, I noticed there were only two voices coming from downstairs, Mother's and Debbie's. Both of them sounded tense. Mother started yelling. Debbie yelled back.

"So where did you find that old man you're goin' out with, anaways?" Mother said with a mean laugh.

"The kids deserve a decent home," Debbie answered in a monotone.

"Well, you might like older men, but you ain't gonna sleep with Swede, so don't even think about it. He might come tomorrow. Remember, he's mine. And don't be wearing any of those tight hot pants or miniskirts around him."

"Yeah, was he worth leaving your kids for?"

"You left home too, before I did, to marry that white prick. And he made you sacrifice my first grandchild. Your father's first grandchild. I covered that up for you. Told everyone you were in the hospital with rheumatic fever. You should be ashamed."

"And where were you? *Drinking!* What the hell else was a fourteen-year-old supposed to do?"

Vern flapped his hand to get my attention. He pointed toward the bedroom window, urging me to look outside. I stood up to see what he was excited about, but something told me I had to get downstairs fast.

I stuck my head around the corner—just in time to see a beer bottle flying towards Debbie.

"NOOOO... MOTHER!"

CRACK! The bottle smashed against Debbie's face, shattering into a hundred pieces. Debbie collapsed into a puddle of beer and broken glass. She lay on her side, not making a sound.

BITTER COLD BURNED my bare face. Everything around me glimmered with hoar frost. Pines lined the street leading up the hill to the hospital, their boughs weighed down by snow.

Wek-ek-ek-ek. Wek-ek-ek-ek.

Three magpies were pecking at a frozen mouse carcass. Every breath became a pillar of steamy vapour in front of my face.

Iodine, rubbing alcohol, burnt toast and coffee. Front desk. "Second floor—third door to the right."

A huge bandage covered the centre of her face—a plaster cast above a reddish-brown gauze plug. The skin around her nose was puffy and blue. Her top lip was swollen. I sat by her bed and took her frail hand. We sat silently, looking at the floor, until Deb broke the silence.

"My nose bled real bad—it's broken." Her voice completely nasal.

"Still hurt, Deb?"

"Not now, but it did earlier this morning. They gave me a pain-killer. And I have to breathe through my mouth. But I'll be okay."

By the third day her spirits were brighter, her colour was better and the swelling was down.

"Wanna play cards?"

"Sure—they have some here?"

"Yeah. And a crib board."

Deb sat on the edge of her bed and rolled her meal tray between us. I shuffled the cards and dealt. Debbie cut the deck.

"I called John this morning, and he says he'll come to get me and drive me home to Calgary. My friend Darlene is covering for me at work."

I flipped the top card—the queen of spades.

"So you won't be staying till you're all better?"

"Ten," Deb opened.

"Fifteen two." I replied, feeling guilty as I pegged my points.

"Twenty for two. Not sure. He's gonna tell me when he can come."

"Thirty."

"One for two." Deb leaned over slightly to peg her points.

"Go. Ten."

"…and fifteen two."

"Wow—you got a good hand, eh?"

"Not bad. Should have a good crib—maybe a run or two."

"Twenty-five. I started learning a song for you."

"Oh, good. CCR?"

"Yup, 'Proud Mary' from the book you got me."

"They say I was anemic from all the blood loss."

"Glad you're feeling better. Swelling's down too, eh? Well, tomorrow I'll spend the whole day with you. The kids say hello. They really love you, Deb."

"Got an ace for thirty-one. I'm gonna peg out. Sorry, Dades."

May the light of Christ, rising in glory,
dispel the darkness of our hearts and minds.

I picked up the guide to Mass from a small table at the back of the church, and we walked past the white lilies, palm branches and giant flickering candles under each station of the cross along both sides of St. Gabriel's Catholic Church. I was proud of how sweet my little sisters Gaylene and Crystal looked in the yellow and white spring dresses we had bought at Robinsons' the day before. Holly had her red dress on, and Travis wore his new white shirt. I seated them in a pew near the back of the church. They looked glum, even though just an hour before we had found and had begun to devour the chocolate animals and the colourful candies the Easter Bunny had hidden for us.

Without being asked, I went to the sacristy. Previous Sundays, I had felt sorry for Father O'Donnell as I watched him struggle through mass on his own. I didn't understand why the locals hadn't volunteered to be altar boys, but I would soon find out.

I knew the role well from my days as an altar boy in Smith: don the red and white cassock and then, during the mass, ensure that I caught any falling crumbs or drops on an oval brass plate as the priest snapped the white wafer in half and poured wine into the chalice. I took it all literally, convinced the miracle of transubstantiation occurred the second I knelt and shook the cluster of silver bells and he raised the Host, then the chalice of wine up over his head and announced: this is the body of Christ; this is the blood of Christ. I would hand the priest the brass plate, and he'd rinse any captured particles or drops into the chalice and then drink the holy water. But Father O'Donnell's hands were jerking from side to side so fast I couldn't keep up. I swerved every which way to follow his movements, panicking about my fate if I let one crumb or drop land on the floor—everlasting hell.

After mass, the church cleared, and the kids went outside to wait for me on the cement staircase. I was about to step into the sacristy to take off the cassock when I heard Father O'Donnell's gravelly voice.

"D'arl, I am just going to put away these heavy vestments—I'll be right back. Can you please kneel by the altar and wait for me? Say a few prayers while y'er at it."

I did what he said without responding, but as I knelt there, instead of praying, I thought about what Mother had told me about a priest bothering Uncle Andy when he was my age, and planned what I would do if things went badly: I would jump to my feet, run to find the kids and never return.

I heard the priest's steps approaching. He stopped right behind me and firmly placed both hands on my head. He began to whisper fervently in Latin. The prayer seemed to go on forever. When he finally raised his hands, I stood up, feeling stunned. I understood that something important had just happened, but I didn't know what.

"You're a good boy, D'arl," he said, his watery red-veined eyes gazing into mine.

"Thank you, Father."

I HAD DRAGGED the kids to church in part to get out of the house, but also because I hoped it would be good for us. Maybe God would help us get out of the nightmarish situation we were living in at home, or maybe some nice couple would approach us—offer to adopt us. I bribed my siblings and cousin Clifford with spending money and a promise to take them to the drive-in diner on the Athabasca hilltop for burgers, fries and milkshakes afterward. Ned had given us money for the weekend the night he arrived for a week-long visit. "Here, T'airl. Hang on to this for me. Take a hunderd for yous, and don't give me nothin' while I'm drinkin'." He turned to Mother and laughed. "He's my little Jew." Ned's words sounded harsh, yet his voice was gentle. I was bewildered, but quickly concluded he must have meant that Jewish people were trustworthy and smart. I smiled awkwardly and tucked the wad into the front pocket of my jeans.

The sun was warm. Freshly arrived spring birds were twittering, and pussy willows had just started to pop out. Usually these things made me dizzy with delight, but today I was numb. After eating, we wandered down to the shores of the Athabasca to see how the spring thaw was going. The river there was even swifter and wider than I remembered it being in Smith. It had overflowed its bank, and last year's spent cattails and the budding red willows were at least a foot deep in water. Chunks of ice bobbed and swirled along with the current.

Back at the house, the usual routine kicked in. I told the kids to wait at the door while I crept inside to see if it was safe for us all to go in, or at least safe enough for us to sneak in together and scoot up the stairs.

There was an eerie quiet in the house. The table was covered with beer bottles, and a green cardboard Pilsner case sat empty on the floor. My guitar leaned crookedly against the wall. What could be going on?

Then I saw her. I gasped and froze. Mother was alone in the living room beside the couch on all fours, naked. She had curved horns coming out of her head, like the devils in the illustrations of hell the Sisters had showed us when we were little, and she was moaning something I couldn't understand.

Satan! She'd become Satan!

I was sure she didn't see me. With one hand I frantically waved the kids in and then climbed the stairs after them, taking the steps two at a time. I ushered everyone into the girls' room, closed its door, then went into mine. I kneeled beside my bed, and the words poured out of me:

> Our Father who art in heaven
> Hallowed be thy name.
> Thy kingdom come.
> Thy will be done
> on earth as it is in heaven.

Then a plea: "Oh God, please take her... please take her!"

By now I was heaving with dry sobs, horrified that I had asked God to take my mother and had meant it with all my heart. What would happen to the kids—and to me? Would the foster home take them back, along with me this time, or would the social workers split us up? Would we end up back in the city? Was Rory's offer of adoption still open? I decided I would write him a letter.

What came out of my mouth next surprised me:

"God, please—oh, please, don't let me *ever* have kids. Never— unless I can be a good father and never hurt them. Please don't let me turn out like Mother!"

I heard the bottom stairs creak. Damn, she was coming up here!

"Gaylene! Momma girl, where are you?"

"Don't answer, Gaylene!" I ordered.

"Where are you kids? Where d'ja go today? I didn't say yous could go anywhere!"

Nobody answered.

"Keep your door closed!" I growled.

"You can't just go out when you want to, Gaylene! Travis—where are you? Holly? Crystal? You kids are gonna get it!"

I opened my door. She was in the narrow hallway, clothed now, grasping Swede's doubled-over black leather belt in her hand. The horns were gone, but her eyes were still glassy.

"Gaylene! Get out here now! You're gonna get a lickin'!"

I stepped in front of her.

"No, Mom. Leave them alone. Please."

"Get outta my way! Now! They need a lickin', Darrel. I'm the boss here. I'm Mom!"

"Then give me a lickin', Mother. You're not touching the kids. You're drunk!"

By now, I could hear the chorus of the kids wailing. Even Clifford was crying.

"Darrel James! Get outta my way! Think you're a big shot *moniyaw,* but yer not. You know that."

She reached for the glass knob on their door.

I forced myself in front of her. She pushed me. I fell over, vibrating with terror, then jumped to my feet and charged at her. When she thrust her arms out to block me, I grabbed them, and we swung in a circle. Once she had her back to the stairs, I pushed with all my strength. She was light, like a sprite.

She flew backwards. I grimaced at the thuds as she did a reverse somersault down the three steps to the landing, then tumbled down the rest of the wooden stairs.

Silence.

"Oh... NOOOO!" I yelled. "What did I do? I didn't mean it. Don't let her die."

I raced down the stairs.

She was sitting on the bottom step hunched over, face screwed up with pain. Droplets of blood were oozing out of a small cut on her forehead.

"Oh, Mom. I'm so sorry. I didn't mean to hurt you."

"Help me to bed, Son," she groaned.

I leaned over, pulled her up and walked her to her dark bedroom.

Back in the living room, I sat in the blue armchair and sobbed. I was upset at what had just happened, but I had gained a new understanding of drunken adults—their amazing physical weakness. I would never again have the same fear around them.

When I had calmed down I went into the kitchen to find the largest butcher knife we had. Holding the knife behind my back, I opened the door to the girls' room. They bustled over, wrapped their arms around me. We stood in a tight huddle for a long time. When they let go, I showed Gaylene and Travis the big knife.

"Listen to me. If this ever happens again, if Mother or anyone comes after you kids when I'm not here, close the door and jam this knife into the door frame."

I thought about Debbie in Calgary. I had to call and tell her this was happening. I was full of remorse.

Why had I come back to live with Mother? Why had I brought the kids back to this? How could I have been so naive—thinking I could change her? How would we get through this hell?

Should I approach Father O'Donnell, I wondered? After all, the priest from Smith had got rid of the Devil at Auntie Rosie's house once by sprinkling holy water all over, burning incense and chanting in Latin.

IN OUR FAMILY, the first weekend in May was an emotional time— Mother's Day and Mother's birthday one right after the other. This year they were on the same day, Sunday, May 9. Debbie and Greggie had sent cards for both occasions. Greggie always picked oversized flowery ones with gushing love poems inside. I wondered where he found them, and if they made Mother think he loved her more than Debbie and I did. Last year I had chosen both my cards carefully, knowing what the competition would be like, only to end up tearing them to shreds in frustration at Mother's behaviour and then being overwhelmed by guilt. What would happen this year? Would Mother celebrate quietly?

Would she go to the bar at the Union Hotel, or would there be a big drunken party at our house? Luckily, I still had enough money to take the kids to the movies. Or maybe that wasn't so lucky: *Love Story* was playing in town that week, and I had already made us sit through it three nights in row.

By the third night, we were all sick of hearing the opening of the schmaltzy theme song and the silly line, "Love means never having to say you're sorry."

After our third viewing, I lay in my bed thinking about that line and the intensity of my reaction to it. Leave *sorry* alone. Sometimes that's all you had to hold on to, like when someone smashed a beer bottle across the face of the person you loved more than anyone; wore your new buckskin jacket to the bar and got it torn to shreds in a brawl; or disappeared for a week at a time, leaving a thirteen-year-old to look after four hungry kids with no food and no money. At least she said *sorry* after each of these things. What if she hadn't?

When we got home on the fourth night of *Love Story*, Ned, Mom, Swede and Uncle Andy were all passed out. The house was a disaster— overflowing ashtrays, puddles of spilled beer and whiskey, a stack of dirty plates in the sink. Johnny Horton's voice sang "Whispering Pines," but the needle was stuck and skipping— *ispering   aines   ispering aines*—probably from Mother dragging the arm across the record back to the beginning. I sent the kids up to their room and asked Travis to sleep in the girls' room that night. I had a plan.

I crept down the squeaky stairs and found what I was looking for: two packs of Rothmans cigarettes and a full bottle of Prince of Denmark wine. Back in my room, I leaned a chair against the door so nobody could come in; lit a paraffin candle left over from the last power outage and set it on the cardboard box that served as our bedside table. I found the cassette on which I had recorded all my favorite 45s, inserted a single earbud and turned up the volume on the portable cassette player Ned had given me. The lowest bass and highest treble notes were fuzzy, but it didn't matter. Holding a restaurant-style juice glass full of blood-red wine, I stretched out on the bed and lit up a cigarette. I tried to inhale deeply, as I had seen Deb and Greg do, but coughed and sputtered. The first cigarette made me dizzy, but I felt grown-up and free.

After a few sips, a warm numbing came over me. Aha! So this was what they liked, Mother, Debbie and Father O'Donnell. This was why they drank. I was getting happier by the minute, euphoric. I stood up, tucking the tape recorder under one arm so I could dance around the room, trying out the moves Greggie had shown me, snapping the fingers of my free hand as I did a partial spin. I heard myself laugh. Whatever had made me think it was my job to protect and feed the kids or to control Mother? And who cared what happened to the six hundred dollars of Ned's that I had hidden in my closet? If they demanded it when they ran out of booze, I'd give it to them—that would mean more booze for me!

My wine—liquid sunshine—splashed away the stress of trying to fit in at school and rise above the gossip about us being poor, being Indian. Of having to avoid Darcy Burtys and Shirley Brown, two redheads who for some reason had targeted me—Shirley with insults and Darcy with kicks to the head or stomach in PE class. If only they could see me now.

I smiled as I thought about last week's public speaking competition: getting up in front of a couple hundred white people, speaking at a podium, dressed in striped bell bottoms and a terry cloth T-shirt while everyone else wore dress shirts and slacks. That had taken nerve, and I won. I stretched out on my bed again and looked over at my new friend—the Prince of Denmark. From now on, life would be a lark.

For two days I stayed holed up like that, sneaking food and bathroom breaks when nobody was around. On the third day, I went to school. That morning, right after the roll call, Mrs. Olsen, my English and choir teacher, handed out a grammar worksheet and then asked me to step into the hallway with her. Her look was intense.

"What is going on, Darrel? You've been my top student, but lately you're failing."

I stood silently, not knowing what to say and afraid I would start to blubber if I even began. Her eyes, solid-blue marbles, held my gaze while she gave me a mini-lecture, pausing between sentences for effect.

"Well, whatever it us, pull up your bootstraps. You can do it. You have to!" she concluded. Her face softened. "I have some good news for you, too. Miss Emmons and I applied for you to attend the provincial music workshop in Camrose this summer, for singing. You're in."

Indian Princesses

THE DAY MOTHER found Greggie's letter, I had run home upbeat and excited, not at all prepared for the scene that awaited me. I planned to practise trumpet for the upcoming Kiwanis Festival before the other kids got home. As usual, I was going to blast out the melodies over and over until I got them right.

Mother was sitting at the bottom of the stairs, holding an envelope in one hand and some papers in the other. Scattered on the step behind her were a few photo strips—black and white, the type we loved to get taken in the booth at the Edmonton bus depot, four for a quarter. I went over and picked one up. My older brother Greg and my uncle Danny were huddled together, smiling. They wore glossy lipstick, puffy wigs and low-cut blouses. Oh. Oh, she had found the letter.

My heart sank. Two weeks earlier, I had opened a letter from Greggie and then hidden it among the folds of the shirts in my improvised clothes closet. I dreaded Mother's reaction, worrying she might have some kind of a nervous breakdown or escape into days of rowdy drinking and partying.

"Ooooh. You found it, Ma. I was gonna give it to you. I was just waiting for the right time."

Taking it from her, I reread the first line of the letter. The flourishes of Greggie's handwriting made me smile, despite the content.

"My name is Trina now, Mom. I hope you can love me for who I am. I will always love you."

"It's okay—I had to find out somehow," Mother mumbled. "Didn't think it would be like this, though. Can't believe it. Jus' can't. *Sosquats*."

"I know, Mom." I held back tears.

"He was just here at Christmas. I thought something was different, but he was dressed normal," Mother said. "Now he's tellin' us he's got *chochos*—he's takin' hormones to grow them."

She rested her forehead in the palms of her hands and rocked back and forth. I sat beside her and took one of her strong hands in mine.

"Cheezus, he's only nineteen," she said, then paused and looked me in the eye. "We havta a-ssept him, Son. It don't matter. We can't discard him."

I gathered up the envelope and pictures and returned them to my closet.

THE KIWANIS FESTIVAL was in Edmonton. Mother was dead set against it at first, but I convinced her to let me stay with Greggie for the weekend. I wanted to see for myself what was going on. And I thought being around family might help him go back to being himself.

Mr. Stychyn, the bus driver, was the father of my bubbly and popular classmate Lori. As I took a seat directly behind his, I understood why she bragged about him: he was so clean and official looking in his Greyhound uniform and cap. I sneaked glances at him, and even stared when I thought he wouldn't see, wondering what it would be like to have him for a father. Would he take me fishing and hunting— help me to become a man? Or would he want the same kind of secret relationship Rory had forced on me? Did Mr. Stychyn, like Rory, have a collection of *Playboy* and *Penthouse* magazines hidden in his bedside table? Did all white men?

I thought about the photo of Rory that I had stashed in my trumpet case. As always, I was overcome with a wave of emotions: bitterness over how he had treated Debbie; arousal recalling his intense touch and scent; rage about how he had looked me in the eye so earnestly and said he could never have an Indian child. I was good enough to touch, but not good enough to be a relation.

The morning bus was full. It was my third Greyhound trip, but the first where I didn't have to hurry to the back to puke from the smell. I opened my wallet to count the spending money I had retrieved from the sky-blue Player's tobacco can—the cache for my paper route money.

As I watched people clamber on and off the bus in the tiny towns of Colinton and Boyle, I wondered what they would think if they saw my brother dressed as a girl. I was thankful that he wouldn't do it around me, out of respect for family. I would ask him about it, though. Why he did it, and why on earth he had sent those pictures to Mother.

THE BUS PULLED into the dimly lit bay. I craned my neck to see if Greg was there. I jumped off the bottom metal step, giddy with curiosity and excitement, and looked around. The bus depot was packed and smoky. Poor white folks, weary-looking seniors, lots of Indians who looked like they could be our relatives, couples and lone mothers with kids, and one black family, likely from Amber Valley, a colony of families whose ancestors had escaped slavery in the United States. Two Indian men stood in the doorway pleading for cigarettes and money.

Then I saw him.

He had hair. Big hair. A lofty bouffant wig, brunette with red highlights. Phosphorescent teal and royal-blue feather earrings hung nearly to his shoulders. And he wore patent leather platform boots—white, with six-inch heels. The boots went up above the knees, revealing black fishnet stockings. Nipples pressed convincingly against his blouse. God, how could they look so real? Falsies? Couldn't be—that was flesh. Yet, through the lipstick, false eyelashes and carefully drawn eyebrows, there he was, my brother. I recognized his chubby face and toothy smile.

But who was the petite figure behind him? She had the face of a geisha, and her hair was a backcombed bubble. She wore a white vinyl jacket and black suede boots with platform soles.

"Darrel—Dades! You made it." Greg sashayed toward me.

I was trembling, unsure how to respond. My mother's voice was a broken record in my head: *Havta a-ssept him Darrel... Can't discard him. Don't discard him.*

Then all at once the petite figure called out the nickname I least liked: "*Lapatak*—Potato!" Oh of course, Uncle Danny. Wherever Greggie went, he would follow. They were only a year apart and had been inseparable since childhood, but they had a relationship filled with jealousy, love and hellish sibling rivalry. Greg fought with Danny almost as violently as he did with Debbie.

Now they shuffled over to embrace me, each placing an arm tenderly around my shoulder.

I glanced behind me. Thank God, Mr. Stychyn was nowhere in sight.

"Hair for days!" I teased as I looked at Greggie.

"You like it, Dades?" He struck a flirty pose.

We gathered up my little red suitcase and trumpet and walked toward the exit. Was this the life I had to look forward to? Would I end up like them here in the city, so openly wild and crazy? I had never wanted to be a girl, but I wasn't tough or girl-crazy like my older cousins, and Debbie always raved about my smooth complexion and long eyelashes. Then there was everything that had happened with Rory.

THE CAB PULLED up to a place called Riverview Towers—exactly the type of high-rise I had dreamed about living in with Debbie.

We took the elevator up to the seventeenth floor.

"Wow!" I felt lightheaded and giddy. "This is amazing!" Plush green shag carpet. A fake crystal chandelier in the dining room. Through the sliding balcony doors I could see the murky North Saskatchewan River pushing its way through a wide and meandering valley.

"Keith stays here with me," Greg said flatly.

"Who's Keith?"

Danny giggled. "Her boy toy."

"And Phil is coming to take us shopping at Hudson's Bay this aft."

I wasn't going to ask who Phil was, but I pieced it together when he showed up. In his forties, I guessed, balding, with a few strands of hair slicked over the top of his head and a gold band on his left ring finger.

Greg puckered to give Phil a noisy smack on the lips. "Look at him. Fifty, but looks thirty-five, doesn't he, and no paunch! Still owns the car lot where I used to work, remember? And oh, you should see the photos of his kids, ever cute. Wanna come shopping with us, Dades?"

I told them I wanted to stay and practise the trumpet, but as soon as they left I put it down and went to Greggie's bedroom. I fumbled through his dresser drawers. Sleek panties, red, black and cobalt blue; fancy bras, corsets and garter belts. Lace trim on everything. Jesus. Who did Greggie wear all this fancy lingerie for? Not one stitch of men's underwear. I stumbled over to his closet: dresses, blouses, skirts and high heels. In the bathroom I threw open the drawers and cabinet doors—foundation, mascara, lip gloss, eyebrow pencils, a tool for curling eyelashes, fingernail polish, feminine deodorant spray, Secret deodorant for ladies, a Gillette razor and a can of shaving cream. Everything Mother and Debbie had, except the dial birth control dispenser and the blue rubber douche bubble with the white goose neck.

I went back to the bedroom and fingered the panties. I let myself enjoy touching everything for a moment. How strange—how exciting that these things could cover a male body and make it look feminine. But was Greggie a guy anymore? It seemed he had put that all behind him.

Then I started to feel afraid. What was I doing, and what could it lead to? There was no way I was going to be like Danny, or my brother—no way in hell. I would become a man like Ned, Swede or Uncle Andy, even though I didn't like the way any of them had turned out. I slammed the drawer and pivoted back to the bathroom mirror. I did look kind of like a girl with my overgrown wavy hair and pretty face.

Did anyone else think so?

GREG'S LOUD CACKLE. The door flew open, and he and Danny strutted into the apartment with Phil in tow. I caught a blast of sweet orange and grapefruit, roses, geraniums and musk. They must have sampled every perfume in the store. Phil set up two new lamps with amber glass bases and large lampshades on the end tables. He stood back looking content, then put his arms around Greg and kissed him for a full minute.

The kiss flustered me horribly. It made me think of the only kissing session I had ever had with Rory, one night while we were lying on the orange sectional couch. I hadn't liked the ashtray taste of his mouth, but the sensation of his lips on mine and his muscular tongue exploring my mouth had excited me in ways I couldn't understand.

Once Phil was out the door, Greg put on music and ordered food from Kentucky Fried Chicken. Soon some other strange and interesting people started to arrive. First there was Monica, in a blond wig, then a tall, full-bodied character who burst in without knocking. A humid waft of fancy perfume confirmed his/her arrival.

"*Bonswah, mes amoouurs!*" she gushed, and swept into the room. Flaming bronze hair—a masterpiece of curls, swoops and waves. Thick but tasteful makeup; a beauty mark to the left of full crimson lips.

"Lisa LaJoie! *Mad'mwazelle* from *parlay-vous*! *Com-on talleh vooo, ma cherie?!*" Greg kissed Lisa on both cheeks.

"*Salut, ma chère. T'es donc belle!*"

"Lisa and Monica, this is Darrel, my little brother."

"*Oh, mon dieu—t'es cute...* such a sweetie! Oh, the girls are gonna love yeee-*ooo!*" Lisa's plump lips smooched first my left cheek, then my right.

I robotically chewed the chicken and fries. Then I excused myself, saying I was tired, and went into the bedroom. I lay down on the mattress on the floor, baffled. What kind of fantasy were Greg, Danny and the others living? Surely it couldn't go on—something had to happen to stop it and bring them all back to reality.

Then I remembered a magazine article Uncle Danny had been obsessed with a few years earlier in Smith: *Ex-GI Becomes Blond Beauty*. There were photos of a glamorous blond who had once been a homely soldier in the US Army. George Jorgensen had had to go all the way to Denmark to become Christine, but that didn't discourage Danny. "I'm going to be a woman one day, marry a handsome man and have lots of kids," he announced to anybody in the family who would listen. The adults, including Mosom, just chuckled. "Oh, for chrissakes, you expecting a miracle or what?" the older cousins would say.

Nobody had ever scolded Greggie or Danny for dressing up as girls and playing house like that, even when they drafted male cousins to play their husbands. None of the kids dared to tease Greg or Danny when an adult was around, but some of them sniped and bullied when they thought they could get away with it.

A FRANTIC VOICE startled me awake. Lisa LaJoie. "Ehhhhh! Look! Hur*ry*—get h'out *'der* on de bal*con*, grab—Dee-*h'ann*! *Vite!* uurry h'up!"

The song "Lola," which I had heard over and over during the course of the evening, was swirling in my head. I didn't really understand the opening—about meeting a woman in a bar in North Soho. Where was North Soho? How could champagne taste like Coca-Cola?

I dashed into the hallway. Saw Greg's pallid face. He covered his mouth and pointed toward the balcony.

"Holy fuck! He's climbin' onto the railing." Keith's voice.

The balcony door was wide open. Monica and some guy were outside struggling with Danny. My uncle was kneeling on a chair that was pushed up against the railing, trying to stand up. The city lights behind him sparkling as far as the eye could see.

"I can do it." His shrill voice didn't sound like him at all. "Let me go-o-o. I wanna *fly-y-y-y*!"

More voices:

> "Whaddaya think he done?" "Speed."
> "Maybe a bit o' rye too."
> "Too much booze." "He smoke any weed?"
> "Dunno."
> "Jeezus—hope they get him down in time!"
> "Fuck—crazy... Never seen nothin' like this!"
> "Fuck it, let her fly..."

The song continued playing in my head—something about boys becoming girls and vice versa. I got the first part, because I had heard Uncle Danny longing for this aloud many times, but the part about girls becoming boys didn't make sense to me. How would that work?

Greggie was frantic, hunched over and blubbering. "Please no—no. Diane. I love you, girl... love you so much."

I thought about the part of "Lola" that said something about being a man—not a very masculine man—still, the singer was glad he was a man, and that's how I felt.

The ruckus and confusion dragged on, but finally they got Danny down. A few people carried him toward the bathroom to run a shower.

He was shouting and crying in a coarse voice, legs jerking, arms flailing, trying to break free. "Leave me alone! Leave me! Lemme go home! Greggie! *Astum! Kwee ah hu!* Help meeeeeee… *niMAMA… niMAMA…* help me!" He was calling for his mother, my Granny Adele. I went back into the bedroom, my head in a fog.

MORNING. THE APARTMENT was quiet. The fusion of odours—spilt beer, stale smoke and sickly blue cheese—put me in a dark mood. Dishes were stacked in the sink, covered with chicken bones, cigarette butts, wrinkled fries and dried ketchup. Greg and Keith sprawled on the Hide-A-Bed, intertwined and snoring. Greg's wig was draped over one of the new lamps.

I grabbed my suitcase and trumpet and tiptoed into the dimly lit hallway. I stepped off the elevator on the main floor, then walked out through the glass doors of Riverview Towers. Spring air and sunshine. When I heard the door close behind me, I realized I hadn't memorized Greggie's apartment number or phone number. Just as well—I wouldn't be back to spend another night as I had planned. Instead, I would take the six o'clock bus back to Athabasca.

At the high school, Miss Emmons was already perched on the high conductor's stool in the band room. It was soothing to see someone normal—a woman wearing a simple blouse, ordinary dress slacks and sensible sandals.

When we heard that our band got an honourable mention in the Kiwanis Festival, Miss Emmons was pleased. She turned to our section and said the trumpets had played beautifully.

THERE WOULD BE other trips to visit Greggie. After a while, I got over the shame of accompanying drag queens and learned to camp it up. Greggie and Danny bought me treats and trinkets. I worried about how they were earning their money. They talked and laughed about it openly.

"I turned an amazing trick last night, girl—gave me twenty bucks extra. Guess I blew his mind!"

"This one trick was wild. Gave it to me rough, but then turned me over, kissed me and rubbed my belly. Said he loves us Indian princesses, our smooth brown skin. Said we're more passionate."

"Princesses? Ha! That's me alright," Greggie laughed. "Princess *Whatta-pity*. Ya workin tonight, girl? Yer sittin' on a gold mine."

During these conversations, I hid my embarrassment and pretended I didn't understand. I wanted to be open and hip too. But most of all, I longed to tell my brother and Danny about Rory. I missed him like I missed my father, even though what we had done was so clearly wrong. Who could I talk to about my feelings if not these two? But I didn't dare.

THE LAST TIME I saw Greg in Edmonton, I was sixteen and travelling from Calgary to Athabasca on a Thanksgiving weekend. I had tried to call in advance to see if I could spend the night, but his phone number was no longer in service. I hid my guitar and suitcase in some brush on the hillside above the river and went to find him. As I had imagined, he was walking along Jasper Avenue. As the traffic flowed by him, some cars slowed. One stopped. Greg, or should I say Trina, went over, stuck his head into the passenger side window, then stood up and guffawed. I scurried over and tapped him on the shoulder. He turned around, fist cocked—ready to fight.

"Greg. Sorry, I mean *Trina*—it's me."

"Who the hell... Oh, Dades! Sorry. You scared me. Don't ever do that!"

He arranged to meet me at Dolly Donuts on Jasper around six that evening, but I waited and waited and he didn't show. I wandered up Jasper Avenue until I came to a movie theatre. After sitting through the seven and nine-thirty showings of *Jesus Christ Superstar*, I staggered out of the theatre dumbfounded; "I Don't Know How to Love Him," sung by Mary Magdalene, had shaken me to the core.

Still vibrating, I walked the few blocks to the bus depot to use the washroom and buy my ticket for the morning bus to Athabasca. I was at the urinal when a tall, good-looking man wearing silver-rimmed glasses came and stood beside me. He peed, but then started rocking his hand until it was apparent he had captured my attention.

"Hi. I'm Norm. Wanna go for a Coke and a ride in my Mustang?"

He was white, well-spoken, with thick auburn sideburns. His Mustang had a new-car smell. I leaned back, wondering if this was how Greg and Danny felt each time they went off with a stranger—a bizarre feeling that it was too good to be true, but also unease about what was to follow, or what might happen if things got out of control.

Norm was gentle and patient. He warned me that we had to keep things secret; he could be in a lot of trouble for being with someone my age. The next morning over coffee, he asked me to read and comment on an article he had written for a social work magazine. It was about the apprehension and abuse of Native youth.

Eddies of the Makhabn

ONE GLOOMY FALL day, a wolf began to howl inside of me. Perhaps it was touching my girlfriend that aroused yearnings I couldn't seem to control. Maybe it was something else. But suddenly, morning, noon and night, I craved the physical intensity I had experienced with Rory. There was no reprieve. It might have been my imagination, but my longing seemed to get worse when the full moon was reflecting off the eddies of the Bow River. I was glad to be back near the Bow, the river I had first admired in Canmore. I was amazed that it didn't freeze in the winter like the Athabasca River did, with a dramatic and scary thaw every spring.

My departure from Athabasca the previous June was deliberate, but it felt impulsive. After Mother had partied for a week at Auntie Helen's house, I gave her an ultimatum: come home or I will go live with Debbie. Ten days later, I repeated the warning. On the eleventh day, when she still hadn't returned, I went to see our social worker and demanded she give me a one-way Greyhound ticket to Calgary, threatening to hitch-hike if she didn't. I left while the kids were at school. One of them, likely Gaylene, would find my tear-stained note of explanation on the kitchen table that day. My five-hour bus ride was filled with anxiety and sorrow. How could I leave them? I was the one who had convinced Mother to take them out of the foster home; who knew what would happen now? What would life be like with Debbie? Was she partying too?

Spring hailstorm, blurry vistas, dead deer, thunder and lightning. Darkness. New bus depot. No Debbie. Pay phone. Taxi. Basement. Drunken Debbie. Foam mattress on the floor. A boot flew through the air. Glass shattered.

GRADE TEN AT Western Canada High School in Calgary. I was astonished to be playing the lead role in the British musical comedy *HMS Pinafore* and dating Lorna, the daughter of a doctor. The summer music workshop Mrs. Olsen and Miss Emmons had lobbied to get me into was already paying off, and life was definitely better in Calgary.

Did my new constant craving cause me to emit some kind of signal to those around me? I didn't know the answer, but opportunities started to appear everywhere with other guys. Girls were attracted to me too, but they were good girls, and the likelihood of having sex with them was nil. Lengthy kisses only led to frustration. Strolling through Central Memorial Park, and on Prince's Island, I noticed guys looking at me the way Rory had. At the shopping centre, men sometimes tried to lure me to hidden corners. At first I wondered if they were undercover security guards, but their lustful looks soon betrayed their intent.

One weekday afternoon, in the grimy downstairs washroom of the Hudson's Bay department store, I was peeing at the urinal when the door to the cubicle at the far end opened to reveal a short, pale man with reddish hair. He blatantly displayed his excitement. I pivoted to leave, but he brushed past me, grabbed my arm and led me to the base of the stairwell. Ushering me beneath it, he began to grab at my clothes and kiss my neck. It turned me on, instantly.

As I wandered home, I wrestled with the guilt. Was I queer? Of course not. Rory wasn't. The guy I had just touched wasn't either— he'd worn a wedding band. He had a wife and probably kids. I had a girlfriend. All I knew was that sex with men was intense and brought temporary solace.

MY NEW BEST friend, Donna Massey, had suggested I try out for the Central United Church choir, where she sang soprano. They needed tenors, and if I got in, the two of us would have more time together. I was thrilled at the idea, but hesitant for two reasons. Donna had told me about Mr. Erickson, the strict choir director who was also the chorus master for the Calgary Philharmonic. And as kids, we had been brainwashed to think that entering the church of a faith other than Catholic was a mortal sin. After thinking it over for a couple of weeks I decided to attend Central United for the music; I wouldn't listen to the preaching, participate in the prayers or take communion, I told myself. Every Sunday morning, I dressed in my best clothes and walked downtown to the church alone.

Magnificent brass pipes on the antique organ with its four keyboards. A dark wooden pulpit that was more like a stage. Gothic-inspired vaulted ceilings leading up to a magnificent dome—and tons of intricate stained glass artwork. So this was why the priests and nuns hadn't wanted us going to such places—this was impressive and inspiring compared to the ominous interiors of the Catholic churches I had seen. No dramatic crucifix of a near-naked Jesus with crusted blood around a piercing crown of thorns. No sad statues of the mother of God to beg to for mercy and kindness. I left with a flyer about a youth group that offered counselling and personal growth retreats at a place called the Banff Centre, which was just twenty-five kilometres from Canmore.

On Sundays after church, Donna always invited me to go for lunch at a little restaurant in the basement of a nearby hotel. I never had money, so she paid. When she found out I was secretly teaching myself to play piano on an old upright in a storage room at our school, she got me a key to a wing of the church where there was a piano I could use.

At school, in spite of strict rules forbidding loitering in the hallways or classrooms, I began to hang out in the music room at lunchtime and after my last class each day, wondering if I would be turned away. Mr. Ferguson, the music teacher, was always there, scanning arrangements for the choir and band and listening to classical music on the high-fidelity sound system. His chalky complexion contrasted with his bushy chestnut-coloured moustache and beard. The intensity of his gaze was shielded by rectangular wire-framed glasses.

The popular kids (or was it the nerdy ones?) were up on a ladder, sculpting images by pressing yellow rope into the grooves between the beige bricks of the back wall. They were all so chummy with each other, and with the teacher. I was too timid to join in their banter and laughter, so I stood off to the side, pretending to study the scores of my solos in HMS *Pinafore*. A couple of times I asked Mr. Ferguson to play difficult parts of the melody on the piano for me, and he did.

Some days after school, Mr. Ferguson motioned for me to join him beside the turntable and console at the front of the music room. "Sit down, Darrel. Have a listen. Tell me what you think of this." One day it would be Vivaldi's *Four Seasons*, the next Pachelbel's Canon or "Clair de Lune" by Debussy.

I felt intimidated by Mr. Ferguson's invitations. What would the other kids think about our close contact? Why had he chosen me for special treatment? I didn't understand classical music, either; I didn't know what I could say after listening without sounding stupid. In the most forceful violin parts, his lively brown eyes would brighten even more, and a blissful smile would cross his face. I didn't understand his reaction, but I knew I wanted to hear music the way he heard it and feel what he felt. During our after-school visits, he soon began giving me private lectures about composers, arrangements, instrumentation and interpretation. I learned to distinguish the oboe from the clarinet, the French horn from the trumpet, the cello from the string bass, major from minor, augmented from diminished. Sometimes I zoned out and other times I was fascinated. Mostly I simply wanted to spend time there, with him and his music.

Mr. Ferguson's hands were smooth, with long, strong fingers, and when he picked up his baton to set the tempo they became hypnotic. I felt at ease with him, but as I walked home I worried. Had he somehow guessed what had happened between Rory and me, and did he think that I wanted secret encounters with him there in the music room?

Then, one day, to my astonishment, Mr. Ferguson asked if I would like to join him as a singer in the Calgary Philharmonic Chorus. "They need good tenors, Darrel. I'll help you with your parts," he offered. Donna was the first one I shared the news with.

Over the next few years, I yearned for even more time with Mr. Ferguson and got it, not only singing together in the Calgary Philharmonic and a church choir, but also playing trumpet in a brass quartet, a concert band and a jazz ensemble and singing in a madrigal group, all under his direction. Christmas carol fests in hotels, shopping malls and department stores; evening rehearsals followed by pizza at Stromboli's. Mr. Ferguson became a mentor and surrogate parent. Without him I would not have made it through high school. But in spite of his calming influence and fatherly company, I still craved and sought out intense sex with strangers.

THE POUNDING OF the timpani beneath the lush vocal harmonies; the precisely timed smashing of the great cymbals; hundreds of voices chanting in syncopated unison—together, they became a river of harmony and dissonance. "O Fortuna" from *Carmina Burana*: I was sure I was learning what bliss felt like. The house lights had been dimmed as usual; there was a dark void above the thousands of concert-goers in Calgary's Jubilee Auditorium. I was impressed by the giant flock of magpies we created as the tuxedoed choir, and by the similarly clad but seated orchestra members. We were completely focused, intently following the movements of the baton wielded by our temperamental conductor, Maurice Handford. The only sad part about the whole experience was that none of my family ever attended my performances. Fortunately, a Cree friend of Debbie's named Marsha often did, and she took me for lunch afterward to encourage me.

I knew it was good for me to be mixing with these well-educated white folks, but I worried that someone would notice my furtive glances at the eye-catching baritones and tenors. Blair, the lead tenor, didn't respond when I said hello. But he was a prestigious lawyer; Mr. Erickson, our choir director, had publicly congratulated him on becoming Queen's Counsel.

Then there was Dale: twenty-five or so, slightly taller than I was, boyish Ukrainian face. He sang second tenor, and I knew he had a good job and owned a condo. He invited me out for dinner, ordered wine even though I was only sixteen and invited me home for dessert and more drinks. I loved the attention and his generosity, even though I knew where it was leading. His kisses were playful, making it less traumatic for me to kiss a man. I felt exhilarated lying beside him, but I went back out to the couch to sleep. I was surprised the next morning when, over a cup of steaming coffee, he told me he was in a long-term open relationship with his roommate Peter.

I was taken aback when I realized that Dale and Peter were proudly gay and that all their friends and family knew they were a couple. They started taking me with them to underground gay clubs in downtown Calgary, where I would tingle with repulsion, dread and excitement. It was shocking to see men dancing together in lines or in pairs, slow dancing and necking. There was whispered speculation all around us of another raid and mass arrest by the Calgary police. But my giddiness mounted as the devil-may-care attitude of the club-goers rubbed off on me.

Repulsion dominated my other feelings, though. The week after a club visit I would plunge myself more deeply into my relationship with my girlfriend, necking with her aggressively in public and directing all my efforts into acting manly.

I didn't talk to Debbie or anyone else about what was happening. She had her own issues to contend with. She had left her truck driver boyfriend, John, and was now involved with Gary, a Cree man, who was violent and almost constantly drunk or high. I was worried my sister might have questions about where I had been, but usually, she wasn't home. When we did have time together, our conversation was lighthearted. She didn't ask me why I let my hair grow long or bought plaid pants and platform shoes with the bit of money I earned from working weekends at the pizza place with her and her friend Darlene.

THE KREBS CYCLE and the periodic table didn't inspire me nearly as much as the jazz band or the madrigal group, so it was biology and chemistry classes I skipped to appease my fierce urges. Downtown there was no shortage of white men in suits, all wearing wedding bands, who were eager to find a dark alcove, hotel room or car for a few minutes of stolen ecstasy.

I didn't understand what was going on with me. What was causing this obsession? At night, as I lay in bed, confusion and frustration welled up in me. Was it a good thing that white guys from a higher social class wanted intimacy with me, accepted me? I thought it was, but then I remembered that Rory had married Debbie and still didn't accept her for who she was. Did lust trump bigotry or aggravate it?

I always felt a blaze of anger as I recalled his words: *I can't have a baby with an Indian woman. You understand, right, Darrel?*

One day when I got home from school, Debbie was gone—her clothes closet empty. A few weeks later, she called to tell me she had decided to go work for her friend Darlene who had relocated to a tiny place beyond the Alberta badlands, called Youngstown, to manage a restaurant and gas bar. I was left on my own at age sixteen. I scrambled to find another part-time job to pay the rent and have spending money: part-time sales clerk at the Hudson's Bay store downtown.

TOM SELLECK'S TWIN came over and wrapped his arms around me, held on. Exciting French cologne flooded my nostrils. His moustache tickled my bare neck in a humid heat exchange: I was still sweating from "dancing in the spirit" to the lively hymn my friend Sherry had just pumped out on the piano for our evening worship session.

"I'm Gresh. Guess I should have introduced myself before the hug." Flashy, perfectly filed teeth, shapely rosé lips, fresh breath.

"Uh, hi, Gresh," I stammered.

"My friend Brenda brought me here. She's been raving about John Hutchinson's fellowship for months. I was skeptical of a group that meets in the basement of a United Church. Looks like I was wrong, though. We have to leave early, but we'll be back."

"Oh, praise the Lord," I responded. "So glad you came, Gresh. This is my girlfriend, Marg."

Nervous exchange of smiles all around.

A gust of warm air surprised us as we stepped outside; a December chinook had blown in. Marg's eyes were brimming. "That was powerful, Darrel, the way you set Psalm 140 to song." I walked her to her bus stop, one hand clasping hers and the other holding the handle of my guitar case. A cluster of pigeons gurgled as we made our way through their feast of bread crumbs thrown onto the sidewalk by an elderly man in a long black parka. A chocolate and vanilla pigeon was perched on his outstretched arm.

I went home to the little basement suite I had moved into right after high school, my sixth home in two and a half years in Calgary. The landlady, a devout evangelical, was thrilled when I told her that I too had "found the Lord." Since my closest friend, Rob, had taken me under his wing and introduced me to John Hutchinson's Pentecostal fellowship, I had decided to be celibate, and I spent a lot of time in prayer and studying the New Testament to keep my mind off sex. I became fixated on Paul the Apostle's first letter to the Corinthians, astonished that the Bible spoke so openly about sex and drunkenness:

> 9 *Know ye not that the unrighteous shall not inherit the kingdom of God? Be not deceived: neither fornicators, nor idolaters, nor adulterers, nor effeminate, nor abusers of themselves with mankind.*
>
> 10 *Nor thieves, nor covetous, nor drunkards, nor revilers, nor extortioners, shall inherit the kingdom of God.*

Initially I was devastated by this searing news. Such condemnation! Not just of me and Greggie and Uncle Danny, but also of Debbie and my mother and all the other drinkers in my family. Not one of my relations, it seemed, could be accepted into the Kingdom of God. Without knowing anything about my life, my religious friends assured me now that when I was "born again" my past had been forgiven. It was my future behaviour that mattered. But even if I worked hard to achieve the same forgiveness for my family, it seemed unlikely that would happen. How could Danny and Greg stop being effeminate? And how could I possibly keep Mother, Debbie and Ned from drinking?

One night as I sat cross-legged on the floor fretting, the telephone rang. I assumed it would be Marg, or maybe another friend from the fellowship. But it was Greggie, calling from Vancouver. At first I was speechless, and near tears. I hadn't heard from him for two years and had become convinced that he was dead.

"Darrel, I'm in a methadone treatment program," he explained eagerly. "I have a really understanding addictions doctor. And guess what—I found a surgeon who has committed to doing my sex change. It's not legal here yet, but he's gonna call it something else. Did you hear?

Danny, I mean Diane, already had hers—it was part of an experiment by the Alberta government. They're doing a hundred sex change operations over five years and documenting what happens to the patients. Diane was a perfect candidate—she had been living and working as a woman for more than a year before she joined the program. And seeing a psychiatrist regularly—well, that was easy."

Great, I thought. The competition between those two would never end. I was frustrated by Greggie's excitement about his operation, and I told him so. He wouldn't take my arguments against it into consideration at all.

"Haven't you heard the latest news about Danny?" I demanded. I took the pause to mean that he hadn't. "He, well, I mean, *she* tried to kill herself a few weeks ago. She drank half a bottle of Drano at Mother's place, but she survived."

"Oh my God, how come nobody called me? She's closer to me than anyone!" His voice was tense and high-pitched. "Don't know why she keeps going back to Smith—trying to live there as a woman. Uncle Andy even hit on her, for God's sake!"

I COULDN'T DO anything about Greggie, but I was on a roll with "witnessing." Along with Marg, a United Church minister's daughter, I had brought two other friends, Sylvia and Gerry, "to the Lord."

I met Gerry while he was panhandling outside of the First Baptist Church one Saturday evening. He ended up staying in my basement suite with me. That was reassuring, because my landlady had become convinced her husband was trying to assassinate her, and she called me upstairs daily to sniff the kettle for cyanide. Debbie was back in Calgary now, and after a month, Gerry and I moved in with her and her new boyfriend, Norbert, in a run-down three-storey house in the city's east side. I was confused by Gerry's pretentiousness and spoiled attitude until he explained that his family owned a large insurance firm in Montreal. His parents had split up and he had taken it hard, ending up doing drugs and living on the streets of Montreal before hitchhiking west. I was too blinded by religion to realize or admit that there was a hot physical attraction between Gerry and me.

We travelled to Edmonton with Debbie and Norbert to spend Christmas with Mother and the kids in the rickety green house she had rented near to downtown. Gerry and I slept downstairs with the kids. He gave me a few back massages, climbing onto my buttocks to rub my back sensually while rocking back and forth. I was ecstatic but embarrassed that the kids were watching, and I wondered if they noticed how flustered I was.

Back at the dilapidated house where we lived, Gerry and I noticed that Norbert had replenished his alcohol supply. On the kitchen counter—unopened bottles of Canadian Club rye whisky and Bacardi white rum. Rebuking Satan, we poured the alcohol down the drain. Then, feeling righteous, we went to bed. While Debbie and Norbert were gone, I had the luxury of sleeping in their room instead of on the floor beside my own bed, where Gerry slept.

I was just falling asleep when Gerry moaned my name from the doorway. I rubbed my eyes and looked over to see his svelte hairy chest, muscular legs and white Jockey shorts.

"Brother Darrel—are you having any weird ideas? Like, I think Satan is after us tonight. I'm lying in bed and these images keep popping into my head—of the two of us making out. It's intense. I'm shoving it in your ass and humping the hell outta you! I don't know what to do."

"Let's pray," I offered. And pray we did. We stumbled into the living room and kneeled in front of the couch. Still in our briefs, we held hands and rebuked Satan in Jesus's name.

A few days later, I decided to talk to him about taking our friendship to another level. "Gerry, we've gotten really close, and I am feeling attracted to you for some reason. I had to tell you."

"What the fuck. I ain't no *fag*, man! You should get help."

EARLY IN THE New Year, I got a frantic call from my sister Gaylene. She had recently turned fifteen and was three months pregnant. Mother was already drinking again, even though she had gotten the kids back from the foster home just months before Christmas. There were tears of sadness and joy all around a few days later when Gaylene and I arrived home after her Greyhound trip from Edmonton. We chuckled as we took pictures of her and Debbie side by side, profiling their tummies; Debbie was four months pregnant.

Although Norbert really cared for Debbie and was generous with her, we were grateful that I now had a stable job with decent pay, working as an operating room attendant at Rockyview Hospital. Sheer determination had landed me the job—six months of weekly calls to the human resources department to see if they had even a dishwasher vacancy. I had checked all the job postings each time I went to visit Debbie when she was in the hospital for a week with anemia. I'd learned that any union job would pay three times as much as the minimum wage I was getting as a shipper-receiver at Hibbert Wholesale Vacuum Parts. Now, friends and family were astounded at my good fortune. I had a great position with on-the-job training less than a year after finishing high school. I humoured their regular requests with both true stories from the operating room and the nightmares I had about working there.

Weekdays I sneaked out of the house at five-thirty, trying not to awaken my two pregnant sisters, Gerry or Norbert as I got ready to catch the bus to the hospital. One blustery morning, still drowsy, I checked the case list to see what equipment was needed for the day: total hysterectomy, inguinal hernia, cataract removal, therapeutic D and C, breast implants and laryngoplasty, reduction of abdominal pannus. As I set out the airways, face masks and rubber tubing for each of the six operating theatres, I reread the procedures on the list and realized that it was a male patient having both the breast implants and the laryngoplasty—gender reassignment surgery at the Rockyview?

I thought of my brother Greggie. He was determined to have a sex change operation. Were those surgeries part of his plan—breast implants and an adjustment of his larynx to make his voice higher?

"Good technique Darrel," Liz, the circulating nurse, goaded me later that day. Beads of sweat had formed on my forehead beneath the pale green cotton cap. I gawked at the shiny purple head of the sturdy penis in the grasp of my right hand. I was prepping the patient scheduled for a hernia operation, but usually the swabbing with gauze sponges dripping with cold clear aqueous hibitane didn't have this effect. I looked around at the masked faces of the surgeon, his assistant and the scrub nurse with their latex-gloved hands held slightly below their chins, palms inwards. They were all straining to contain their laughter.

"Maybe you should watch, Liz—could you use some pointers?" My voice echoed in the operating theater as I glanced at her—icy daggers.

The surgeon laughed. "Way to fire back, Darrel. That'll teach you, Liz," he called after her as she ducked into the scrub room for a tray of instruments. I scrambled out of the theater as fast as I could, mortified. How could this happen to me, of all people, in front of the doctors? Did they know? Did they think I was trying to bring on that reaction?

IT WAS A sunny Saturday morning, and for once Rob, Ron and I were all home. The three of us, buddies from high school and church, had decided to become roommates, renting a large old house at the edge of downtown Calgary. Debbie had abruptly ended her brief relationship with Norbert and moved back to Youngstown to live with her future husband Brian, the father of baby Joseph. Gerry was sharing a room—and a bed—with Barry, a nymph-like guitar player with flowing waist-length hair.

As usual, I was the first up and made a large pot of Mocha Java, anticipating a jovial chat in the cozy kitchen. Instead, with coffee in hand, my roommates herded me toward the wingback chair in the living room, told me to have a seat and stood on either side of me as if to block my flight. I had never seen such intensity in Rob's brown eyes, and I was sure I could smell Ron's anger. I felt myself stiffen.

"There's something we've been meaning to talk to you about, Darrel. Ron and I have both discerned this. We think you're demon possessed."

"Me? Possessed?" I heard myself say this and laugh, but I was thinking something different. Could it be true? My obsession with having sex with men had become stronger since I had been celibate, but I hadn't acted on it. Had they somehow guessed my attraction to Gresh? Could they read my mind?

"It's not funny, Darrel. This is very serious. We think you are possessed by the demon of homosexuality, and you need to deal with it if you want to stay in this house," Rob continued.

"Wow! That's incredible. Well, I don't *feel* possessed. What do you think I should *do*?"

"That's up to you."

"Okay. Well, I'll talk to John," I offered, hoping to placate him. After all, although another friend had brought me to the Lord, it was Rob who had introduced me to John Hutchinson, in fact, to the whole charismatic Christian scene—prayer fellowships, speaking in tongues, dancing in the spirit—and Rob had always been so caring. I still cherished the hours we had spent holding each other in his sporty blue Toyota Celica after he drove me home from prayer meetings and band rehearsals, my head resting on his quarterback-sized shoulder and my right hand in the middle of his chest, twitching in its eagerness to investigate other places.

I retreated downstairs to my bedroom, upset and bewildered. A week earlier, John had asked me to become an elder in the group, but now Rob was telling me I was demon possessed. As soon as I had the house to myself, I put another pot of coffee on and opened the back door wide. The sunshine warmed me as I sat on the porch steps. The tweets and chirps of the soprano songbirds, *whee, whee, whoo, wheet deet deet deet, wheet deet deet deet*, cheered me up.

THE BUS RIDE to the far end of Calgary's south side felt interminable. The air chilled my face as I stepped off and glanced around to get my bearings. The Husky Tower looked so tiny in the distance, an orange mushroom cap with an elongated round stalk. I located the house quickly and hurried toward it, slipping on the layer of crimson leaves the wind had blown onto its cement walkway. I stood at the door for a couple minutes before ringing the doorbell. I looked at my watch— four o'clock. The man had said it would take about an hour. Was this it? Would there really be no more sex with men after this? I took a deep breath and rang the doorbell.

I don't know what I thought an exorcist would look like, but the man was taller and more robust than John Hutchinson, with thinning grey hair and a large round face. He introduced himself as a dentist might, ushered me into his sparsely furnished office and closed the door. He motioned for me to take a seat on a stackable metal chair as he got right to the point: "John told me what the issue might be. Do you ever have thoughts about having sex with other men?"

"Well, yes. I do. It occurs now and then. I've been celibate for a while now, though sometimes I have wild dreams about sex with a guy," I mumbled. I debated whether to tell him about being sexually abused by Rory, but didn't.

"Okay, that's all I need to know. John *did* tell you about my fees, right?"

He pulled another metal chair directly in front of me and sat down, took my hands into his, which were much larger, and leaned in until our foreheads were almost touching. I could feel his body heat and smell his spent deodorant and Old Spice aftershave. A sudden shiver. He closed his eyes, screwed up his face and launched in:

> SATAN, WE COMMAND YOU IN THE NAME OF JESUS TO LEAVE THIS BROTHER. IN THE NAME OF *JESUS*, WE CAST OUT THE DEMONS OF HOMOSEXUALITY. BY THE BLOOD OF THE LAMB, SATAN, WE CAST YOU OUT! YOU MUST LEAVE, NOW! JESUS, WE ASK YOU TO FILL THE VOID THAT THESE DEMONS LEAVE WITH YOUR SPIRIT. MOVE IN, JESUS, AND FILL OUR BROTHER WITH RIGHTEOUSNESS. JESUS, I ASK THAT YOU HEAL BROTHER DARREL FROM THE DEMONS OF HOMOSEXUALITY AND FILTH. PLEASE TAKE CONTROL OF HIS BODY SO THAT ANY TIME HIS MIND THINKS ABOUT SEX WITH A MAN HE WILL BE DISGUSTED AND VOMIT. VOMIT RIGHT THEN AND THERE, LORD. IN JESUS'S NAME, BE IT DONE. AMEN!

We sat for what seemed like an eternity while he murmured in tongues. I began to get irritated, wondering how I had let myself be talked into this. This is a farce, I wanted to yell—an hour-long bus ride and a fee of a hundred dollars for nothing. I wondered if my head would twist around backwards before he had finished.

I had known all along that I wasn't demon possessed—that wasn't the issue. I felt I had to go through with the exorcism to placate Rob, who had become as close as an older brother. But something didn't sit right with me about considering same-sex attraction or love to be the work of the Devil. The whole process—the conflict with Rob and Ron, the forced confession to our religious leader, John, and the contrived and expensive exorcism—caused me frustration and stress, and I soon began to act out even more than before, frenetically seeking intimacy with strange men.

THE DAY AFTER the trip to the exorcist, I was at the house alone when I got a call from Mother. Her speech was hesitant; I could tell she was close to tears.

"Darrel, Uncle Danny, uh, *Diane*, died last night. He took an overdose. Your cousins found him on your Granny Adele's grave." She paused, and then continued. "They say she was dressed as a man. In fact, they say she wore men's clothes the last week before she died." Her voice broke. "Some of your cousins and them white people. They just couldn't accept her, Son."

I was sickened by the image of Diane lying in the graveyard, clad in grey wool socks and a red lumberjack coat, hair recklessly hacked into a man's cut. I understood why she had kept trying to make a life back home. She was seeking the acceptance and love she and Greggie—Trina—had experienced as young boys when dressing up, playing house and doing girls' chores. Perhaps if they had remained crossdressers, the acceptance would have been there. But complete gender alteration—a surgical sex change—was new territory for our people, and our culture had shifted. Catholic values had replaced the tolerance that our Cree great-grandparents and our older aunts and uncles had shown regarding sexuality and gender identity. Auntie Rosie and Mother had always been solid in their support of Diane and Trina, but others struggled with it or outright condemned them.

Trina was devastated by the news. She told me her doctor had doubled her dosage of methadone, and she didn't go to the funeral. But she cherished the photo that Auntie Rosie sent each of us of Diane in her coffin—her young face nicely made up and pretty. She was dressed in a delicate blue-and-white crocheted sweater with a frilly collar.

FINALLY, I WAS going to see a psychiatrist, the one Mrs. A., the head nurse in the Rockyview OR, and her friend the head anaesthetist had referred me to. October 30, 1976: ten a.m.—Foothills Hospital, Calgary. What with my childhood trauma, family problems, gender identity issues and alleged demon possession, I must be insane, I thought. Anybody would be, wouldn't they? It had been an arduous process to get here—interviews with medical students, residents and researchers; IQ and other psychological tests. Alone in the waiting room—the first patient of the day, I guessed—I was too anxious to peruse any of the magazines. I sat on my hands, staring at the doorway, thinking back to how the whole process had begun.

One day at work, Mrs. A. had noticed I wasn't myself. She took me aside and asked what was wrong. After a long conversation in the empty surgical theatre that she used as an office, she offered to refer me for counselling. The social worker at the Rockyview, with her kind smile, sympathetic eyes and gently wrinkled complexion framed by mauve-tinged grey hair, wept. A few minutes into my story, she had reached over, put her hand on my forearm and sobbed, "I'm so sorry, Darrel."

"It's okay, Mrs. D. It's okay." I put my other hand on top of hers and smiled to calm her. Later, she told Mrs. A. that I needed much more help than she could offer. When Mrs. A. and the anaesthetist asked me what the issues were, I went on at length about my family—but my pressing concern was really my sexual orientation and gender identity: the grave fear that my destiny was to follow in Greggie's footsteps. The two of them secured me an appointment with this renowned psychiatrist and gave me time off for all of the assessments leading up to it.

My mind raced. This was it. The psychiatrist was going to tell me that I was screwed—confirm Norm the social worker's crass assessment after our month-long clandestine fling that I would require a penis as a pacifier for the rest of my life. I had read the section on homosexuality in *The Merck Manual*, the go-to medical guide for doctors and nurses, and the text clearly said it was a permanent disorder characterized by rampant promiscuity, which of course led to venereal disease, anal warts, hepatitis and eventual depravity. Or would he tell me that I was like Greggie, a woman trapped inside a man's body?

"The doctor will see you now, Darrel."

My knees wobbled as I walked toward his office.

It felt like we were in a movie. The psychiatrist sat behind a vast mahogany desk in his white lab coat: shoulder-length salt and pepper hair, an untidy greying beard and beady eyes that peered at me through wire-rimmed spectacles. A shiny wooden pipe leaned against the can of Marcovitch Black & White tobacco. Would he ask me to lie on the posh leather couch over by the window?

"Sit down, please," he said as he motioned toward the wooden chair opposite him. He didn't smile, but as he spoke I noticed his teeth were stained grey.

I wondered if he would notice how jittery I was—surely that would make his diagnosis even worse. I clamped my legs together, scrunched my toes and wrung my hands beneath the overhang of his desk.

The doctor pulled his chair closer, leaned forward and looked into my eyes.

"My team has spent a lot of time with you over the last six months, Darrel. I have your complete file here. I've reviewed the notes and read the team's recommendations—and I agree with them."

I felt like a tongue-tied actor standing in the spotlight. What had they recommended? Lithium salts? Psychotherapy? ECT—shock treatments?

"You know, you are going to be fine."

Tears started to form, but I blinked them back.

"You do your own work, my friend. You've weathered the challenges life has thrown your way, and you've held together. You're smart, and you know how to get help. Keep doing the same, and you'll be just fine. Do you have any questions?"

"I'm fine? That's it? Nothing wrong?"

Outside in the bright daylight, I wondered if I should head back to the Rockyview or go home. There was fresh snow on the Rockies along the distant horizon. I had been so happy when we first moved to Canmore, where I had been sheltered by the Three Sisters and Mount Rundle and stirred by the Bow River, which I now knew the local tribe called the Makhabn. What did it all mean? How could they say that I was normal and healthy when I felt so confused and lost?

Maybe I should have told them about Rory.

Pîhpîkisîs: The Sparrow Hawk

KNEW I was in trouble the day Gresh and other friends from our Christian fellowship came to visit Rob, Ron and me in our rented house in downtown Calgary. After we completed the tour of my space in the basement, and everyone else had traipsed upstairs, Gresh lingered in the dimly lit walk-in closet off my bedroom. When I went to see what he was doing, he gently pulled me in and closed the closet door with his foot. Holding my arms at my sides, he kissed me—tenderly at first. When my lips didn't resist, his tongue started to probe. Then we stopped and looked at each other, eyes open wide. Without speaking a word we knew we had to get out of there before things went any further and our friends got suspicious.

Gresh was the same age as Debbie—twenty-six—and he was a head-turner. Wherever we went, both men and women would eye him up. In the early days of our friendship, after church on Sunday mornings Gresh would often offer to walk me home. I showed him my favourite route—a meandering dirt path through the cottonwood and spruce trees along the Elbow River. I didn't want him to see the rundown shack I then lived in with Debbie, Norbert and Gerry, so I would suggest we stop in a secluded stretch of the river valley to chat. Gresh would sit cross-legged, lean against a river boulder and pull me over to sit in the hollow of his embrace, wrapping his arms and legs around me. Spooning me like that, he would patiently listen to my latest lament about my family situation: two pregnant sisters, an alcoholic mother, younger siblings in and out of a foster home, and a drug-addicted older brother who wanted a sex change. I was embarrassed that I couldn't hold back the tears. After all, I wasn't looking for pity; I hated it, from anyone.

The weekend following our closet encounter, Gresh and I set out on a road adventure. Usually, the vast prairie vista knocked the life out of me, but now it fascinated me, neutralizing the excitement and anxiety that intensified during our hour-and-a-half drive along the arrow-straight highway.

I tried to make intelligent conversation without sounding phony. Religion was a safe topic, yet awkward; wasn't our intent to engage in sinful acts that weekend?

"Do you believe in the gifts of the Holy Spirit, Gresh, like speaking in tongues and prophesying?"

"I believe in dancing in the spirit. That's what first caught my eye— seeing you bouncing up and down that night at John's fellowship."

I blushed and smiled.

We stopped at a nondescript motel with a restaurant a few miles north of Red Deer. I got jittery as reality sank in—I was about to spend the night alone in a motel room with this man. How could he be attracted to me, especially after all I had told him about my family? And how would I react when he made the moves to initiate sex? Would I suggest prayer as I had with my friend Gerry the night he came to my bedroom door in his underwear? I had learned a valuable lesson from that experience—Gerry went on to sin with others, having a fabulous time, and I had been left out in the cold. So would I finally let myself go with the flow?

At dinner we raved about the food, even though it was simple fare. Afterward, Gresh suggested we go for a stroll. We walked the gravel lane that cut through an endless wheat field. After glancing around to be sure no one could see, he took my hand in his. In the distance a cluster of crows emerged from the sea of gold, forming a scatter pattern and open *V* shapes against the denim-blue sky.

The suspense ended as soon as we stepped into the motel room. Gresh made his move swiftly and confidently, and I was overwhelmed by the tide of new sensations—his fragrance, *Eau Sauvage,* his hot breath on my neck, the whispering in my ear. Despite everything I had been through with other men, I felt innocent and naive.

I was taken aback by some of the things Gresh wanted to do, but I couldn't say no, not to him. Waves of pleasure sedated my overactive mind, soothing the guilt and fear that lurked there—or was that the Holy Spirit trying to protect me? The Holy Spirit was the wise voice within us, Pastor John preached. This time it was telling me to relax and enjoy the ecstasy.

I felt relieved when it was over, not because I hadn't liked it, but because of what it meant: finally, I had a lover, and not just anyone—a caring, handsome and smart *moniyaw.* There were many differences between us, and I hadn't expected my first real lover to be a man, but it didn't seem to matter. We could work it all out, I was sure.

But as I lay beside Gresh that Friday night, too electrified to sleep, fear returned and began to displace my bliss. What would he do when he learned about Rory and realized that I was damaged goods? And what would happen once the infatuation wore off and he grasped that he had an Indian pauper sleeping in his bed?

The next morning as we cruised along the highway, Gresh grabbed my neck and pulled me toward him, turned his head and forced a deep kiss, relying on his peripheral vision to keep us from crashing into oncoming cars.

That afternoon at Sylvan Lake, when I told him I was sure the other bathers were watching us with suspicion, he lifted me into the air, then pulled me underwater and forced a breathless kiss. I opened my eyes to see his hair wafting in the water and a stream of bubbles rising from his nose. When we surfaced, I knew we were a couple.

To my surprise, that night we ended up in Youngstown, the tiny prairie town where Debbie now lived. By coincidence, Gresh's friend Doreen taught school there, and on the spur of the moment, Gresh made a decision to visit her. Together, the three of us prepared a dinner of linguine with chicken slow-cooked in a creamy mushroom sauce. Gresh slept on a foam mattress on the floor in the living room, and I slept on the couch. Once he was positive Doreen was sound asleep, he called me over for a dramatic and mostly silent lovemaking session.

The next morning, I was flustered. I thought about paying Debbie a surprise visit, but how would I explain Gresh? My sister knew me all too well, would guess something was going on between us. And then there was the tiny house she lived in. How could I have taken Gresh there?

On Sunday evening, as Gresh dropped me off at home, I noticed a pair of robins hopping about in the rose-coloured twilight, pulling worms out of the ground. I sat on the front steps to watch them. My mind spun a web of questions: Had I really let him do all of those things to me? Was I in love? Was I now officially queer? What would I tell Marg, my girlfriend? Could I still be Christian? And what would I tell my family—could Gresh accept them? What would they think of him? I focused for a moment, concocting a story of how Gresh and I had spent the weekend, then I went inside, hoping that Ron and Rob wouldn't ask too many questions or notice my new glow.

THAT FALL, GRESH and I moved into a spacious two-bedroom suite near Mount Royal: a two-bedroom because optics were important. We didn't want anybody, including our evangelical Christian landlady, to suspect that we were a couple. Gresh went back to teaching after a hiatus of a couple of years, and I kept working as an operating room attendant at the Rockyview. I made less money than he did, but my pay was decent, and I liked my job. My paycheques were now mine, too—Debbie was in Youngstown with Brian, and Gaylene had taken baby Jennifer to live with Mother in Edmonton.

Gresh and I slept separately most nights, and this frustrated me, as did the fact we had to keep our relationship a secret. The apartment we shared felt foreign to me—the white walls, the IKEA and Woolco furniture, the bookcase he was so proud of and the artwork carefully suspended at eye level, instead of higher up as we had done at home. A limited-edition print from a West Coast Native artist that one of Gresh's ex-lovers had given him hung opposite the chrome and glass dining table. Following Gresh's specifications, the apartment had to be spotless.

We quickly settled into a routine: broiled codfish with plain rice and salad for dinner on weeknights; cleaning and laundry on Fridays, followed by dinner out; baking Saturday morning, then lunch and a shopping trip to a suburban mall; and of course church twice on Sundays. To relax, Gresh would listen to Barbra Streisand or Roger Whittaker. I would play my guitar and sing songs like "Feelings" and "You Are So Beautiful" along with sappy Christian songs we learned at John's fellowship—"This Is the Day That the Lord Has Made" and "How Great Thou Art."

Many days I thought I was happy; other times I felt empty and isolated, even from myself. I didn't know who I was anymore.

I never made the mistake out loud, but sometimes in my head, I would call Gresh "Rory." Each time I held his perfectly manicured hand, I felt guilty about where my mind would go—*Rory, Rory, Rory*—and I would squeeze Gresh's hand tighter. Much later, I would see it made sense for that to happen. Gresh picked up where Rory had left off, advancing my sexual development, correcting the way I spoke and lecturing me about etiquette. He taught me the meaning of *ubiquitous*.

One day, on sale, I bought a chic amber leather bomber jacket and a parka lined with otter fur. I was thrilled to show Gresh my haul, but seeing them made him angry. "They're too showy. I'll never walk alongside you wearing either of them," he snapped. I stashed the coats in the closet.

Sometimes I thought about Clara, Auntie Helen's oldest daughter, who in her late teens had married a Ukrainian man and moved to the city. Whenever Clara came to visit, dozens of us would go to Auntie's house to catch a glimpse of her. She was beautiful—carefully styled hair, light makeup, cat's eye glasses, a tight knee-length skirt. Her husband, with his blond crewcut, looked strong and handsome beside her. But other aunties and female cousins would whisper *moniyas skwew*, barely loud enough for Clara to hear. I felt sad for her—this was the worst insult one could utter, but she *did* look like a white woman now, a complete stranger.

After a few months of living with Gresh, I felt white too. When drying myself off after my daily shower, I would study my hands and feet—sure that like Clara's, my complexion had become paler. What would my cousins think about the way I looked—the way I talked? Mother had accused me of talking and acting differently after my three years with Rory and Debbie. *"Sosquats.* He's stuck up and talks like a *moniyaw* now. *Wah wah,* doesn't even fart no more," she had announced one day in front of two aunties, laughing.

I often wondered how Gresh saw me, too. At times he would jokingly serenade me with the song "Indian Love Call," and we would laugh, but one day we were in a nearby restaurant having pizza when a group of local Indians walked in. He commented on the longing look in my eyes upon spotting them; then his face got serious. "Stay away from people like them, Darrel—they'll drag you down and get you in trouble."

THERE WAS ONE front on which I had more experience and success than Gresh: guilt suppression. After lengthy lovemaking sessions that began on the couch, moved to the floor and then to the bed, Gresh would kill our pleasure, saying that we would go to hell for sure if we didn't repent and beg for forgiveness. I would try to calm him so we could hold onto each other a few moments longer. "Gresh, now is not the time. Relax—puh-leeze, my man."

His remorse after intimacy began to worry me, though. After all, he was older and presumably wiser. Wouldn't he know what kind of behaviour would take us beyond redemption—send us to hell? *Hell.* I felt such dread at the mention of it. Could it be true that all of my Cree ancestors, who could never have known Jesus, were in hell, as the Bible seemed to imply?

In spite of our fears, or perhaps because of them, Gresh and I kept going to John's prayer group. Our fellow worshippers adopted a "don't ask, don't tell" approach, even though they knew that earlier, at Rob's behest, I had gone through an exorcism. Soon, however, a drastic decision by John and a group of elders convinced us that the group had become heretical.

Like me, my Québécois friend Gerry did a lot of sinning, but with women instead of men. His exploits weren't anonymous, either. Instead, they were with women of the fellowship, both single and attached. During our Sunday evening confession circles, when it was his turn, Gerry would raise his hands to cover his bearded face, then shake his head and say that he hoped that the Lord Jesus had a lot of patience, because he had sinned again—this time with sister X. His hazel eyes would then brim with self-loathing, as sister X either dropped her head or jumped to her feet and scurried out of the room.

The last time it happened, I had been the only one to object to John's proposal to invite Gerry to a special prayer session where, through the laying on of hands, we would deal with the situation once and for all. I was concerned that Gerry would suffer the same humiliation I had endured through my exorcism. In the end, though, I decided that as the group's youth elder, I should go. After all, I had convinced Gerry to accept the Lord and invited him into the fellowship.

I arrived early, at the same time as Norma, an elder who had been motherly to both Gerry and me. I was sure she would make a last-minute plea to stop the session, but her face was stern. Jim, a new elder, came in on her heels. I hoped that Gerry would sense the danger and stay away, but he arrived a few minutes later. John directed him to take a seat in the single chair in the middle of the room and motioned for Norma, Jim and me to approach.

Gerry must have felt the sudden warmth of a cluster of hands on his shoulders. John swooped in last and placed his giant hands on Gerry's head, then screwed up his face and began to speak in a booming voice. He opened in tongues.

"*Gulpto frots minda brenthit. Hroda snter wolta blut. Ogulto westla vine blet.* Brother Gerry. We have been patient, and have tried every-thing in our power to help you. You have led more than a few of our sisters into sin, sisters who were submitting unto their husbands and following the Lord faithfully. As your elders, we have decided that our only option is to turn your soul over to Satan for the destruction of the flesh."

I felt Gerry slouch under the weight of our hands, and I thought his face would explode. My face was burning too, and I was short of breath. I had to speak out before things went any further. "John, I'm sorry. I object. I can't continue—what makes you believe you have the authority to do this? And how can we pray to Satan? Is he not the enemy? If we are going to turn Gerry over to anyone, it should be to the Lord."

"Brother Darrel, I've explained to Brother Gerry that it's for his own good. We have to act swiftly so that his soul may be saved in the day of our Lord Jesus—First Corinthians Five."

I squeezed Gerry's shoulder and then removed my hand. "I have to go. This is all wrong. So very wrong."

I raced up the stairs to get out of there. I waited outside the church, hoping that Gerry would join me, but he didn't. I ran the ten blocks home.

When Gresh came home, I told him what had happened. We agreed it was heresy. Who did Pastor John and these people think they were, judging Gerry and appropriating divine power and authority like that? Did they not realize how cruel they were being, condemning him as an irredeemable sinner? We decided that the same fate would await us once word got out about our ongoing transgressions, so we never returned. We decided to join First Baptist, across from the gay bar on Fourth Street, instead.

I LONGED FOR Gresh to meet my relatives, my enduring Cree aunties and spirited cousins. But each time I considered talking to him about it, the idea brought on panic. I tried to imagine how he would react to the swarms of raucous children, the muddy streets, the bleak surroundings and the modular homes and trailers that my relatives lived in. And I worried about mealtimes. We would have to visit the houses of each of my older cousins to eat. What would he think about our delicacies: bannock, boiled moose tongue, dried moose meat, deer stew, fricasseed rabbit and potato and hamburger soup seasoned with black pepper?

And what about the way my relatives spoke, their lilting accents, abrupt fragmented sentences and endless teasing? It would have driven him crazy. But the clincher was this: I didn't know how I could explain our relationship. My cousins liked to ask blunt questions; they knew about Trina and Diane, their queer lifestyle as teenagers before they began dressing as women full-time, and about Diane's suicide, so they would be onto us right away, and it wouldn't be fun. I could hear my cousin Lady goading me, "*Mah*, ever ugly—if yer gonna go with men, why'd you pick *that*?" She would then tilt her head back and extend her lips to point in Gresh's general direction, a defiant smirk on her face.

Gresh's closest friend, Brenda, was a cheery, voluptuous woman with a milky complexion, bright-red lipstick and a bouncy black afro. She had a master's degree in counselling and worked as a senior administrator at the local branch of the Canadian National Institute for the Blind. Brenda must have noticed my increasing sadness and isolation—she invited me along to movies and dinners with the two of them. I was thrilled with this until one day Gresh threw me a zinger. "You are such a social climber, Darrel," he said. "Brenda is *my* friend—back off."

His words smarted as much as the backhanded slap Rory had given me one day when he was unhappy with how I had cut the lawn. I had yelled at my brother-in-law afterward, my cheek stinging and my nose numb, saying it took a big man to hit a kid, but I didn't know how to respond to Gresh. Why would he say that? What did he want for me—to stay poor, uneducated and marginalized? I wondered if he had any sense of the loaded message he conveyed with his words: Who do you think you are, Darrel? Remember your place in society and your destiny. You aren't one of us and never will be. Go back to the bush.

The trouble was, even if I had wanted to, I couldn't have gone back to where I came from. Mosom's cabin in Spurfield no longer existed; neither did our home in Smith. Worse, our family had disintegrated. Now that I had left John's fellowship and become distanced from my friends there, Gresh was my only bridge into society. And a precarious drawbridge he was turning out to be.

GRESH NEVER MET my aunties or cousins, but one day he did meet my mother. During a road trip in the late fall—this time to Edmonton to visit friends from his U of A days—I decided to pay a surprise visit to Mother and the kids, who were living in a rental house close to downtown. She had managed to get the kids out of the foster home again and was doing well, I believed—being the mother she was capable of being. But when Gresh and I pulled up to the house on Sunday afternoon, I spotted her staggering along the street, with the kids nowhere to be seen. Mother's permed black hair was dishevelled, her clothes loose and she looked as if she hadn't slept in days. As we stepped out of the car and approached her, she flashed us an angry look and growled, "Are you here to fuck my daughters too?"

I felt instant rage. What did she mean by that—had she prostituted my sisters, or was she trying to protect them from two men she didn't recognize? Whatever the case, at that moment I knew—my expectations and wishes for Mother were unfulfillable.

"Mom, it's me—Darrel. And this is my friend Gresh."

A hollow stare. Then a look of recognition that shifted to horror, followed by a burst of tears. She sat down on the cement steps of the front porch and buried her head in her hands. I asked Gresh to go back to the car, and I stepped past her into the house.

There wasn't a sound. I felt as if I had stepped into a time warp back to our little house in Smith, the day all the dishes had been smashed on the kitchen floor, or to the house behind the pool hall in Athabasca, where I sat up night after night listening to Mother's stories. I remembered the time I had accidentally pushed her down the stairs, after stopping her from hitting the kids with a belt, and the time she threatened to destroy the house with Ned's chainsaw. I had to assuage the flood of gut-wrenching memories. "Hello," I called out. "Are you guys home?"

My little brother, Travis, appeared out of nowhere, jumped up and grabbed me around the neck. "Darrel—Brother, thank God you're here." Gaylene stumbled up from her hiding place in the basement, holding baby Jennifer in her arms. Holly and Crystal lumbered after her. After convincing Mother to go to bed and settling the kids down, I promised them I would get them into a safe place quickly. My worry at leaving them that afternoon was tremendous. I justified my actions by telling them—and myself—that I had to work the next day and needed to catch a ride home with Gresh.

I observed Gresh's profile as we drove back to Calgary. I needed to see how he was coping with the horror we had just witnessed; *his* mother was a complete teetotaller and had been all his life. At first he was silent and distant, but after a while he softened. He shifted his body toward me, then drove with his left hand at ten o'clock and his other arm over my shoulder. I stared straight ahead, plotting what I had to do next.

That evening, after hours on the phone first with Debbie and then with the kids' former foster parents, I called Alberta Children's Services and insisted that my siblings be apprehended and put back into foster care as soon as possible. After hearing my threats to call the *Edmonton Journal* and city police in response to her reluctance to investigate, the social worker agreed to act. I was sure I wouldn't be able to sleep that night. I felt morose about having convinced Mother to take the kids back. How could I have been so naive and selfish as to think that she would quit drinking and become the devoted mother that I had known as a toddler—the mother I wanted my sisters and little brother to know and love? My fantasy of a happy family had brought them to this.

IN MAY 1977 a letter came from the University of Calgary, telling me that I had been accepted into general arts and sciences. I leapt around on the green sculpted carpet in our apartment, cheering and waving the letter.

That evening Gresh and I had a tense conversation over our broiled fish and tea. He asked why I had registered for science courses, and I answered that I planned to be a doctor. Perturbed, he launched into a lecture, telling me that I would never be a doctor and that I should train as a teacher instead. I was angry and perplexed. How could he say that, when the doctors and nurses at work had been so encouraging? Mrs. A., the aging head nurse, had told me I was smart—could succeed in any career.

I was exhilarated to be studying at the U of C, but the experience was exasperating. I loved navigating my way through throngs of energized youth, but most days I felt out of place as I wandered from one sterile building to another. It was as if I had just been transported there from my *mosom*'s trapping cabin.

My interpretation of what I was learning was different from the usual student's. For example, Ernst Haeckel's theory that "ontogeny recapitulates phylogeny" simply confirmed what my great-grandfather had used to say—that we are all related, the two-legged, the four-legged, those that fly and those that swim. My zoology professor was amused by this.

Charles Dickens's *Great Expectations* gave me hope that I, like Pip, could find a way out of poverty, although I knew it wouldn't be through a benefactor—I would have to work for anything I got. Geoffrey Chaucer's *Canterbury Tales* confused me, and in panic before an exam I asked Gresh for advice about how to interpret the text. He suggested that I consult Coles Notes; I did, and my reward was a mediocre but passing final grade.

THAT FALL, AFTER settling into my new routine at the U of C, I began to miss the people I had worked with in the operating room. So I was pleasantly surprised when one of the doctors, Jim, called, saying he wanted to see me. I had visited him at his mansion on Elbow Drive a couple of times before meeting Gresh. Jim was in his early thirties and Chinese, but had grown up in the Philippines. He was handsome, rich and charming. I knew he was interested in me, and I was attracted to him too. At the time, though, I had been concerned that he wasn't a born-again Christian and that he surrounded himself with flamboyant men he had met in Calgary's new gay bar. One day when Gresh picked up the phone first, and I explained who Jim was, he became incensed that a doctor I had worked with was calling me and insisted that this was paramount to harassment and stalking. That night he initiated a dramatic lovemaking session and afterward said, "That Chinese doctor won't get his hands on you—not as long as I'm around." The next day, he went to Jim's clinic to warn him to leave me alone. I was outraged. I hadn't written Jim off as a friend or lover, far from it, and Gresh had been very clear that he and I couldn't have an ongoing relationship.

Leading up to exam week, another incident made it challenging for me to focus on my studies. After dinner one evening, Gresh had something to tell me. As he leaned forward to speak, a look of deep concern crossed his face.

"Darrel, we have to talk. Damien came over this afternoon, and we did something. It happened so fast. He lay on the floor, I unzipped his jeans, and, well…"

His second confession cut even more:

"When Brynn came down from Edmonton and stayed with us last Easter, he snuck from the couch into my bedroom after you were asleep, and I screwed him."

I pulled on my parka and boots and fled the apartment. I leapt off an embankment onto the sidewalk, my coattails flying behind me. When I saw that an oncoming car was speeding, I dashed into the street, as if daring it to hit me. It honked and swerved. And right behind it was a city police car. The officer stopped and called for me to approach through his bullhorn.

"What's going on?"

I hesitated, but then blurted out the truth, defying him to arrest me.

"I just had a brutal dispute with my lover."

The policeman looked puzzled for a moment, then looked into my eyes and said, "Well, take it easy. Don't do anything you'll regret, alright?"

He drove away slowly, watching me in his rear-view mirror.

I wandered the residential streets of Mount Royal, mumbling to myself and occasionally yelling and swearing. If someone had seen me they would have thought I was crazy, but it didn't matter. In fact, I think I was hoping someone would report me.

After a couple of hours I returned home. I was leaning against the door, pulling off my boots, when Gresh came over and forced an awkward hug. He was crying.

"I'm sorry, Darrel. I didn't make out with Brynn. Or Damien. I wanted to see how you would react. Needed to know if you really love me."

An hour later, he confessed again—the Brynn part was true, but the Damien story wasn't—they had just petted. I wanted to throw myself down and pound my fists on the carpet, but instead I jumped up and strode to my bedroom, sure that Gresh would follow to comfort me. When he didn't, I cried for hours alone, stunned at how callous he had become.

Later that night, he gave me notice; he wanted to live on his own.

A MONTH LATER, Gresh was living on the eighth floor of a high-rise on Fourteenth Street. I was in a studio townhouse with a beautiful cathedral ceiling made of cedar. I lay on the couch with a box of Kleenex nearby, getting up only to eat and go to work. Each night I fell asleep to Jim Croce singing "Operator" and "Time in a Bottle" or to James Taylor's mellow tones: "Fire and Rain" and "You've Got a Friend."

Over the summer, I found an escape from my despair. I reconnected with high school friends who were musicians and decided to study alongside them. I worked up the Italian art song "Sebben, crudele" with Mrs. Higgins, my former singing instructor, and auditioned for the U of C School of Music. I was accepted as a voice major and became immersed in music once again. I joined the U of C chorus and returned to the Calgary Philharmonic Chorus.

Often I became emotional while singing passages from works like Verdi's *Requiem*, Berlioz's *Symphonie Fantastique*, or *Miserere* by Allegri. I didn't understand why, but I felt energized and lucid when the music ended. In high school I had learned about classical music from Mr. Ferguson, but I didn't understand the Latin, German or Italian lyrics. I still didn't grasp the complexity of the music. I was a twenty-year-old Cree guy. I decided that as long as the music moved and inspired me I should continue with it, and not feel I had to explain to anyone why I was there.

I attended recitals, listened to all kinds of ensembles, from baroque brass to barbershop vocals, and went to receptions and after-parties. My family couldn't relate to what I was doing, but Debbie and Gaylene listened patiently on the phone as I tried to tell them about it. One day while Debbie was visiting, I decided to practise my vocal scales and arpeggios in the bathroom. As I stepped out, Debbie got a dramatic look on her face, opened her mouth wide and loudly echoed my *wah-ah-ah-ah-ah-ah-ah-ah-ah*. We stooped over with laughter.

SHORTLY AFTER I moved into my own place, Mother came to visit. I wasn't sure where she had been living, but after a couple of weeks it became clear that she had no place else to go. I was still aching with loneliness from the breakup with Gresh, so I welcomed the company. At first we were thrilled to be together, but then the drinking took over again.

Gresh's brief visits, for tepid, mechanical sex that frustrated us both, had dwindled over the summer, and they didn't happen at all in September. I began to panic—did this mean it was completely over—that's it, that's all?

One morning in mid-October I called Gresh at the elementary school where he was teaching Grade Four. My voice was edgy, and I mumbled something about suicide. He coughed and said he had to get back to his class. He called me back on his lunch break.

"Darrel, I want to see you this evening. Let's meet on the Seventeenth Avenue hill. I'll bring Jim."

What was going on, I wondered. Had my reference to suicide scared him? Was he going to try passing me off to Jim, after consistent efforts to disparage him?

That evening I drove my little Toyota SR5 along Crowchild Trail through heavy rain and pounding thunder. The bronze city lights in the distance calmed me. I put the car in second gear to climb the slick dirt road to the top of the Seventeenth Avenue hill. Streaks of lightning lit up the blackened dome overhead.

Normally, the rhythmic *whik awhuk whik awhuk* of the windshield wipers, along with the millions of raindrops drumming the roof, would have lulled me to sleep. But now I was vigilant, waiting for a single pair of headlights to come bouncing up the road. There it was, unmistakable, Gresh's car.

Jim opened the driver's door and stepped out, opening a large black umbrella. Why was *he* driving? He flashed his smile; I had forgotten about the gold fillings. He was still dashing—maybe this was going to turn out okay after all. Seconds later, Gresh stepped out of the passenger's side and huddled beside him. I leaned against the hood of my Toyota and crossed my arms, raindrops splashing off my face. Jim started the conversation in the slight accent that I had always found appealing.

"Hi, Darrel. How are you? You know I think you're a great guy. I'm so proud of you—going to university now. How's it going, really?" Before I could answer, he continued, "You might be wondering what I'm doing here. Gresh and I have something—"

"We're seeing each other," Gresh interrupted. "We're moving in together at the end of this month."

"We'll live with my family in the house on Elbow Drive," Jim said. "You were there, remember?"

"Yes, of course I remember. It's beautiful." Without another word I turned and got into my car.

Reeling with frustration and anger, I drove around for at least an hour before parking near the Tenth Street Bridge. Would the water of the Bow bring peace, wash away my pain? Rain was pelting the windshield. I stumbled out of the car and down to the rocky shoreline, then pulled off my shoes and socks, waded in. My feet sank into silt as slippery pebbles gave way. The icy current pushed against my calves. I looked downstream, then upstream; the lights of the Calgary skyline bounced off the ripples. Standing waves and swirling eddies close by. Dripping wet from the rain, I bent over and pulled water up onto my forearms and face, like I had seen Mother do every time we went down to the shores of the Athabasca.

I THREW MYSELF into my studies after that. I was now back in sciences, after one term in the Bachelor of Music program. A few of my music professors wanted to be mentors, and would have become friends, but what I saw of their lifestyle scared me. Cutthroat competition to get a seat in the Calgary Philharmonic and maintain it. Concerts and recitals in the evening and on weekends, relationship problems and financial insecurity. Then there was the head of the choral program, who I had encountered in the second-floor washroom of the psychology building the previous year before switching to the music program. Blotchy complexion, grey hair, dandruff-dusted shoulders. As we stood peeing, he tried to get me to glance down, but I wouldn't. He followed me out of the men's room, but I ducked into a nearby classroom to lose him. When I walked into my music history class the following September, there he was. One day after class, he informed me that it was mandatory for all vocal performance majors to sing in his chamber choir; rehearsals were at his house on Thursday evenings.

So instead of studying the circle of fifths and music history, I was back poring over diagrams of molecules and algebraic formulas. Evenings and weekends, I was either in a science lab or waiting tables at a restaurant called Pardon My Garden. Mother must have felt abandoned. I could tell she was out of place in the modern apartment we had moved into in Silver Springs, with its dishwasher, fireplace and wall-to-wall beige broadloom. She no longer used the simple Cree phrases and words I understood and cherished. She began to travel to Edmonton, where she stayed for two or three weeks at a time. "You're so *phisticated* now," she would tell me when she phoned from there, drunk. "*Wah wah moy miyosin*, my son."

The Eviction

IT MIGHT HAVE been a coming of age thing. Maybe revenge drove me to do it. I wasn't sure. But one day that February, when the icicles on the eaves were thick and long, I asked her to leave. In my smoke-filled Toyota SR5, we drove through blustering snow to the Greyhound bus depot in downtown Calgary. It crossed my mind that I could have waited for the weather to shift, for a milder sunny day—a chinook, perhaps. But I feared I would lose my resolve. After all, it was Mother I was evicting.

Silence for the half hour or so it took us to get across town. Her scowling, worn Cree face—masked by a thin layer of foundation, rouge and rushed red lipstick—dominated my peripheral field. I didn't dare look directly at her, but I could feel her sideways glances. She was trying to read my mood—see if I was weakening or about to crack.

I caught a glimpse of my face in the rear-view mirror and saw the intensity in my eyes. I should have discussed this with Debbie. We had always been close, and since she was my older sister, her opinion mattered. But what if she had asked me to wait? Maybe she would have offered to take Mother in. No, she had enough on her hands with two rambunctious little kids now, Joseph and Jaime, and a shaky marriage to boot.

I had gone over my rationale so many times. Mother was spending two weeks out of every month partying in Edmonton, coming back to collect her cheque and recover a bit before heading out again. We'd had some heart-to-heart chats and belly laughs at first, but now, after a few months of living together, all she did when she was there was roll cigarettes, sip coffee, do crosswords and sleep. Why didn't she love me? Had she ever?

We had both been miserable ever since she had mentioned her plan for my two younger sisters and niece, Jennifer:

"I'm thinkin' of getting the girls out of the foster home again, Darrel."

I was on my way out to work, but my eyes popped open and I froze. "I should be back around midnight tonight, maybe one o'clock if customers linger."

"I wanna do it before it's too late. They're already teenagers."

"I will fight you tooth and nail if you even try," I growled. I stomped out of the apartment, trying not to slam the door.

Goddamn! Hadn't those poor kids been through enough—fleeing drunken brawls and threats of lickings only to end up sleeping under eighteen-wheelers where they would have some protection from the snow or rain? In and out of shelters and foster homes. My pulse pounded in my temples and ears.

Then, at Christmas time, I had paid Trina's airfare to come to Calgary from Vancouver, just so Mother would stay. The day she arrived, Trina shook me down for money for cigarettes and bingo to boot. By Christmas day, the two of them had stopped speaking.

Now I was in in the driver's seat, taking Mother to the bus depot. She would likely call me that night, drunk. What would I say to her?

SOSQUATS MAGA MINA pasquats! I coulda never kicked my own mother out like that—and in the middle o' winter. He forgets, I'm Mom—*Okâwîmâw*. Can barely see outta these frosty windows. Can't cry now—other people aroun'. *Mahti poni mahto esquieu.*

Well, at least I have hot coffee and fresh Rothmans to smoke, and he bought me a new book of crosswords. Feel like I wanna puke. It's the smell on these Greyhounds, the toilet. The water for flushing, blue like berries, makes me sick, and Darrel is the same way. Cheezus, look at that snow whirling all around us.

Hope Herb lets me stay at his place. Helen is shacked up with some German guy, and she don't drink now. Can't stay at her house no more. Don't know what got into him, my Lapatak. It was probably Gaylene. Flashes those blue eyes, gets teary and then people fall for whatever she wants. I knew I shouldn't have married her dad. Lots of younger men were after me, but Ned was Sonny's cousin, and Sonny asked him to look after me and the two kids when he died. I was big with Darrel then. Ned had women chasing him like crazy too, even though he was fifty, and that was part of the problem.

Oh, here's another *esquieu*, lifting her green garbage bag of things up to the overhead bin. She's gonna join me.

"*Tansi.*" She wants me to shake her hand. Brown and strong. Warm. Her shiny paisley kerchief came undone—is gliding down her arm—hope it doesn't fall to the floor. Oh, she got it. Good.

"*Mah, kinehiyawin ci? Manando, igwa kiya.*"

"*Key'ops ekosi. Tanti toot'i' h'en?*"

"Edmonton—my boy just kicked me out."

"*Wah wah sosquats. Maga mina.* Ain't like it use'ta be, eh?"

"Don't know where I'll end up. Can stay with a friend, but not for long."

"I got a room downtown—you can stay with me. Be cheaper for both of us."

"*Tapwe ci?*"

"*Tapwe.*"

MAH, SOSQUATS. WHAT am I doing here anyways. Slept outside last night—so damn cold. Shouldn't'a listened to that old *scanak*. Stayed with her three months and now here I am on the Edmonton skids cause o' her. She locked me out last night—or maybe she didn't even get home. Gotta get a place—get on welfare—nodody's gonna hire me now, a down-and-out *esquieu*. No way.

Spring is coming but the ground hasn't thawed. And my mind ain't right—I start out thinkin' *Nehiyaw*, then switch to English, then *Nehiyaw*—Cree again. What the hell is goin' on. Jus' nodded off a little last night sittin' upright, and dreamt about them nuns—the one that bothered me when I was little and the one who gave me and Margaret bread and water two days for talking *Nehiyaw*.

What did they give me to drink las' night, anyways? My head is poundin' and I got the shakes. Mouth tastes so sour. They jus' passed it around in that brown paper bag, burned bad goin' down. Gotta get to Herb's today. He'll let me stay a couple o' nights.

Gotta move around to try 'n keep warm. Maybe that laundromat on One Hundred Twenty-Fourth Street still stays open all night. Nobody'll kick me outta there. How'd I end up here, on the skids?

Mah, what's that car doin'? Went around the block three times now 'n keeps slowin' down when he passes by. There he goes again— wait a minute, he's gonna stop. *Mah*. I recognize that guy. I seen his picture in the papers and on TV. City coun'sler, mayor or somethin'. Geez, what was his name? He's stoppin'.

"Are you alright? You need a ride somewhere or you just need to warm up a bit?"

"Ah, yes. Yes, I need to warm up."

Four in the afternoon 'n here I am back on the street. The coun'sler dropped me off at Herb's, but Herb wasn't home or wouldn't answer the door, not sure which. Maybe's he's in the hospital. That *esquieu* is gone—maybe back to her family in Hobbema, or maybe she died like so many *esquiewak* these days. Jus' disappear 'n nobody knows or cares. Tried to tell a cop—wouldn't listen. Wish I could'a at least got my things from her place.

Good thing the coun'sler gave me a few bucks and a hot meal. I got to have a bath and he was gentle in getting what he wanted. Who the hell would ever believe a city coun'sler picked me up for some *mus-awey*? *Wah wah, nâpewak*. They'll do anythin' for *timih-kwan. Kohkôsak*.

Least I can make a fire in this old barbeque behind the Chongqing Inn with twigs and scraps of wood I find here 'n there. Less food since them *sekipachwaw* closed the place and left. They were good people. Set food out at night for us here behind their restaurant, leftovers. Pretty soon the others will show up, mostly *Nehiyawak*, but sometimes one or two *Moniyawak* and a *kaskitewiyas* from Amber Valley too.

Jus' can't get warm today. I feel so much better when I camp down by the river, but I don' make it there every night. When I do, *wiskipôs*, the one *Moniyawak* call whisky jack, keeps flyin' around me with its raspy chatter and whistles. Must be tryna lead me away from this place, this way o' life. Saw new leaves on the trembling aspens the other day. Made me think o' Slave Lake and how I used to love the way they fluttered 'n danced in summer. Oh, and them crows, so many of 'em. They got things to say to me, but I don't wanna hear 'em right now.

Wonder who'll show up tonight 'n what they'll bring to drink. There's always a bottle or two to pass around. Ah, here comes someone, up the alley. Two new guys, both *Nehiyawak*. *Wah wah*, ever rough, but looks like they each got a twen'y-sixer.

AWIYÂ! MY HEAD'S gonna burst any minute. What time is it anaway? Barely daylight. My hand is throbbing so hard—what in the hell? These flies. So many. Goddamn. Oooohhhhh, my hand! Hurts worse than a toothache.

Oh my God—*wah wah sosquats*! My finger! They cut off my finger. Stole my ring! Lapatak gave me that ring—ten-karat gold 'n had a *B* in the middle.

Awiyâ! Sosquats—those bastards. What in the hell they put in my drink? They knock me out, then rob me. What else did they do? Doesn't hurt anywhere else, but I gotta get to a bathroom, wash up 'n clean this wound. Maybe I can find a small Kotex somewhere to wrap around my finger. I'll try that Mohawk gas station close by. Damn. Knew I shoulda gone to the river last night. Have to find some T3s or somethin' for the pain.

Maci manitowi—sons o' bitches. Geez, my voice is hoarse.

Mah, everything's spinnin'. I'm gonna black out.

YOU HAVE TO stop that, the nuns warned us. *Arrête donc!* That language is from the Devil. Talk English. *Et les hommes*, they *crient et dancent* while pounding on that loud *tambour*. That too is evil. Paint their faces with *blanc*, yellow, red and black stripes. *Pis les costumes et les plumes!*

This is why I have such bad luck, livin' on the skids 'n everything. That's why my kids are sufferin'. Supposed to not talk Cree, not even *think* Cree. Language o' the Devil. Language of the Devil, but I can't help it. Mosom and Cucuum always talked Cree. It ain't the same in English. I didn't teach the kids Cree—that's gotta count for somethin'. Least they won't go to hell. Can be normal 'n live as good as white people, *Moniyawak*. You'll speak English, be somebody when you grow up, I would tell 'em. Worked, but now they don' understand me, think I'm crazy, a crazy squaw. They're ashamed o' me. I know it. Can't even explain things to 'em in Cree 'n some things you jus' can't say right in English. Like your feelings—like love.

Damn, I know I shoulda given up that bundle a long time ago—sweetgrass, sage 'n tree fungus 'n other things Leo gave me. Always hid it. Never talked about it with Debbie, Greggie or Lapatak, only to my sisters, 'n they were scared of it. Kids thought my medicine man was their uncle. That's all they knew. Uncle Leo came around for visits, and I sent them outside so they wouldn't see, wouldn't be affected. Used to be you got caught with that stuff, or drummin' 'n dancin' with a group, ya'd go to jail. Leo didn't charge me much—jus' some food or *mosoyas*—moose meat—if I had it. He was a good man.

Wish that doctor would hurry up. *Mah*—won't give me nothin' for the pain anyways. They know me here. Think I'm here for drugs.

MIDDLE O' SUMMER. Don't know how they found me, but they did. So here I am in this huge dim room somewhere in the West End, sittin' around this table with my kids. Some kinda family celebration— jus' Travis 'n Greg ain't here. Debbie brought this dress she thought would fit me. I never wear pink, too girlie, but I don' mind it, and she got me a nice flower to pin on. She washed and set my hair in her room at the Eastglen. She took her time, massaged my scalp. So many memories o' when I done that for her, then braided her hair, every day for years. *Wah wah*. So ashamed. I look rough, tired 'n wrinkled. She must see it too. Must've hated watchin' my face in the mirror as she worked and made small talk. Glad she didn't ask about my finger.

Mah. That's Elvis Presley singin' "All Shook Up." I used to sing that song with Sonny. Everyone's pretty happy. They're gettin' up to dance. Gotta behave myself now or else. Debbie doesn't leave my side.

"Where ya stayin' nowadays, Mom?" Her voice is so soft, like she's afraid.

"Herb's place. Helpin' him out. His wife died 'n he got his leg cut off."

"You're lookin' worn. Need to take it easy. Should come for a visit this summer—get to know the kids. Make your cinnamon buns 'n bannock. Strawberry shortcake."

"*Tapwe*, this summer, Debs. We'll pick berries."

I say I'll go, but she knows I'm foolin' her. Can't work—we end up drinkin' together, and the last two times it got real bad. She kicked me out that time in Canmore, and then, in Athabasca, I hurt her. Didn't mean to. Darrel was there both times, upset and yelling.

Here comes Darrel with some drinks. So handsome in his beige suit. My God, think I'm gonna cry... No. Not here. *Nomoya mahto esquieu*. Looks like me when I was that age. Got his dad's ears 'n laugh. Shoulda never told him his dad was a crazy Frenchman—that he was conceived behind a woodpile, when I phoned him the night he kicked me out, but I couldn't help it—wanted to hurt him. Yes, he's Sonny's boy. So proud.

He smiles at me and takes my hand, then Debbie stands and takes the other one. "C'mon, Mom, let's dance—as a family." They pull me over ta the dance floor. Holly joins in. She got my eyes and my chin. She's tiny like Ned's mother Cucuumy. Gaylene sees us and dances over. So pretty, my blue-eyed Indian in her flared blue dress with that tiara of daisies in her blond hair. Reminds me o' when she was little— at Debbie's wedding. *Katawasisiw*. Did I jus' say that out loud or think it? Damn, I'm losin' it. Now Crystal gets up. Everyone's smilin' 'n laughin'. Little Jennifer, Gaylene's girl, is dressed like a princess. So beautiful, all of them. Cheezus, can't cry here. Have to laugh along with 'em. Be happy, *esquieu*. Laugh.

How can I tell 'em I got nowhere to go? No food. No money. Don't want their pity. After all, Darrel evicted me. He always did hate me drinkin'—guess he couldn't take it no more. Gaylene never forgave me for takin' off with Swede. But they all turned out good. What if we stayed in that small town, Smith? Gaylene woulda had five kids by now 'n Darrel never woulda gone to university. Woulda ended up down-and-out alkies like me. Damn, I wanna get drunk—get wasted. Wonder if Debbie's got any codeine, 292s or T3s. Gonna tell 'em I gotta go early. *Namoya. Cheskwa esquieu.* No, stay. Who knows when I'll see 'em again. Maybe never. At least we're all laughin' together 'n dancin'.

EKOSI MAGA. I have a place. I got on welfare. Good thing, it's fall and getting chilly. Maybe get the girls back now. Stayed at Herb's for a week and got cleaned up 'n straightened out. He's a good man. The coun'sler picked me up again. He said he really liked me, wanted to help me get off the street, but I done it on my own. I'll go for one last drink with those guys—say *ekosi*, goodbye. Some of 'em were good to me. There they are, they're passin' around three green bottles, maybe lemon gin. Can't stay long.

Code 99

HAD FIGURED that my first shift as an orderly in Emergency, the day after I completed CPR training, would be eventful. Even so, I froze in disbelief at the announcement over the hospital intercom. *Code 99 ICU, Code 99 ICU*—that means you, Darrel, you're on. I hustled up the stairs behind the emergency room doctor, feeling important but inadequate. You can do it, I told myself: You passed the CPR training with top-notch results. I was back working at the Rockyview after completing my third semester of sciences at the University of Calgary. My seventeen-year-old sister, Gaylene, and her daughter, Jennifer, were living with me by then in the apartment in Silver Springs. Mother was gone.

At age twenty-one, youth seemed to be the only thing I had in common with the boy who lay on the ICU bed. He had a blond crewcut, a stocky athletic body. Tubes everywhere, running out of his nose, mouth and penis, and an intravenous line in each arm. Somehow I could tell he was from a privileged family. I navigated my way past the respirator, pumps and IV poles and stepped onto a stool to position myself properly. Find the sternum, place your palms two fingers above its base. Use your body weight, but not too much pressure.

I was surprised by the clammy feel of his pink skin. When the doctor nodded, I began the compressions. After a few minutes, he checked the pulse.

"You're getting good perfusion—keep going."

My adrenaline level must have been off the charts. I was astonished this was happening. Back in Athabasca or in Edmonton, it would have been unfathomable to have a local Indian boy on such a highly skilled team, caring for white patients. Focus, I reminded myself. One one thousand, two one thousand, three one thousand. Focus.

I did, but to no avail. When the head nurse read out the blood gas results, the doctor ordered us to stop. His voice cracked as he announced, "Time of death: 11:05."

The tension was palpable, the humidity suffocating. We had failed this young man and his family in spite of our best efforts. Tranquil baby face, purple lips, blue fingernail beds. Dead? Just like that? Gone forever?

In a daze, I helped the nurses remove tubing, catheters and needles to prepare the body to be viewed. Then I fled the ICU, past the doctor who was in the hallway speaking to the distraught parents, downstairs and outside. I plunked myself on the banks of the Glenmore Reservoir, gazing at its ripples. The chirping and whistling of the songbirds seemed out of place.

A better future than I could ever hope for had awaited this boy, I was sure, but it had vaporized as his spirit shifted into another dimension. I had overheard the ICU nurses discussing his case in the cafeteria the day before: on his motorcycle, he had rear-ended a car, flown over it and landed on his helmet, which was shattered. His neck was broken.

It was the first time I had seen a person die. This was so different from seeing a dead robin or butterfly or one of the laboratory rats I had to dissect in zoology class. I didn't understand the emptiness and sense of panic I was feeling, and there was nobody I could discuss it with. Mosom had passed away years earlier, and I didn't know where Mother was. There was no way I would be able go back to work for the afternoon.

As I drove down Crowchild Trail to my apartment building on the northwest edge of Calgary, I wondered what my future really held. Could I handle the stress of being a doctor if one death upset me so much? My first set of grades hadn't been strong enough to get me into medical school, but I had to keep trying. That was my ticket out of poverty—not for me alone, but for my family. As a doctor, I would earn enough to help all of them over time—Mother, Gaylene, Trina, Debbie and the younger ones still in the foster home. There were other considerations, too. I would be fulfilling a lifelong dream, and in doing so I could prove that I was as smart as any of the white kids who had scorned and tormented me in Smith and Athabasca.

My thoughts returned to the white boy at the hospital. Other than Father and my great-grandfather, Mosom, nobody in our close family had died in my lifetime. Even though we had problems, we were still alive. I would talk to Gaylene about our good luck in this regard when I got home. She would agree; she always did.

A year after giving birth to Jennifer, Gaylene had her daughter placed in the foster home she herself had grown up in, so she could complete high school and train to be a nurses' aide in Edmonton. When she dropped out, her funding was cancelled, and she could no longer stay with Granny McLeod. I brought her and Jennifer to Calgary to live with me.

I opened the apartment door to a surprising scene. Debbie was there, and she and Gaylene were sitting at the kitchen table smoking. Their eyes were red and puffy. What was going on? Had something happened to Travis, or Greggie? To Ned?

"Gaylene has something to tell you, Darrel."

I braced myself, looking from sister to sister, trying to guess what was going on.

"I'm pregnant," Gaylene sobbed. "I was so ashamed. I didn't know how to tell you."

We stood in the dining room in a three-way hug. I was already analyzing the situation, trying to figure out what this meant for me. The next week, I increased my hours as a waiter at Pardon My Garden, Calgary's trendy seafood restaurant and jazz bar.

BETWEEN EMERGENCY CASES at the hospital, my coworkers and I had time to sit at the nursing station and chat. A couple of the nurses, Barb and Pauline, befriended me and wanted to know more about my life. I shared my past with them in small packages, testing their reaction as I went.

First, I told them about Mosom, who had only spoken Cree, my hero and idol; how he had taken Mother, Debbie, Greggie and me to live with him in his two-room trapping cabin after my father died. I described how he had provided for us by hunting moose, deer, beavers and rabbits, hauling firewood, gathering teas and herbs, selling furs and buying us clothing and food with his treaty money. When they smiled and agreed he was a wonderful man, I opened up more and told them about a traditional Cree woman Mother respected a great deal, Honorine. It was a lovely name that the locals twisted to O-la-rine. Honorine had somehow eluded residential school and also only spoke Cree—and the legend was that she had killed a bear with an axe to defend herself. She lived alone in a cabin in the woods; had long, thick unkempt hair adorned with a colourful bandana. The Smith towns-people feared her. Mother said Honorine spoke high Cree and knew a lot about herbs and medicines, tanning moose hides, sewing buckskin clothing and doing beadwork.

Again, the nurses found this story fascinating. What I couldn't tell them about was my life with Mother. How she had appeared to me as the Devil, or how—in an incident I had blocked from my mind but had begun to have nightmares about recently—while drunk one Sunday morning, using gasoline she had sent Debbie and Greggie to buy at Hugo's Garage, she had tried to set the house on fire with us kids locked inside. Or how Rory had exploited me as a vulnerable boy while I was in his care. These stories of being Indian I still couldn't share with anyone.

One day a woman who reminded me of Honorine—the same thick black hair, beautiful dark complexion and proud manner—pushed a man in a wheelchair up to the triage desk. His left leg was raised and loosely wrapped with a blood-soaked pillow case.

"His name is Peter Falls-With-An-Axe. Been shot in the thigh and foot," she announced. I whisked them to a treatment room so the nurses could stem the blood loss and set him up for the doctor to examine. When I returned to the desk, I overheard the nurses' conversation.

"Another drunken Indian with gunshot wounds. I wish they would get it together," said a nurse named Sue.

This nurse had always been kind to me—almost motherly. I was speechless for a moment, but then I spoke up.

"Sue," I said, "I'm Indian too, you know."

"Yes, but you're different." She looked me in the face. "You're a credit to your race. These local Indians are losers."

"Wonder what they have for lunch in the cafeteria," another nurse interjected.

My friend Curt, an orderly, came over and put his hand on my shoulder. "Let's go down to the lake a bit before lunch, my friend."

THAT SUMMER, BARB surprised me by inviting me to go on a trail ride in the Rocky Mountains with her and a couple of friends. I knew I couldn't afford it, and that it would mean leaving Gaylene and Jennifer alone for a week, but I went, and it was spectacular. We rode for eight hours a day, and by the time we arrived at each new idyllic site, the lanky cowboys had our teepees all set up. As my horse plodded along the dirt trail, I spotted tiger lilies and Indian paintbrushes. Alongside them were more delicate flowers that only grew in the highest alpine meadows. I held my horse back from the others, then let it gallop along the crest of the mountain top to catch up. I wondered if other riders thought I looked Indian, sitting on my horse with its head thrown back, the wind in my hair. Mosom had talked about hunting on horseback near Rocky Mountain House. He must have loved it.

We spotted birds I had never seen before; someone said they were mountain chickadees. Someone else pointed out the ospreys circling overhead. I loved our coffee and pee breaks by gushing mountain streams. I could never resist taking off my riding boots and wading in. It all took me back to the magical moments I had spent in Canmore, living under the careful watch of the Three Sisters mountains—a time when the mountains themselves had seemed to become my grandparents, a source of strength that allowed me to stand up to the teacher and refuse the strap. It was a time when I had truly been in touch with my own spirit, before the years of confusion with Rory. Was this latest stay in the heart of the Rockies helping me to re-emerge, to find myself again?

After six nights of sitting around the campfire sipping brandy and singing folk songs, the stress of university, of working two jobs and of having my sister and niece living with me had dissipated. It all rebounded in a flash when I arrived home.

Gaylene and Jennifer were gone, along with their clothes and belongings—no note or message. I was devastated. I had thought things were going okay with Gaylene. Jennifer and I had bonded so sweetly. She would block the doorway with her little body and demand I stay home each time I went to leave; I had to pick her up and give her a kiss to get out the door. Disconsolate, I scanned the phone bills and found the number Gaylene had called most often—her friend Helen in Edmonton.

Helen had been sworn to secrecy, but she took pity on me and told me where Gaylene was—in Edmonton, living with the parents of Jennifer's teenage father, John. I drove to Edmonton that afternoon.

As soon as I entered the smoky basement suite, Jennifer ran up to me, grabbed onto my legs and wouldn't let go. Gaylene sat in an armchair, teary eyed. A few days there had made her realize that there was no way things could work out. She and John couldn't afford their own place, and although his parents were kind, the place was just too small for four adults and a toddler, not to mention the baby on the way. She stood, walked over and gave me a hug.

"Gaylene—I think you should come home."

"I know, I know. I'm sorry, I'll get our things."

I hated to admit it, but I felt fed up and ashamed of my family: my teen sister who was pregnant for the second time; my mother, probably on skid row in Edmonton; and my brother Greg, now Trina, a recovering drug addict. Debbie seemed happy, but drinking was a bone of contention between us. I had never found a way to calm Mother when she was drunk and angry, but I would hug Debbie and tell her that I loved her until she relaxed and went to sleep. It worked every time, but I hated going through the experience. God knows I had been through it enough with Mother in my childhood years.

By chance, though, a new dimension had opened up in my life: gourmet food. The staff discount at Pardon My Garden allowed me to sample French crepes with a seafood Newburg or coquilles St. Jacques filling, filet mignon grilled to medium rare, tangy ratatouille or braised beef ribs with garlic mashed potatoes. People often ordered expensive red wine and left half of it. I tried it all, but as with other pleasures, I couldn't tell any of my friends or family. After all, who did I think I was, going around using fifty-dollar words and eating like that? The waiters and chefs delighted in seeing how dazzled I was by the menu items they recommended. The bartender gave me samples of exotic mixed drinks and smiled at my *oohs* and *aahs* as I sipped them. A couple of evenings when I finished work early, I stayed to listen to jazz in the lounge. I admired the talent of the trumpeter and saxophonists, but I felt out of place among the well-heeled patrons. I couldn't relax enough to appreciate the music.

Each evening, as I poured expensive French wine and served elegant food, I observed the diners carefully—their fashion sense, their menu choices and the personal confidence that bordered on arrogance. My determination gradually solidified—someday, somehow, I would experience that lifestyle; I would become a pleasure-seeking diner and wouldn't let guilt stop me. After all, there were no songs about gluttony in our catechism classes.

In any case, religion was dropping to the background for me. One evening I went to work at Pardon My Garden with a small gold cross and white dove pinned to the lapel of my blazer. At the end of the shift, the manager called me into his office to ask why I had worn them to work. I knew what my Christian friends would say—this was an opportunity to witness my faith, to tell my boss about Jesus. But I didn't. Instead, I told him a half-truth: they were gifts that I was wearing out of nostalgia.

BETWEEN MY MORNING shifts in Emergency and my evenings at the restaurant, the range of emotions I went through daily was at times incredible. Take the afternoon the black phone rang and Barb fielded a simple question: "On a bet, a friend swallowed two tablespoons of rat poison. Will he be okay?" Barb advised the person on the other end to call an ambulance immediately. Minutes later the red phone rang—the ambulance carrying the poison victim was on its way.

I met them in the garage and opened the back door to see a slim, balding Caucasian man in his thirties. His voice was anxious.

"What the hell is going on? Can't you guys do something to stop the jerking in my legs?"

As soon as we got him onto the treatment table, the man started thrashing from side to side, and his face was twitching. Within minutes he was gasping for air, and the pattern on the cardiac monitor showed he was in ventricular fibrillation. I knew my role.

I climbed onto the table beside him; I leaned directly over him and initiated chest compressions. His eyes were wide open, and I fell into their depths—mesmerized, but unsure what I was seeing there. Was it the trepidation of dying? Was he getting a glimpse of what was on the other side? I guessed it was a desperate yearning to stay alive.

One one thousand, two one thousand, three one thousand. His chest got rigid. I had to use more pressure; I heard a rib crack. Damn.

Within minutes an anaesthetist strode into the room, oozing self-importance. After a brief exchange with the emergency room physician, Dr. B., he loaded syringes of varying sizes from glass vials. He drew a golden viscous liquid into the largest one. I thought I was going to faint. "We're going to induce a coma," the anaesthetist announced. Within seconds, the patient's face relaxed. Once he was completely out, Barb and I wheeled him up to the ICU.

Another afternoon, Barb answered the red phone. I heard her pleading with the ambulance dispatcher not to send an unconscious baby, since the Rockyview didn't have a pediatric ward. She hung up the phone. "They're coming." A flurry of nurses bustled to sterilize the pediatric trays.

I pulled opened the double doors of the ambulance to see a distraught paramedic with a baby cradled in his left arm.

"Ready to take over?"

Before I could respond, he had passed me the baby. A familiar baby smell wafted into my nostrils, and I could feel the peach fuzz of its head against my bare bicep. I had never ever expected to use the two-finger chest massage technique we had learned for babies or toddlers, yet here I was, massaging a real live baby instead of a doll. In a frenzy, I strode down the hall counting out "one and two and three and" to pace the massage. The child's elastic sternum bounced back after each compression.

As the team started IVs, inserted a tiny catheter and ventilated the baby, the paramedics told us what had happened: the father had slipped on a flight of stairs to the basement, dropping the baby before he himself tumbled. The father was en route in a separate ambulance; someone was trying to track down the mother.

After an hour, the doctor pronounced the baby dead. I had never felt so much emotion and tension in one room. Everyone was speechless and pale; some were in tears. The doctor left the room cursing under his breath.

I focused enough to help the nurses tidy the room a bit, since the mother would likely burst in at any moment. Then I snuck to the staff bathroom behind the nursing station to hide and get control of my feelings.

The paramedic who had handed me the baby pulled open the bathroom door and brushed past. An acrid odour; his vomit in the sink made me gag, too. I sat on the toilet and put my head in my hands, but tears wouldn't come. I began whispering to myself: deep breaths, deep breaths. I knew I was shirking my responsibilities, and I had to pull myself together. Then I heard a nurse's voice outside the door. "Darrel—there's a call for you to go to the morgue. A family is here to view a relative, and they need you to help set it up."

I had never been to the morgue before. The stench announced its location before the sign did. Formaldehyde, methyl alcohol, bleach, perhaps, and the unmistakable stench of death. The bodies were zipped up in shrouds or body bags and refrigerated, but still the vapours seeped out and pervaded the basement.

Gordon, a retired medic from the British Army, led me to a dimly lit lab at the back where the rigid body of an older Caucasian man lay uncovered on a morgue table. Coarse stitches outlined a huge U-shaped incision below his chest. Large formaldehyde-filled jars lined a stainless-steel trolley—I recognized the shapes of the kidney and heart, and I was sure the smaller jar contained his brain.

"Okay—help me to slide him over to the stretcher, so we can set him up. You support the head."

The daunting odour and the sight of the disembowelled cadaver were making me woozy. I reached up to support the head, but my hand slipped into a moist cavity.

"Oh God! My hand is inside his head!"

"Oh, fuck. Guess they haven't stitched it up yet. Sorry about that, mate. Must have run out of time."

Shaking, I pulled my hand away and hastened to the sink to scrub it. My thoughts were frenetic. Death and more death—everywhere around me, it seemed. Was it some kind of omen?

ONE SUNDAY EVENING at Pardon My Garden, the manager burst through the kitchen doors to tell me I had an urgent phone call. It was the Foothills Hospital—Gaylene had arrived there by ambulance. Her water had burst, and they expected she would give birth that night.

I was angry that Trina hadn't called me right after calling the ambulance. At my request, she had come to Calgary to look after Jennifer. We went through strained negotiations about the terms and conditions of her visit: a return airline ticket and spending money at least equivalent to the amount she would have received on welfare in Vancouver. We'd had hellish fights ever since her arrival.

I heard Gaylene screaming as soon as the elevator doors opened. Following the sound, I zipped to her room, and there she was—alone and in distress with an IV and some sort of baby monitor attached to her.

"Oh, thank God you're here. The baby's coming—I can feel it."

She had yanked her call button out from the wall, but no nurse had appeared. I ran to the nursing station. "My sister Gaylene is freaking out. Her baby is coming!"

A young nurse strode over and smiled at me. "I know she has that sensation, but I measured her dilation a few minutes ago—the baby will be a while yet."

"She's beside herself. Can you please come and check again?"

I hurried back to Gaylene's side. Her nurse came in a couple of minutes later, lifted the blankets, let out a shriek and then called, "We have to get her to the birthing room now!"

As we pushed Gaylene's bed past the nursing station into the birthing room, the nurse shouted for someone to get the doctor—stat. We slid Gaylene onto the table; she was moaning and gasping, trying hard not to yell. The doctor appeared, scrubbed and gloved, wearing OR greens.

I was there when Magdalene was born. Gaylene had given me the honour of choosing the name. We called her Maggie.

I CARRIED THE letter around for a week without opening it. The following Saturday, as I sat in the car outside Pauline's place, waiting for her to come down so we could head to the emergency room staff Christmas party, I finally tore it open. Bad idea. The letter informed me that my student funding had been cut. The reason given was a weak employment market for Bachelor of Science graduates.

I stuffed the letter into the glove compartment as soon as I spotted Pauline coming toward the car. At Dr. G.'s house, I felt my face stretch to smile as I shook the hands of the doctors and nurses and their wives and husbands. My mood was dark, but I still knew that what was happening here was extraordinary. These accomplished white professionals had invited me to party with them. They were treating me as an equal. In Edmonton, the first question would have been, which neighbourhood do you live in, Darrel? My answer, the West End, would have brought an abrupt end to the conversation.

It was supposed to be a fun occasion, and it indeed seemed to be for everyone else. There was lots of cheery banter and laughter. I tried to cheer myself by sipping Chivas on the rocks and chatting with Curt, but later, all I would really remember from the party was the perfectly decorated Christmas tree and the giant cheese ball in the middle of a platter of other fancy cheeses. To maximize our party time, Barb and Pauline had arranged for us to spend the night in Emerg. That way, we would be on site for work at seven a.m. the next day.

I hardly slept that night. I lay thinking about the letter, doing mental calculations of my income from my two part-time jobs versus my costs. How could I continue to support Gaylene and the girls and pay tuition and rent, not to mention car payments and credit card bills? I was sure the next phone bill would be the worst yet. Leading up to Christmas Gaylene had been calling her friends a lot, and I didn't blame her. She had no company other than her two girls. I knew for sure now that Mother was living on "skid row" in Edmonton. Some cousins had seen her there.

The next morning, I pretended to myself that everything was fine, that I was still on track to head to medical school. I listened intently when Dr. B. gave me his usual tips about suturing wounds, smoothing bone fragments and re-inserting displaced joints. I heard myself laugh along with everyone else at shift-change report when the night charge nurse told us about the couple in treatment room C. The husband had a vibrator stuck in his rectum, all efforts to get it out had failed, and he was booked for the OR. But my laughter was hollow. Dominating everything was my looming sense of doom.

I didn't discuss my situation with anyone. Secretly, I started a job search and booked a trip out to Vancouver to see Trina for early January. She was back living there, and she had been nagging me to join me.

THE FOLLOWING WEEK, a Calgary chinook provided a reprieve from the frigid weather. Everyone at work was cheery. We were sipping coffee and enjoying Black Forest cake when a call came through on the red phone about a serious motor vehicle accident involving a motorcycle on Glenmore Trail.

The paramedics had begun CPR, and I continued the chest massage on the patient as they wheeled him down the hallway. He was a ruggedly good-looking man with dark blond hair, a short-cropped beard and sideburns, probably around twenty-five. I felt myself getting anxious, pleading silently, please don't die; please—you have to get through this.

Once things settled down slightly, I was distracted by something sharp poking against my left thigh.

When Dr. C. asked me to pause so he could check for a pulse, I lifted the sheet and saw the jagged edge of a pearly-white stick-like object jutting out at a thirty-degree angle—the man's fractured femur had pierced his skin. The tension in the room was mounting, and something was happening to me that I didn't understand. My chest was tightening, and my thoughts were colliding. This beautiful young man was dying, and here I was feeling sorry for myself—gawking at the doctor and mourning the fact I would never be in his position. Then I realized I was praying, but not to Jesus. Instead, it was an open prayer to the universe—please let this man live, and please help me to get through all of this.

What was so mesmerizing about this man's face? Why was I getting so emotional?

The doctor stopped the process after twenty minutes and made the pronouncement.

"My son... Where is my son?" A desperate male voice in the hallway.

"We'll take you to see him in a minute. Let's have a seat in the quiet room down the hall. Let me get you some water or tea." The smoky voice of the nursing supervisor, Mrs. R.

My hands were shaking, but I tried to appear calm as I discontinued the IVs, removed his urinary catheter, and washed his bristly pallid face, his flaccid arms and hands.

"I want my boy. Need my boy!"

In he came, the father, his face as twisted and white as the bedsheets.

"Ohhhh... ohhh, my son!"

I fled to the chapel down the hall and knelt beside the front pew. When I closed my eyes, I saw the young Italian's face, and then, to my surprise, my father's. I had contemplated his face for hours in the few photos that Mother had, trying desperately to will him back to life. He was about the same age as the young Italian when he died, and they looked so much alike, even though Father was Métis.

Suddenly, I got it—the magnitude of Mother's loss when Father died, and why she had never recovered. I recalled the stories she told about how Debbie had gone into shock after Daddy's death, and how Greggie's personality had changed completely. I had never known Daddy, at least not directly, but now I was sure he had sung to me and rubbed Mother's swollen brown belly every day for six months, until the pain of cancer completely devastated him.

Finally, I felt the magnitude of my own loss, and I wept. With my future up in the air and my family in ruins, I needed my father more than ever. And the volatile man-to-man love I had experienced— in the perverse connection with Rory, in the clandestine encounters in dark corners of shopping malls, in my passion with Gresh—had I been searching for my father, his scent, his touch, his voice? Getting into medical school was to be my salvation, our escape from the rut of poverty and despair his death had plunged us into. So what did it all mean? What now?

Footsteps in the hallway. I dried my eyes, stood and turned to see Barb's silhouette in the doorway.

"Darrel, are you alright? Your sister Gaylene called. She needs you to pick up diapers and milk on the way home."

L'Échappatoire

PACKED MY belongings and crammed them into my Toyota SR5, strapping boxes to the roof to begin the journey. I had planned to leave earlier in the day, to avoid driving into the night, but it was one delay after the other, as if I was postponing my departure. Gaylene and Jennifer were excited about their new life with Jennifer's father, John, Gaylene's junior high school sweetheart, but saying goodbye to Debbie over the phone was emotional.

As I passed the Calona winery on the outskirts of Calgary, I turned the radio up to full volume. "Heart of Glass," Debbie's favourite song, was the first that grabbed my attention. Then, interspersed with songs I didn't know, "Knock on Wood," "YMCA" and "Funkytown." My thoughts were intensifying, and fear started to creep in. Why was I leaving all of my family except Trina behind in Alberta? Would things work out in Vancouver? I would be sleeping on Trina's couch until I could afford to get my own place. No savings, credit cards at their limit. I knew it was all over between Gresh and me, now that he was living with Jim, but this move would make that more final, too.

On a recent visit, I had secured a job at the Vancouver General Hospital. After two weeks' orientation, they would certify me as an orderly and pay me thirty percent more than I had earned at the Rockyview. Yet it was a far cry from being a doctor. Was this the best I could do after two years of university? Would I ever get back to my studies? From my few trips to visit Trina in Vancouver, I had the impression that people were different on the West Coast—flaky, with a wild streak—at least on Davie Street where she lived. How would I fit in? Would I become more like the alternative types I saw there? Trina was already pressuring me to grow my hair long. She herself seemed to have settled down. She was studying nursing, and her friend Arlene, who had turned tricks with her at the Blackstone Hotel on Granville Street, was training to be an X-ray technologist.

Debbie was upset that I was moving. She didn't like or trust Trina, and she saw this as a move, on my part, into Trina's camp. The two of them hadn't spoken for eight years, ever since Trina and Diane had paid Debbie a surprise visit at the truck stop where she worked in Calgary, dressed in full drag. Debbie pretended she didn't recognize them, then told them to leave and never return. Trina often talked with rancour about Debbie's rejection of them. Trina's life since her operation had not been easy, either. Both times I visited her in the year following her operation, we had spent a lot of time in doctors' offices—she'd had complications. As we sat waiting or went for coffee after her appointments, she shared intimate information that left me disillusioned with her choice and the result. She had sacrificed the chance at bona fide orgasms for the psychological gratification of being frontally penetrated by a straight man, she confided. Then there was the hormone replacement process, which in the long term would leave her with osteoporosis and degenerated discs in her back and neck. She hated having to sleep with a prosthetic penis inside of her every night. To make matters worse, shortly after her operation she had discovered that she could not have intercourse because of the pain. All too quickly, the giddy carnival of Greg/Trina's youth had turned into a desperate march from one medical clinic to the other, urinary catheter in hand. The final insult was medical receptionists and nurses glancing up from behind their desks to say, "Can I help you, sir?"

I stopped for gas in Canmore, pumped myself up with coffee and made a mini-pilgrimage to a spot where I had spent time as a kid admiring the Three Sisters. There was a new subdivision, but I went to the edge of the creek and lost myself in the presence of the three magnificent peaks. Cascade Mountain, just inside the gates of Banff

National Park, was as regal as ever, adorned with jutting ice sculptures that were waterfalls in the summer. A flock of bighorn sheep lingered at the turnoff to Lake Minnewanka, their breath forming a cloud of steam. By the time I stopped in Golden for more coffee, it was dark outside. The caffeine made my head buzz. After an hour or so back on the road, I decided to stop for a pee and a nap in a rest area. Ten or fifteen minutes later I awoke cold, the car blanketed by powdery snow. Instantly alert, I started the engine and returned to the highway.

The snowflakes got fuller and heavier. I was slowing down when I saw a luminescent red sign saying WRONG WAY. It was as if a heavy fog had descended over me. I pulled over to get my bearings. Was this an omen? Was some invisible force attempting to block my escape from the Alberta side of the continental divide? Alberta had always felt like a trap to me, in part due to stories I had heard from Mother. For years I had been convinced that our family was under a curse, because more than once Mother spoke of an incident that had occurred a couple of generations before I was born. In a suspicious hunting accident, the father of the current chief of our tribe had shot the man who was hereditary chief at the time, a distant relative, and stolen the chieftainship. He made himself leader for life and conspired with government officials to make his immediate family the only registered members of the Indian band. Following this, the self-appointed chief had paid a powerful medicine man to place a curse on the descendants of the deposed chief and his followers, including our family, to prevent us from sharing the wealth that would accrue from the lands and resources of our territory. As a teen, I had asked Mother and one of our aunties for more information, but instead of answering my questions, they got stern faces and told me to never raise the topic again. My life had improved dramatically after I converted to Christianity, so I deduced that Jesus had blocked that curse, at least for me. What would shield me now?

THE FIRST FRIEND of Trina's I met was Jean-Paul, a francophone originally from Montréal. He invited me to go for a swim and sauna in the basement of their high-rise. I was cute, he informed me, but my body type was too much like that of a Chinese person. The kinky black hair on my fingers and toes was a turn off, he added, and he wondered aloud if I shared another trait that many gay men believed to be common in Asian men—a small penis.

A constant carnival was the best description of Vancouver's West End: an around-the-clock shuffle of drag queens, transgender people and flamboyant gay men, all camping it up in a tacit contest to be the most hilarious or outrageous of all. Hookers and their pimps were everywhere, unabashedly going about their business. One evening when I was out for a walk, a petite Filipino drag queen approached me, saying, "You look sweet. Would you like some company?" I was put off, and that made him more determined. He followed me for a block, calling, "Come back, baby. Why are you so uptight?"

The Vancouver General was twenty times larger than the Rockyview and was a more comprehensive facility that included advanced cardiac care, a state-of-the-art burn unit, short-term psychiatric assessment, a renal unit and a hyperbaric chamber. There was also more death. I dreaded being the on-call orderly, because it was likely that at least once during the shift I would get called to take a patient to the morgue. But I made new friends among the other orderlies my first week at VGH: Réjean from Québec City, Robin from Northern BC, Guy from Newfoundland and Jean from Montréal. Three of the four were gay.

Sex was available everywhere, with gay men, bisexual men and those who were straight but curious. Walking on the beach at English Bay or Kitsilano brought requests for intimacy. The pretexts varied: I just broke up with my girlfriend; I have always wanted to try this; it's a phase I'm going through; or, I just bought this container of ice cream and I'm looking for someone to share it with. But the fun was short-lived. When word got around about a disease that was spreading like wildfire amongst gay men and drug addicts, the era of carefree sex came to a halt. My friend Réjean died of AIDS within weeks of being diagnosed.

Jean-Paul and a few of Trina's other friends raved about Trina's Croatian neighbour, Milan: how attractive he was, but strictly straight, unattainable. Trina, Milan and I spent hours together in cafés, on the beach and at her place. I began to bump into Milan regularly on Denman Street, and he invited me to join him for coffee at the beach, just the two of us. Milan was as amazing as people said, piercing blue eyes, a wide smile with an intriguing space between his front teeth, and an air of aloofness and sophistication. As time went by, our relationship deepened.

One afternoon in late April, I was sunbathing at English Bay with Trina and Milan when the idea popped into my head that I had to resume my studies, and for some reason I felt I had to act that very day. When I got out to the University of British Columbia, I learned that I had missed the registration deadline for science courses, so I signed up for intensive French and Spanish courses as electives. I bumped into Robin, my orderly friend from VGH, in the long lineup. He was taking advanced French courses, and he spoke Spanish well from having spent time in Colombia. He would become a mentor, showing patience as I tested my beginning French and Spanish on him.

From my first day at UBC, I knew the experience was going to be different—the place had a gentler vibe, and the hostility and officiousness that I had felt at U of C were missing. I was pleased when my French professors told me I had a refreshing perspective on books like *L'Étranger* by Albert Camus, *Huis Clos* by Jean-Paul Sartre and *Liaisons Dangereuses* by Pierre Choderlos de Laclos. Several of them insisted I continue studying languages and literature, and one day, after I made a bold comment in class in French, the professor responded that he thought I was *très intelligent*. I walked a bit taller as I headed to the cafeteria for my mid-morning coffee and cinnamon bun.

Initially the principles of existentialism disturbed me, but with time they provided relief. What if there really was no heaven or hell, and I had only to live in the present and make the most of it—accept responsibility for my own happiness and well-being? I loved the notion that I could choose whether or not to believe in Christianity without living in constant angst of going to hell. These new teachings assuaged the recurring sadness and fear I'd had about my unsaved family members and ancestors who had practised their so-called pagan rituals, chants and dances. They weren't being eternally punished after all.

I related to the notion of people making daily life hell for each other. Rory, Gresh and my mother knew something about creating hell for others. I also learned that white people, in particular European aristocrats closely aligned with the Catholic Church, hadn't taken the Church's teachings seriously at all. They had sinned more deliberately and in wilder ways than I could ever have imagined. Religion was simply a way of keeping underprivileged people like us oppressed, fearful and poor. Voltaire's *Candide* and Jean-Jacques Rousseau's *Confessions* helped me to understand my misgivings about Christianity and the Catholic Church, and they made me more determined in my rejection of both.

One day on campus, I stumbled across a cultural event put on by the UBC Native Indian Teacher Education Program. I was drawn by the *bohm bohm* of a traditional hand drum—the rhythm Mosom used to tap out in the mornings and evenings to accompany his *haeey hai* chant. I snuck in and heard an elder explain that this rhythm is an echo of the sound a baby hears in the womb: the mother's heartbeat. Hearing the drum awakened something within me. There was no going back to Catholicism or Pentecostalism; I knew I had to learn about traditional spirituality and begin to practise it. I accepted Mosom's spirit as my guide and decided to pray to him and my ancestors in much the way I had prayed to Jesus.

I initiated conversations with my new Vancouver friends about being Indian; they encouraged me to learn more about my culture and shared articles and books they came across. I devoured everything I could find about traditional Cree spirituality.

Joseph Campbell's *Power of Myth* and Bertrand Russell's essays, like "Why I Am Not a Christian," helped me to weasel my way out from under the black cloud of fear and guilt. After reading passages that held meaning for me, I would sit still, eyes closed, and feel relief wash over me.

A YEAR AFTER I had completed a degree in French language and literature, I was in teacher training and living in a high-rise near Stanley Park. I was at home one night, in the thick of designing learning modules and scanning children's books, when the phone rang. "Hello, Darrel." Gresh's sultry baritone. How could anyone sound so seductive in just two words?

I almost dropped the receiver in the torrent of emotions. I did manage, though, to ask how he and Jim were doing.

"Oh, I'm fine, and Jim's okay, but working too much. Listen, we both miss you, and we want you to come for a visit. We'll pay your way and spoil you rotten. Everyone calls me Gresham now, but you can still call me Gresh," he said with a laugh.

The monologue went on. "I was fed up with doing everything with Jim's brothers, sisters, nieces and nephews, Darrel. Our new house is huge—way more than we need, but it's not as ostentatious as the mansion. My family felt uncomfortable visiting us there."

I was pleased to realize that I held no grudge against Jim. Instead, I saw him as a kindred spirit who had also become entangled in Gresh's web of seduction. If anything, I pitied him. I knew it was just a matter of time before Gresh's crazy-making would start to erode Jim's sanity, as it had mine. I was touched by their invitation, however, and thought that perhaps we could actually be friends, the three of us. I accepted.

As soon as I arrived, Gresh hung my coat in the foyer closet and took me on a tour of the house. It was expansive, with an old-world classiness I had seen only in movies. Gresh's one piece of art—the salmon print—hung in the hallway, dwarfed by large original water-colours and oil paintings that belonged to Jim. I didn't see any of the IKEA or Woolco furniture that Gresh had so proudly assembled and displayed in the apartment we shared. The elegant wooden furniture, alongside extravagant sofas and wingback chairs, I was sure had been selected by an interior decorator.

I couldn't help but notice the thick gold band with a glittering diamond on the ring finger of Gresh's left hand. Over a few glasses of wine, they filled me in on their summer trip to London, offering a detailed description of their room in a four-star hotel and explaining how the room had sat vacant for a week, even though it was prepaid, because Gresh decided he wanted to see Paris instead.

After a while, Gresh asked me to go upstairs with him so we could chat as he sorted the dry cleaning that had been delivered that morning. Standing in his spacious walk-in closet, I watched as he inspected his Hugo Boss and Armani knit shirts. "Damn, they didn't put the collars down properly," he complained.

Later, over dinner, the three of us had an amiable conversation until Jim started asking questions about my life. "Is your mother still drinking? Why isn't the federal government paying your university tuition? Are you paying taxes?"

I recognized the expression on Gresh's face; he was about to explode. He poured more wine. By nine o'clock, Jim had passed out on the couch. Gresh helped him up to bed, and I started to clean up the kitchen.

I was at the sink rinsing pots when Gresh came up behind me. He wrapped his arms around me, rotated me to face him and pressed me up against the fridge. He began kissing me—gently at first, then forcefully. His trademark kiss became deeper; his embrace tightened as my body relaxed. He unbuttoned my shirt; I drew in a deep breath as his lips singed my neck—gasped as he latched hard onto my left nipple. His cologne prompted a deluge of memories. I was melting, and he knew it. He pulled back for a moment and looked at me. His eyes glistened.

"You're the one for me, Darrel. I love you. Ever since I first saw your little Indian butt jumping up and down at church. Jim and I—we're not meant for each other. He's an alcoholic."

Thanks to having analyzed *Les Liaisons Dangereuses* in one of my French literature courses, I understood the dark intrigue that was taking shape in Gresh's kitchen, and also the *enjeu*, what was at stake for me: my sanity, my dignity and my blossoming relationship with Milan. Gresh was my Vicomte de Valmont, the hero and villain from the book. Love and seduction were like a chess match for him. He tested the naïveté of his adversary with his no-holds-barred seduction; the weaker victims would suffer greater humiliation, but in a show of mercy, he kept in touch with them. Gresh didn't love either Jim or me, but he needed us to confirm his superiority. And, like *le vicomte*, he had been spurned by a conquest with whom he had fallen in love—while we were living together—a real live Ken doll, a man who actually carried the name.

I broke from his clutch, terrified. I wondered who would be on the receiving end of his lies the next day: Jim, me or both of us.

"I'm going to bed, Gresh, alone."

AFTER SOME TIME, I reluctantly resumed visits with Gresh, at his invitation. How could I tell him about the changes in my beliefs, and how would he react? On our first visit, at the Eau Claire Market on the banks of the Makhabn, I was as nervous as I had been the first weekend we spent together. I had arrived early, with the hope of buying some new clothes that would fit me better. I spent twenty minutes in the bathroom of my hotel beforehand, arranging my long hair, torn as to whether I should wear my gold rings carved by Coast Salish artists and wondering if I should tell Gresh about my BMW. Would he think I was even more of a social climber than before? I knew I would have to avoid any conversation about religion.

He took a glance at my ponytail and carved rings and muttered, "Why do people choose to emphasize one side of their heritage over the other?" For our entire brief visit, he wore a scowl, which confused me. (Years later I would understand what he was getting at—what about my Scottish and French bloodlines—why wasn't I honouring those?)

We stayed in touch for the next few years, and in the second week of July, like clockwork, a birthday card would arrive in the mail, signed *Love, Gresh*. Sometimes there would be a carefully folded letter in his neat handwriting with an update on his life: career changes, travel, family events. In one letter he told how his father's suicide had motivated him to get trained in suicide prevention and set up a program in Calgary.

Another letter caught me completely off guard. Gresh told me that he and Jim had split up and sold their white house on Elbow Drive. Jim had moved back into his mansion, and months later had a tragic accident. One night, in the wee hours, he had slipped and tumbled head first down the huge spiral staircase in the foyer. He died—and he didn't leave Gresh anything.

I was in Calgary regularly, and Gresh and I met up often. There was no sexual innuendo or seduction, and I came to appreciate him as caring, intelligent, evolved and accomplished. He was eager to tell me how much he loved his adopted niece, whom he said was "Native," and how through his work in suicide prevention he had learned much about First Nations culture and beliefs. Gresh had a long-standing partner, an artist, and was working as a highly specialized school psychologist. I thought our friendship was finally on a strong and healthy track. But on our last visit, Gresh suggested we walk to my hotel to have a drink and make dinner plans. As he was chaining up his bike, his voice took on a naughty tone. "Let's have a race, Darrel. The first to arrive at your hotel gets to give the other one a blow job." I rolled my eyes—he hadn't changed a bit.

FOR YEARS I had kept the secret of my sexual contact with Rory to myself. At age eighteen I told Greggie about it, but I swore him to secrecy. Later, I told a few gay friends. Both Greggie and my friends smirked with amusement at first, thinking I was bragging—recounting a fantasy that many guys seemed to hold about making out with a straight brother-in-law. Their faces sunk into a look of consternation as they realized that it had been a situation of abuse—that I was only eleven when the intense contact began. Then they condemned it outright, and some friends advised me to go after Rory with criminal charges or a civil suit.

For the most part, I managed to live a double life, with my secret—and my guilt—intact. I threw myself into my education and my work. Working half-time at the hospital and studying full-time at UBC allowed me to avoid intimacy with family and friends. But when I was twenty-nine years old and in my second year of teaching, something shifted deep inside, and I came to see the biblical proverb that had so tortured me, about being ensnared in evil, in a new way.

FUCK   COCKSUCKER   DICK   BALLS   PRICK
        SLUT   PUSSY   GIVE HEAD   BLOW JOB
    .CUNT   SCREW   CUNTLAPPER
            BOOTY   CORNHOLE
PENIS   VAGINA   INTERCOURSE   ANAL SEX   FELLATIO
CUNNILINGUS

I froze in the doorway of my Grade Four classroom. My eyes were fixed on the chalkboard, where all these words had been scrawled. I dropped my dripping umbrella by my desk, threw my coat onto my chair. Good grief! What was going on? Had someone played an awful prank? Who would do this, and in my classroom—why target me? I wondered what I should do next—make an issue of it, or erase the words quickly and pretend it had never happened?

I was making for the blackboard when a group of students burst into the room. Several pointed at the words on the board and started to giggle. When a girl named Nella saw the look on my face she came over to me and explained, *"Monsieur McLeod, c'est Madame Hickling qui a écrit ces mots au tableau."*

"Merci, Nella."

I'd known that Meg Hickling, a respected sexual health educator, was going to be visiting my French Immersion class, but I hadn't put two and two together. When Meg sauntered into the room with her sassy short-cropped greying hair and cat's eye glasses, she gave me a disarming smile. "It's a little exercise we do in the *Feeling Yes, Feeling No* sessions. We replace the slang vocabulary with the proper terms, then discuss why some people think sex is dirty or sinful."

I took a deep breath. My overactive imagination already had me in the principal's office, or, worse, the regional superintendent's office, explaining how those words had come to appear on the chalkboard in my classroom.

"Wow. Well, what a surprise! I think I'll stay for the rest, if you don't mind," I said.

As I sank into a student desk near the back, Meg strode to the front of the class and continued her presentation by describing how some exploitive adults initiate sexual contact with children. Children will likely feel, intuitively, that the touching is wrong, she explained, and should feel free to say to the person, "Please stop, those are my private parts, that doesn't feel right."

"But what if you like it?" A boy's voice.

Giggles. Sideways glances. A couple of students blushed. One girl sat solemn, staring at the floor. Jarret had asked the question, and now his face was bright red. He liked to be the class clown, but was he serious this time—talking about himself? I was breathless as I waited for Meg's response.

"Often," she began, "in fact all too often, the abuser will be a person you know: an uncle, a neighbour, a grandparent, a step-parent or a father or mother. And it may indeed feel good. The child may very well think he or she likes it, but it is harmful and can lead to serious problems in teen or adult life. Abuse is not the child's fault, not ever. If this is happening to any of you, seek help. You haven't done anything wrong or bad. Talk to an adult—an authority figure you trust."

I felt I was suffocating, and my mouth was parched. I *was* an adult—the teacher—but I felt as if she was addressing the little Darrel inside of me, the innocent eleven-year-old. It wasn't my fault. What had happened with Rory was not my fault. I felt my head might explode as the new understanding of my situation took shape in my mind.

I had never been able to talk to anyone in my family, other than Trina, about what had happened with Rory. Until that day, the remorse I felt about having sex with men was debilitating; I would spend days alone at home afterward and avoid people. I'm sure others perceived me as distant and aloof, when in reality I was withdrawn and depressed. "You're always so serious," Milan and my other friends would say.

Now, finally, I could see what had happened through the eyes of a responsible adult and an expert in the field. Rory had groomed me, prepared me for his plan.

"Are you okay, Mr. McLeod? You look pale," Meg called out from where she stood.

I swallowed hard and stifled the tears that were forming in my eyes. I couldn't speak to answer her; instead I nodded emphatically.

As I walked down Trafalgar Street to the apartment I shared with Milan in Kitsilano, I made a resolution: I would track Rory down to bring charges against him. He was the wicked and ensnared one, not me. He was the one who would be caught fast in the cords of his sin.

From then on, I looked Rory up in the phone book whenever I passed through Calgary or Edmonton. I thought about setting a trap, then pouncing when the time was right. Eventually I called him. He was back working for Alberta Highways in Calgary, he said. Politely, he asked about Debbie, then suggested we meet for a drink the next time I was in town. I was shaking and felt helpless as we spoke. What power did he still have over me? My reaction to hearing his voice shocked and scared me, but after a few days, my resolve was back.

I wanted to see him, all right. I imagined hiring a few Cree or Stoney men to corner and beat him while I confronted him about what he had done. Or maybe I should wear a recording device and trick him into admitting the sexual abuse. The second option was more realistic and wouldn't land me in jail. But after that one phone conversation, Rory seemed to disappear. He was no longer listed in the phone book, and my calls to directory assistance led nowhere.

Summoning up all my courage, I called the Calgary police and told a constable my story. He referred me to the RCMP. The officer there listened for a few minutes, then said it would be difficult to prove what I was saying; it would be Rory's word against mine. He asked if I was willing to live through the scandal and frustration that charging Rory would bring. For the time being, I wasn't.

Rory had influenced my life in powerful ways. I was attracted to men who resembled him: his dominant masculinity, his intense personality and his looks. When I looked at my face in the mirror, I knew I sat astride a razor's edge between acting and being myself. The spirit of that fun-loving and vibrant boy Rory depredated still thrived in me, and in fleeting moments, when a beautiful man or woman caught my eye, I lamented what might have been if I had been allowed to develop normally. After years of psychotherapy, a university education and intensive healing work, I was still searching for physical and emotional intimacy with a man who had Rory's hands.

Mistikosow: The Frenchman

THE FRENCHMAN LAY in bed with his head and knees elevated. Strips of gauze framed his puffy purple face. His eyes were so deeply recessed that I couldn't tell whether he was awake or asleep. Salt and pepper stubble accentuated the wrinkles around his mouth. Great, I thought, I get to spend sixteen hours with a depressed semi-conscious patient.

Still, I was glad to be working a double shift as an orderly after completing my first full year at UBC. The hours of one-on-one care would drag by in the dank room, but the money would contribute to my summer travel to study Spanish in Mexico. The trip was all I could think about that spring—even though I felt guilty about planning two months away at a time when my family needed me. I picked up all the shifts I could, going home just to sleep and shower.

I perused his chart. Philippe was forty-five and from Paris; he owned a French bookstore on Robson Street. His Canadian-born wife of five years had left him for another man. After threatening suicide several times, Philippe shot himself in the head, but the revolver slipped, and the bullet grazed his skull.

The longer I studied the man in the bed, the angrier I became. There was really no treatment plan for him—keep a suicide watch, offer food and drink, and invite him up for walks. Was this the best the system could do for someone in crisis? My thoughts grew darker, and my anger couldn't find a focus. One second I was angry about how society failed people like Philippe, and the next I was angry at him for being such a wimp. Then I was angry at myself.

I couldn't let myself think about that now. Concentrate on Philippe's daily care and on Mexico, I told myself, and soon you'll be there. Be strong, and don't forget to call Mother on your break—just hope she doesn't cry again.

With no training as a counsellor or psychologist, I went with my instincts in these situations—right or wrong. But what came next was a surprise, even to me. I had something to say on the subject of suicide and death, and I decided Philippe was going to hear it.

I fixed my gaze on the floor and summoned my deepest voice.

"You know, suicide is a completely selfish act." I threw in some French for effect: "*C'est égoïste, mon ami.* What about the people who love and cherish you? *Pensez à votre famille, à vos amis proches.*" Did he think it would have been easy for them to find his body, I asked, the top of his head blown off, blood and grey matter spattered on the wall like an abstract painting, face disfigured and arms flailing in a grand mal seizure? Or maybe already dead, lying in a pool of thickening blood?

"Imagine them frantically brushing away the blowflies that had already begun to colonize your body—laying eggs in every crevice—crawling in and out of your nose freely."

I glanced over at him. I was sure his nose twitched, but it might have been my imagination.

I kept going. I told him I wasn't sure why he'd used a gun. Others choose a noose, maybe tied to a rafter somewhere. The results either way were grotesque: face ballooned, tongue jutting out, a puddle of urine and maybe semen on the floor below. "I don't know if there is an elegant way of killing yourself, *mon ami*, but I wouldn't recommend you try that either."

Then I mentioned the smell. More like a bouquet of smells. *L'odeur de la mort*: potent and unmistakable.

"*Et, c'est final.* You can't change your mind and go back. I know—I've seen it first-hand."

As he lay there, immobile, I described what happens to a body at the point of death. How when the heart stops, the body convulses and gasps for air, producing a muffled rattling sound in the throat. Ears chill as the blood turns acidic. When the circulation stops, what once was a person turns into a mannequin—rubbery skin, a chalky pallor, clammy and cold. The pupils deteriorate, resembling those in a glass eye. Blood pools in certain areas of the body, making them reddish-blue. Then the muscles give up. "Bladder—your bladder and bowels release their contents—oh, the stench. Later, your pupils cloud over completely."

Again I checked for a reaction. I could tell he was listening, though his face revealed nothing.

"Then you meet the undertakers. They pump chemicals into the veins and body cavities of your corpse to delay the natural rotting process. They're simply postponing the inevitable, masking the stench so that your family and friends can look at your cadaver without vomiting and dashing out of the room, so they can caress your face and say their adieux. Then they put you into a box."

Was that a tear on his cheek? I couldn't be sure—the lighting was so dim. Damn, my voice was getting thick. I took a deep breath, fixed my gaze on the floor again. I was about to continue when the door opened, startling me. A Filipina woman in a blue uniform entered and set a food tray on the bedside table. Something deep-fried; probably chicken cutlets with boiled vegetables. I hoped that soon a nurse would be along to replace me for a dinner break, even though I had no appetite. I regarded the Frenchman closely. Why this pang of sadness? Was the black amoeba of his depression engulfing me too?

From the payphone downstairs, I called Mother at Brian and Debbie's place in Youngstown. Again she pleaded with me to spend the summer with her, Brian and the kids, Joseph and Jaime. I hadn't told her about Mexico.

Once back from supper, I saw that the man's head was turned to one side. The nurse had tried to feed him, she told me, but he hadn't opened his mouth or eyes even once. I pushed the door shut and went to sit at his bedside. I fumbled in my backpack to find the *Vancouver Sun*, took it out and glanced at the headline:

HMS *ARDENT* SUNK IN THE FALKLANDS—THATCHER VOWS REVENGE

"*Je comprends*. You don't want to eat—but you have to. You want to get out of here, right? To get on with your life… or end it. You know you can't do *either* here, *mon ami*."

I raised a teaspoon with small pieces of chicken and carrot up to his mouth. "Okay, *ouvrez*."

When he didn't budge, I gently pinched his nose; he grunted. As his mouth opened, I popped in a few morsels. He grunted again, then made a chewing motion. Just as I was congratulating myself, he took a noisy breath in through his nose and spewed the food particles, engulfed in a wad of saliva, onto the bedspread.

I pushed the tray towards the door and flopped back into the bedside armchair. Fine, I said to myself—we can't make you eat or drink, *Monsieur*, but I can talk to you. Just wait.

That night, I hardly slept. At six thirty the next morning, on an empty stomach, I made the fifteen-minute bike ride to the Vancouver General in just ten, barely noticing the clouds of cherry blossoms or the wall of red camellias alongside the Heather Pavilion. I took the stairs two at a time up to the nursing supervisor's office to confirm my assignment—another double shift with Philippe.

His breakfast tray sat undisturbed. I coughed to announce my presence, said *Bonjour*. I added sugar and cream to his coffee and sipped it while I pulled together my thoughts.

"*Mon ami*," I said at last, "someone close to me committed suicide last fall—eight months ago. My oldest sister, Debbie."

His face remained frozen, but I knew he was listening.

"I loved her with all my heart." I swallowed hard, then sat quiet for a few moments. But all at once I felt restless, and I decided to try another tactic.

"*Vous, mon ami*—you're still alive. *On va marcher*."

As I cranked the head of his bed into a near-upright position, he opened beady blue eyes to see what was happening. Sliding his legs to the edge of the bed, I leaned forward into a near embrace, then slipped my hand under his back and pulled him upward. His body odour and the fermenting-fruit vapour of his breath almost swamped me. We stood side by side next to his bed, with his arm slung over my shoulder, but he wouldn't take a step forward. I eased him back into bed.

"We'll try again later. *Alors, je reprends mon histoire…*"

I had travelled to Debbie's funeral with my other two sisters, Gaylene and Trina. We had gotten a special deal from Air Canada. ("Oh, you might wanna mention that in your next suicide note, *mon ami*—some airlines have bereavement fares.") As the stewardess set down our rum and Cokes, we each lit up a cigarette. Gaylene speculated aloud whether Travis, Holly and Crystal would find their way to Youngstown from Boyle to say goodbye to Debbie. After a half hour of sombre conversation and another drink, we shifted into Indian survival mode—humour. We took turns clowning around and telling jokes.

Debbie's best friend, Darlene, had arranged for someone to pick us up at the Calgary airport and drive us to Youngstown. The ride through the badlands in a smoke-filled crew cab truck was the longest three hours of my life, and the melodramatic country music made it worse. "My God, I thought I was going to burst when Emmylou Harris's velvet voice came on singing 'Beneath Still Waters,'" I told Philippe.

I had all the time in the world, and so did the man in the bed. So I went on, monitoring the steadiness of my voice and checking his face for a reaction. For minutes at a time, I forgot he was there beside me. I described what it had been like to stride into Debbie's little house, eager as usual to see the kids and look at the family pictures on the wall. The sorrow I felt when Joseph and Jaime ran up to me. I was overwhelmed, but couldn't cry, not in front of them. My loss was huge, but theirs was a hundredfold worse. I'd had twenty-three years with their mother, Joseph five and Jaime only two. Vacant smiles. Their toddler faces stupefied—a look I imagined battle-weary soldiers would wear. A blue cloud of pungent cigarette smoke hung over everything.

"I mumbled some excuse to flee outside, *mon ami*. I banged my fists on the roof of the closest car, swearing and yelling. I stayed outside until I was sure someone would have put the kids to bed. Then I ventured back into the house, my belly aching and grumbling.

"That night, someone, maybe a neighbour, drove us the thirty kilometres from Youngstown to the next biggest town, Oyen, to some nondescript concrete building they called a funeral home. I sensed death as soon as I walked in. The zombie-like undertaker ushered us into a dim room with dust-covered plastic flowers all along the walls.

The casket sat on a chrome stand, like the ones they give you for your suitcase in a hotel.

"*Mon ami*, without a word, the undertaker flipped the casket open. There lay the corpse of the person I loved more than anyone, my sister Debbie—inanimate—contracted and cold. She must have been in a blinding depression for some time for it to have come down to that—hurting in a way that only someone who has been there could comprehend."

I told the man beside me how I had felt when I looked down at the preserved, ashen body, smelled the pasty makeup on a face that only vaguely resembled hers and grasped her rigid right hand.

"I couldn't cry—that would have been easy. I heaved. I yelled. I swore. Then, in desperation, I grabbed the hand of her best friend, Darlene, who seemed even more devastated than me, and together we muttered the Lord's Prayer. I know. I should have been able to do better—an improvised prayer from the heart or maybe the *haeey hai* chant I had heard Mosom, my great-grandfather, sing with his hand drum, but neither came to me.

"What would you have done in my place, *mon ami*? And what if it had been you lying there? What do you think your family would have done—recited the *Je vous salue Marie*, or something more imaginative?"

I knew that if Mosom had been there things would've been different—he would've led a ceremony. He would have burnt sacred herbs like sweetgrass, sage and tree fungus. He would've beaten his drum and sung sacred songs to help my sister find the way out of the place someone goes to when they take their own life. Maybe my aunties or my mother knew what to do, but they had been so brainwashed by the Catholic Church that they'd gone along with the white way.

"I can't tell you how strange it was, to be in that desolate town without my sister, the only person who could have convinced me to go there in the first place," I said.

I moved my chair closer. I took his hand in mine and held it, praying that nobody would come in and see us like that.

We sat in silence for the last few hours of my shift.

DAY THREE SHIFT change report on Philippe: "Flat affect, still refusing to eat or drink. Not a word spoken in three days. Continue suicide precautions."

When I entered his room I saw that someone had shaved him. He looked younger. I set my large cup of coffee down on his bedside table. *"Bonjour, mon ami. Comment allez-vous? Ça va un peu mieux?"*

I settled into the big armchair and thought about what I would say today, even though I felt sure he must be fed up with my monologue. I knew the tack I was taking with him was extreme—not just the talking, but the force-feeding, which I had done several times, and the involuntary walks twice each shift. It occurred to me that my actions might be seen as abusive, or even borderline illegal, but I didn't care.

Someone pushed the *play* button again. I heard my voice droning:

"Let's see—where was I? Oh yeah—we were in Youngstown, in the middle of an alkali belt, where the water was so salty that it was undrinkable."

I told him how our relatives from the Cree side had arrived the day after I got there: Auntie Margaret and her oldest daughter, Mable, Auntie Rosie, Uncle Charlie and Uncle Andy. "I'm sure that small town was blown away to have so many Indians in their midst. The neighbours and friends who came to the door with cakes, casseroles and toilet paper were all fair; our relatives looked black alongside them."

When we got the news about Debbie, we'd had to call the Edmonton police to find Mother. Sitting at Trina's dining room table, shaking from stress and caffeine, I dialled the non-emergency number. They patched me through to a constable who worked the downtown core.

"What's her name? What does she look like?" From his voice, I imagined he was middle-aged and experienced.

"Bertha Dora Villeneuve. She spends time at the King Eddy and the York. A native woman around forty-five years old. She is missing her right ring finger."

When he answered, his voice had a softer tone. "Oh, that sounds like Red. Yes—I know where I might find her."

MOTHER HAD ARRIVED at the church a few minutes before the funeral, her thick black hair hacked into a Mohawk cut and her brown skin taut over her high cheek bones. When she caught sight of me she began wailing and sputtering so badly she could hardly breathe. I panicked. I ran to find Auntie Margaret, her oldest sister, to hold Mother and calm her—I couldn't do it. I suppressed the feeling each time it arose, but in my heart, I blamed her. Her, and myself.

I glanced at the man in the bed. Still no response.

"Your mother was likely just as distraught when she heard about you, *mon ami*, but she probably didn't chop her hair off to mourn your loss.

"Anyway, as you can imagine, I wasn't myself that whole week. I usually take charge of situations, especially when my family is involved, but I felt like I was watching scene after scene unfold around me. I couldn't intervene or participate. I went through the motions of playing with the kids to distract them, and that was fine as long as they didn't speak to me or look at me directly. When that happened I jumped to my feet and raced to the bathroom.

"Someone had decided Debbie would be buried in Youngstown, instead of in the Smith cemetery with our father, grandparents, aunts and uncles, and one little brother who was stillborn. So they buried her on the vast prairie—and there she rests, alone, *pour l'éternité*."

I stood and turned my back to him. Through the window I could see that the copper-coloured VGH streetlamps had come on. I closed the door to his room completely and leaned against it.

"*Mon dieu*, I got carried away. But it's fair game. You want to kill yourself, so you should know what those around you will go through if you actually succeed. I'm not angry at Debbie for taking her life at thirty-one. She suffered so much: fatherless at age six; watching our mother go from teetotaler to hard-core alcoholic; growing up poor and Indian in a racist town; abused by our favourite uncle at age twelve; married at fifteen to escape the hell at home, and then beaten by her husband Rory, who sent her to work in Bubbles car wash instead of back to high school. Another turbulent marriage, while living in a redneck hamlet, was the final straw. But it was still selfish of her to take her own life. There had to be a better way. What was your life like, *mon *ami*—what did you go through to get to this place? It had to be more than losing your wife to another man. No one is worth sacrificing your life for."

A white-and-grey seagull with massive wings landed on the ledge outside the window. It spotted Philippe's egg salad sandwich on the windowsill and tapped its hooked orange beak against the uneven antique pane, then squealed with frustration.

"They chalk it up to mental illness, or even a genetic disorder, and maybe it is. But surely there are other ways to deal with a personal crisis. *Dans ton cas, mon ami,* if you think you were punishing your ex-wife for her affair, think again. She would have inherited your bookstore and your wealth; squandered it on her new man and lived blissfully ever after.

"I can't judge my sister or you, *mon ami.* I've never been to that extreme place where I wanted to die. *J'y ai pensé*—but only as a fleeting thought. If I were ever in such a desperate state, I hope I'd try other things before killing myself: make a lengthy bucket list and start checking it off; sell everything and travel to Brazil; smoke pot; hire a gorgeous personal escort for a week; go to a sensual massage parlour for a happy ending or two; sky dive; move to Spain; go wild and crazy. Call the universe on its bullshit."

Philippe's gaze was fixed on the floor. I was tempted to try making eye contact but was afraid I might lose it if I did—so I stared at my feet instead. We sat silently. Anyone walking into the room would have felt the incredible tension, but nobody entered.

"Well, enough of that." I looked over at him. "Do you really want to die, *mon ami? Veux-tu mourir?*"

He held his breath but peered into my eyes for a second.

"That's what I thought. Then let's get on with your life, for God's sake."

The next afternoon I wasn't assigned to work with Philippe. But on my supper break, I went to see him. His mother was with him, and there were hints of life in his pale blue eyes. He held my gaze for a moment. When I grasped his pudgy hand, I felt him squeeze.

A MONTH LATER, I was sitting in my apartment in Kitsilano, going through photos and slides of Debbie. I wanted to organize them in chronological order and store them in a safe place before leaving for Mexico. The phone rang. I was hesitant to stop what I was doing to pick it up, but I did.

It was Philippe.

Speaking haltingly, with a thick French accent, he told me he was back home in his condo. His mother had stayed with him after his discharge but would return to Paris the next day. To my surprise, he invited me to join him for supper the next night at a French restaurant called Le Crocodile. He wanted, he said, to celebrate his survival.

After hanging up, I hurried to the bathroom to look into my eyes. I wanted to see if the joy was back—the joy that hadn't been there since the day I learned about Debbie's death. Sure enough, it *was* back. It looked different than it had before, but there it was, unmistakable and real. I was looking at my real self again.

A FEW OF the slides captured the dinner we'd had the last night of Debbie's final visit to Vancouver. I had invited Trina, Milan and Gaylene. Debbie had insisted that I prepare Alaskan king crab with drawn butter, make a baked Alaska for dessert and serve white wine. She wanted us to dress up as if we were going to a fancy restaurant— she wore her new black dress suit and a frilly red blouse. I recalled the night so vividly.

After our feast, Debbie asked me to play guitar and sing "The Rose" by Bette Midler. The lyrics were melodramatic, but I could relate. I had seen the delicate spring reeds be swamped by the flood waters of both the Athabasca and the Makhabn, as had Debbie. It seemed there was no hope for the fledgling plants, yet they would survive. And, in my first year of university, I cut the heart out of a frog with a razor-sharp scalpel, and left it to bleed—the heart continued to beat on its own in a petri dish, independent of the host body. Could love be equally cruel? I set up a makeshift stage in the living room, with an overhead lamp to shine down on me as I sat to strum and wail.

After dessert, we snapped photos, each taking turns posing with Debbie. After everyone else left and she had put Jaime to bed, Debbie and I sat down at the kitchen table. I knew it would be the last chat of that visit. She had to leave early the next day to catch her flight back to Calgary. I was expecting small talk, but Debbie started a conversation that got me squirming in my chair. She asked if her ex-husband, Rory, had hit me during the few years I lived with them. I was gobsmacked. Surely she knew about the incident in Canmore—the time he back-handed my face so hard it changed the shape of my nose. It had bled for hours. She must have been getting at something else. I knew that what she really wanted to ask was if he had *bothered* me—sexually abused me. But she didn't know how to raise it directly, and I wasn't ready to flip open that box on my own.

At the time, I still blamed myself for what had happened with Rory. I carried a crippling shame that I had betrayed her, my closest sister, in the worst possible way, and I was terrified about how the conversation might end if I opened up. I knew things would never be the same between us. It didn't occur to me that our relationship could have gotten even stronger, that there might have been healing for both of us. We were both victims of the same man. Rory was twenty-four when they met in Smith, and Debbie was only thirteen when he began to sexually exploit her. I was ten when he first touched me.

I think my sister understood all this. That was why she was reaching out. But I couldn't speak, and after a few moments she said that I should have told her about Rory hitting me. That she would have done something. We sat in awkward silence for a long time.

THE DINNER WITH Philippe was difficult, but a celebration nonetheless. He had a scar and a permanent bald patch above his left eye, but otherwise looked healthy and relaxed. His warm gaze put me at ease too. And I was heartened that he didn't resent how I had behaved toward him in the hospital.

I hadn't been to such a fancy restaurant since my days as a waiter at Pardon My Garden. I was dazzled. After the waiter cleared our dinner plates, the light-hearted conversation ended. Philippe looked me straight in the eye and told me that he was grateful for how I had challenged him. My story had helped him to comprehend the selfishness of what he had done, he said, and to reflect on death—how final and brutal it is. Then he got teary eyed and said, "*Je suis désolé. Je sais que le suicide de Debbie était un coup dur pour toi et ta famille.*"

At least it had gotten Mother off the street, I told him. And it was true. The day she found out about Debbie's suicide, Mother quit drinking cold turkey.

I WAS VERY excited about my Mexico trip. I would spend a week on the beach in Puerto Vallarta, then travel to Cuernavaca for a six-week Spanish immersion course. I would call Mother and the kids as often as I could, send them postcards and bring back souvenirs, but I had to go, that was clear. First, though, I wanted to better understand what had happened with Debbie. I made an appointment with my own doctor, bringing with me the coroner's report and the photos from our last supper together.

My doctor read the coroner's report thoroughly before commenting. Debbie had sought help for unexplained headaches and depression, and the country doctor had prescribed chlorpromazine, usually used only in a hospital context. She had stockpiled it until she had a lethal dose.

"She had a plan, Darrel," he told me. "She had already decided her fate before she came to see you; the trip was to say goodbye. She seemed happy because she probably genuinely was. She had an out, an escape from her situation, and visiting you was an important step in that process. We often hear about this with suicide victims—a quasi-euphoria in the days or weeks leading up to their death."

WENDY, A NURSE from the neurosurgery ward, drove me to the Vancouver airport the splendid July morning I departed for Mexico. She and a few other nurses had befriended me and been supportive following Debbie's death. Wendy and I had dated a bit, and she gave me an artsy early birthday card over coffee at the airport. A message written inside asked where the two of us were going as a couple. How could I tell her about Milan? No time to think about that now, I was caught up in the excitement of the adventure I had planned. Milan had agreed to meet me in Puerto Vallarta for the final week of my trip.

Palm trees lined the sides of the simple runway that led to the customs inspection hut. Buy pesos, find a place to stay, call Milan in

Vancouver, then phone Mother and the kids in Youngstown. It was working, my strategy to escape sorrow.

"*Mas despacio, por favor.*" I repeated the sentence over and over to the brown faces who spoke Spanish way too fast for a beginner to understand. My first night in Puerto Vallarta I went out dancing with the Canadian couple who were my neighbours at the hotel I had found. TEQUILA GOLD SHOOTERS 50 CENTAVOS read the sign in the disco bar. We laughed, danced and drank until the swirling room and my wobbly legs told me it was time to go back to my hotel. I fumbled my way out to a waiting taxi.

The next day, after an eight-hour bus ride to Guadalajara, panic set in. What had I done? Why had I come to Mexico, and alone at that? When I got to the motel I'd booked, I locked myself in my room. I should have been more responsible, used my savings to buy Debbie a gravestone and gone to spend the summer with Mother, Brian, Joseph and Jaime. For the next twenty-four hours, all I did was cry.

Beyond the Athabasca

I JUMPED OUT of bed, instantly alert, and I knew: today Mother would die. I could hear a bird clunking around in the enclosed deck downstairs. It must have been large, given all the racket it was making. The blue numbers on the alarm clock read six a.m. Shaken, I lumbered downstairs and flopped onto the couch. I rested my head in the palms of my hands, hoping the bird would find its own way out.

SWOOSH   CLUMP CLUMP   SWOOOOOSH

I opened the balcony door. It was at the far end—an owl, just like the ones I had seen in Stanley Park, with a rounded head and no ear tufts. The bird panicked when it became aware of my presence and began flapping around more vigorously than before, bumping up against the window and the cedar wall.

The message had been conveyed; there was no way to undo it. Still, it was urgent to guide the bird out. I held a folded blanket in front of me and approached the owl. The resistance of its wings surprised me as I gently pulled them down and helped the bird through the window. It flew off into the dawn of the grey Vancouver sky, towards the sparkling lights of Grouse Mountain.

I paced the apartment for a few minutes, in a frenzy, trying to calm myself. Get a grip, Darrel. You helped the bird find its way out, now clear your head. Get ready for work. Mother had always talked about bird messengers, but it was a myth, and why would one come to you?

I was thirty-two, living with Milan in Kitsilano. I was glad that he was away and not there to witness the scene or see the state of mind I was in.

Trembling, I flopped back onto the couch. I pictured Mother as I had left her lying in her hospital bed two weeks earlier: her gaunt brown face turned to one side, her strong hands motionless, an IV line running to her arm and a line from a morphine pump that went under the sheets to her belly. She was no longer in pain, but it had been clear from her face that she wasn't at peace, either.

THAT AFTERNOON, THE school secretary's imperious voice came over the intercom. It was two p.m., a sunny day in October. I was at the front of the classroom, sketching the solution to a math problem on the chalkboard.

The usually rambunctious preteens fell silent.

"Mr. McLeod, you have an urgent call. Mr. Girdler will come to your classroom to relieve you."

With each deliberate step along the waxed green tiles, the haze descending on me got heavier. The secretary motioned for me to take the phone in the back office.

"Hello."

"Darrel, it's me, Gaylene." I could hear the heaviness in her gravelly voice. I knew what she was going to say. The message from the bird was real.

"The hospital called an hour ago. Mom died late this morning."

The haze deepened. I gathered up some personal things from my classroom and wandered home through the cool autumn air.

Back at the apartment, I stretched out on the couch where I had spent so much time cuddling and watching television with Milan. The haze had become a fog. Was there anything that could cut through it? I turned on the television for company. *Fantasy Island* was on—but I was in no mood to laugh. I sat there feeling empty inside.

Great, I thought—back to Edmonton, and then onward to Smith. Once again, I would leave the safe haven of the coastal mountains, rainforest and ocean to be exposed and vulnerable in the city where Mother had lived on the street. "Fucking Indian" was still a common catcall on Eighty-ninth Street then. In Vancouver, the parents at my school called me "First Nations."

THE NEXT MORNING, bleary-eyed and exhausted, I leaned back in my airplane seat and put my headphones on. Grouse Mountain, the Lions, a snow-capped Mount Baker—the coastal mountains felt close and intimate through the small windows. I closed my eyes knowing I would be safe for a while yet—we still had to fly over the desert of Kamloops, and then the Rockies.

Pachelbel's Canon and the *Moonlight Sonata* soothed me until I was nearly asleep. Then the dissonance and the persistent sixteenth-note runs of Vivaldi's "Autumn" perked me up. The haze lifted for a few minutes as the music found its way into me. I got a whiff of brewing coffee and suddenly craved some.

I usually kept my love for classical music a secret. Of all of my friends and family, only Milan knew how much it meant to me. I was afraid others would think I was pretentious. I pictured Mr. Ferguson, my fatherly high school music teacher, and recalled the years of singing in choirs and playing trumpet. How could I have known then that classical music would be such a treasure—the only thing to bring me solace at times like this?

As I stared at the giant cumulus clouds below, I wondered again if things would have been different if Father hadn't died the year I was born. Mother didn't seem to ever stop loving or missing him; it was at least part of the reason she drank. And for most of her adult life she had mourned the loss of her own mother, who had died at age forty-eight. What would life have been like if the two of them had lived? If we could have sat around visiting in Cree, strong in our culture? Mother had preferred Cree—she spoke it whenever she could, but she taught us English because she felt she had to. Whenever I asked her how to say something in Cree, she would lecture as she wagged her large index finger at me. "You'll speak English—you're gonna be somebody some day!"

With Mother gone, what connection would I have with my relations and culture?

Then I thought about Debbie. Her death had shocked Mother into a new reality, allowing her seven sober years.

The seatbelt warning sign blinked and then stayed on; the pilot announced we would experience turbulence over Kamloops. The arid rolling hills I could see out the window tugged at me—I would have to explore them one day. I reflected on my last flight to Edmonton, to see Mother after she first told me she was sick.

Trina had picked me up at the airport in her white turbo Mustang with its posh garnet interior; she had driven from Vancouver to Edmonton when she learned Mother was ill. She was moody as always. Ever since her sex change operation, she had struggled with obesity. Now, months after having her stomach stapled, her hair was platinum blond and cut into a provocative shag, and she popped T3s eight at a time. She filled me in on the drama between her and Mother since her arrival two weeks previous. They hadn't spoken for a week, even though Trina went to the hospital every day.

Mother had looked terrible. Her hair was a mess, and she was scowling; her face was more emaciated than I had ever seen it. I found her hairbrush, a towel and a face cloth and began to groom her; I felt her relax at my touch. A few tears slipped over her cheekbones.

A tap on my shoulder startled me. The flight attendant told me to remove my headphones and stow my Walkman for landing. I peered out the window—flat brown fields and pavement as far as I could see. There was no escaping it now. The desolate horizon where the steel-blue sky touched down kept repositioning itself, and the dreadful emptiness in my chest was back—I felt it every time I was on the prairies. I wouldn't understand it until years later, when I read about the massacre of the buffalo: reduced from thirty million to around three hundred in eighty years. It was part of a bigger government plan to force the Plains Cree into submission; starve them. Bad medicine.

I WASN'T SURE where things stood between my sisters and me now that Mother was gone, but I called Gaylene and Holly to see if they would help with the funeral preparations, or at least spend some time with me. They were both pleasant on the phone, but it was clear there would be no assistance and no visits. They were still bitter about their experiences with Mother. I didn't blame them, and I was convinced that they must hold a grudge against me, too, for taking them from a safe and secure foster home. Alone in Mother's apartment that night, I agonized over this for hours, remembering a discussion I had had with the psychologist at Edmonton's Cross Cancer Clinic concerning my family.

I had watched the psychologist's face closely as I recounted my childhood. I wanted to be sure she was taking in what I said but wasn't overwhelmed by it, like the social worker at the Rockyview had been. I told her about Mother's binge drinking and the violence that happened when she was drunk. I told her about the Sunday morning when I was eight years old, when Mother locked us in the house, then poured the gasoline all around and lit it on fire. It was only Ned's quick action that had saved us from dying in an inferno. I told her how Mother had broken Debbie's nose by throwing a full beer bottle at her; she had done the same thing to me, but fortunately her aim was off. I had other memories of drunken and violent scenarios at home, but I had blocked the worst ones out. I simply did not want to relive them.

My quandary, I told the psychologist, was this: how could I possibly still have feelings of love for a person who had done all of this?

"There's no explaining the incredible loyalty some children show toward a parent in spite of abuse, neglect or abandonment," the psychologist told me, with a sympathetic gaze.

If that was intended to console me, it didn't. In fact, it made me bitter. Throughout my life, I had been naively devoted to Mother, when everything and everyone around me indicated my hopes and expectations of her couldn't be met.

I was also the one who stood by my mother and helped her through her illness, making sure she ate well and giving her daily bed baths once she was immobile. Some days I struggled with being there, wondering if some sort of heart-to-heart reconciliation was possible before she died. To my surprise, on her last day at home, it happened.

At my request, the paramedics had come to take her to the hospital. Once she was strapped to a stretcher, I leaned over her to apologize—to say I was sorry she wouldn't get to die at home, as she had wanted.

I opened my mouth to speak, but something silenced me. With her helpless doe eyes locked onto mine, she raised her hand to caress my unshaven cheek and chin. We were like that for only a moment, but for that time, it was just the two of us in the world. We connected in such a profound way that nothing else mattered.

The minute Mother had been wheeled out into the corridor, Trina pushed her way into the dimly lit apartment hallway and came right up close to my face. "Darrel, what did you do with her meds? We all know that money is what matters most to you. You can have her savings, just give me the morphine." It was too late. I had already given it to the paramedics.

MOTHER'S YOUNGER SISTER Auntie Rosie and her husband, Charlie, arrived in Edmonton the day after I did. When I heard their voices, I hastened to open the door to Mother's apartment. There they stood, side by side, looking the same as they always had. Uncle Charlie slightly taller, his shiny brown complexion a shade darker than Auntie's, his thick black hair in a crewcut, hers in a short feather cut. Her slow gaze. His constant smile. I had always felt Auntie could see into my soul, and here she was, doing it again. I didn't have to say a word about how I was feeling. Uncle Charlie didn't say a word, either. His presence said it all.

"*Tansi.*" Auntie took my hand and held me still, directly in front of her. "You'll be okay, Tairl.   We'll make it."

"*Manando, egwa kiya…*" My lips were trembling, but I was determined not to cry. "So glad you guys came."

I brewed some coffee, and we sat down at the dining table. After ten or fifteen minutes of comfortable silence, the conversation began.

"What are you gonna do? How are you gonna get your mother home to Smith?   We'll organize everythin' once she's there. We'll do the awake fer three nights."

I stared at Auntie, caught off guard by how much her voice sounded like Mother's. Her face and hands made me think of Mother too. The slow cadence of her words and her lilting voice comforted me at a deeper level than anything else could have, but nothing eased the dread about what I knew would follow: the trip back to Smith, the wake and the funeral.

"Oh, Auntie. Maybe we *should* do three nights, but I discussed it with my sisters and brother, and we don't think any of us could handle three nights without sleep," I lied. I hadn't raised this with anyone, but I knew that none of my siblings would participate in one night, let alone three. And I couldn't bear the thought of three sleepless nights filled with Catholic prayers.

"It is really hard on a person, but it's to help their soul get to the other side, like the priest says—through purgatory. We'll do one night then, but our family will keep prayin' for her for two more days."

The mention of purgatory took my breath away. My mind flashed back to a scene that had played out with Mother on the grounds of the Misericordia Hospital late one morning. Song sparrows and wrens were twittering away, and the leaves of the weeping birch trees flashed in the breeze. I was pushing Mother in a wheelchair from one building to another when we came across a group of Catholic priests—a murder of magpies, except that the white patch was around their throats. The pungent smell of burnt toast.

I got a sudden shiver, and Mother's head dropped—I thought she had fainted. When I moved in front of her, I saw tears were streaming down her cheeks. "Mother, what is it? What's wrong?"

Her face was screwed up with emotion. She couldn't look at me.

"I'm going to hell, Son. I know it—I'm going to hell."

The day she had appeared to me as Satan leapt to mind—and now she was talking about hell. How strange. What was it that was upsetting her? Did she actually remember the things she had done while she was in a drunken stupor? I had never confronted her about them, and I was sure nobody else had either. We all wanted to move past the terror of those moments as quickly as we could. Was it the visit she and Swede had made to Canmore she was thinking about? The time she had spent the entire day in the bar, drinking with Rory and Debbie, while I waited out in the car, hoping to at least catch a glimpse of her? Or was she afflicted by memories of the ways, in an alcohol-fuelled rage, she had injured and maimed Swede, the boyfriend she had left us for, a man she had truly loved?

"There is no such thing as hell, Mom. Did Mosom or Cucuum ever talk to you about hell? Of course not. It doesn't exist—don't believe the nuns and priests!"

"Please take me back to my room, Son. Just let me go to bed."

I tucked her into bed and held her hand for a few minutes. After she had calmed a bit, I took a break to sort out my feelings. I felt sorry for her, but there was nothing I could do. Mother had to go through whatever it was she was going through. Nobody could save her from it, not even Jesus.

When I got back to her room, she was awake but incoherent. Worried, I pushed her call button. The nurse arrived quickly. She was the one Mother liked. The one with the kind smile and gentle touch.

"I'm concerned about Mother—she's changed so much in the time I was gone. She was upset earlier, about dying, but now she's confused and talking gibberish."

"Well, yes, she was anxious, so I started her on Ativan," the nurse explained.

"I wish you had discussed it with me first."

"Listen, you need to understand—your mother's well-being comes first, and she was very distressed."

I struggled to contain my anger. Somehow, I knew that there would be no more lucid conversations with Mother. She couldn't cope with what was going on in her head, and the nurse had responded by giving her what she needed to escape it. Gradually, she slipped away. For a week, she was unconscious with only a few waking moments. One day an elderly nun, who had stopped by to visit against my wishes, asked her something in Cree. Mother answered in Cree, but I didn't understand any of it. I sat by her bedside for another week, alone, trying to read and listen to music, before I decided to return to work. Two weeks later, the same day Uncle Andy had gone to visit her, she died. Great-aunt Eva said my uncle's visit was what she had been waiting for.

THE FUNERAL HOME wanted two thousand dollars to drive Mother to Smith. When I told them about the wake, their fee jumped another thousand dollars, for a second return trip. I didn't have that kind of money—I was a beginning teacher and had just taken four months off without pay. Auntie Rosie, Uncle Charlie and I looked at each other, perturbed. Then an idea came to me.

"Well, Auntie, I could rent a cargo van and drive her to Smith myself. It's *Mother*."

Auntie Rosie gave me one of her penetrating gazes. "Good idea, Tairl. Uncle and I will ride with you. We'll bring her home together. She always did like a car ride," she said and then giggled.

I got a white cargo van with air conditioning. That afternoon, we drove to the funeral home to view Mother's body. The bright fragrance of fresh-cut roses and Stargazer lilies floated in the air of the foyer, barely masking the stench of death and embalming chemicals. The undertaker led us past a showroom of coffins and urns and a tacky chapel lined with plastic flowers, then through a swinging double door.

I had handled dead bodies when I worked as an orderly. The procedure was simple enough: remove IVs and catheters; a quick once-over with a face cloth; tie the identification tag on the big toe of the right foot and wrap the corpse neatly in a bedsheet or shroud before sliding it onto a trolley. I had even stomached a full autopsy. None of that prepared me for what came next.

I froze in front of the stainless-steel refrigerator with its square doors, shiny pull handles and sliding drawers. I couldn't believe the undertaker was going to do that now—slide the tray holding Mother's body out of the cooler for us to have a look, with no niceties. I knew this wasn't the way things were supposed to go. I had set up viewings at the hospitals in Calgary and Vancouver, and it was never this callous—this disrespectful. The throbbing in my head intensified; my emotions numbed. I was sure I was going to throw up. He did it: he opened the door and pulled out the sliding tray that held Mother's body, covered by a white sheet.

Auntie Rosie took one of my hands. Her large, warm fingers were identical to Mother's, which were now cold and still. Uncle Charlie filled the undertaker in on our plan.

"You're supposed to have a permit to move a body in Alberta. That could take some time, so we simply won't say anything." The mortician faked a smile as he glanced past me, and I thought, right—there's that attitude again. Anywhere else, this whole process would have been more dignified. My mind was fuzzy, but my thoughts were clear in that moment. She's my mother, for God's sake. Are they going to arrest me for transporting her body?

The next morning Auntie Rosie made breakfast: bacon and eggs sunny side up with pan fries and toast, like she had made for Uncle almost every day for more than thirty years. We went through three pots of coffee as we sat around Mother's kitchen table, with the familiar blue cloud of cigarette smoke floating in the air. Uncle broke our easy silence.

"So what kinda Cree they talk out there in BC? I hear those Indians are pretty rough," he said in his soft-spoken, singsong tone.

I laughed. "They're not Cree, Uncle. Quite a few different native languages in BC."

"We're related to some of them up there. Three Cree brothers went there from Wabasca to trade horses, stayed and started families there," Auntie commented.

"Reeeeally, eh? Don't talk Cree there, eh? That's somethin'." Uncle shook his head and gave me one of his slow, wide smiles.

We drove back to the funeral home in the early afternoon. I thought my head was going to burst; a headache would have been a welcome reprieve. I signed some forms. A new person, the mortician's assistant, handed me a document entitled *Death Certificate* in bold black and helped us to load the coffin into the van. "If the police stop you—show it to them. There shouldn't be a problem."

THE BRANCHES WERE completely bare on the trees that lined the streets leading out of Edmonton. Weeping willows swirled in the wind like horsewhips. On the highway the wind of passing eighteen-wheelers rocked us, so I accelerated.

As we drove, I searched the landscape for solace—an eagle or a bear, a natural-looking cluster of evergreens, a herd of buffalo, maybe even silos or grain elevators—but the exasperating fields went on forever. I recalled that same road in winter—somehow the scene was less melancholic under a giant blanket of snow.

Panicked jackrabbits did their zig-zag hop pattern along or across the road, scarlet blotches and patches of brown fur every few miles. Soon their fur would turn white. I looked in the rear-view mirror at the metallic gray coffin, then glanced at Auntie Rosie and Uncle Charlie sitting beside me on the bench seat.

I couldn't believe this was happening. I had fantasized about a return to Smith that was filled with triumph, with Mother showing me off and bragging. This is my son—he went to university; he's a teacher now, *mamaskatch*—but instead I felt humiliation and shame coming on. Tongues would be wagging and clucking. *It's Bertha Cardinal, remember her? She's the one who rode through town naked, on a bicycle. And that's her boy, what was his name? He looks healthy; are those his real teeth? Her oldest girl committed suicide and her oldest son, Greg… well, he had an operation to become a girl—took some weird name like Katrina.*

Heavy grey clouds. The wind had picked up—was it going to rain?

Out of my side window, I caught a glimpse of the ditch. Four crows settling onto a deer carcass.

The speedometer read 110. I lifted my foot. There was no hurry.

"Who'd have ever thought we'd be doing this?" I turned briefly to Auntie.

"*Tapwe.*" She smiled and nodded as she lit another cigarette. The sulfur from the match tickled my nose.

"I hope Mother doesn't mind riding with us like this."

"*Mah.* Well—better than in one of them hursts with them weird men in purple suits," Auntie answered.

"That's for sure. I know she'd rather be with us," I said with a dry chuckle.

Uncle Charlie laughed. "You guys are crazy."

"Well, Mother always did see the funny side of things."

We passed the sign for Rochester. My Grade Nine debating partner, Diane Sasnowski, had lived there. I wondered if she would remember me.

Soon we would pass through Athabasca. I loved the rolling hills with their thick cover of spruce trees just before town. So many days I had taken the kids for walks through there and down to the water, to escape. As we watched the muddy river glide by, I fantasized about taking them to a place Rory and Debbie had taken me once: its source in the Rockies, where the runoff from the Athabasca glacier fed into an exhilarating turquoise stream in Jasper National Park. I wondered if Mother had ever gone there.

Then a torrent of bad memories. The time I had won the public speaking contest at school but forced the kids to watch *Love Story* four nights in a row to avoid the drunken craziness at home. Oh my God, I had pushed Mother down the stairs there the year Debbie gave me my first guitar. And the spring day I abandoned the kids. I had cried on the Greyhound all the way to Calgary.

I wanted this trip to be over so I could get on with my life—my beautiful life on the West Coast. Athabasca, Island Lake, Hondo—then Smith. Smith. Two nights there—that's all I could take—then a day in Edmonton—then home, back to Vancouver. I fixed my gaze on the road.

I thought about *L'Étranger,* the novel by Albert Camus that had shaken me in my second-year French course. The book's opening sentence was "*Aujourd'hui, maman est morte*"—today Mother is dead.

Would I be like Meursault, the main character? He didn't cry at his mother's wake, and he went out partying the next day. The only thing that made sense to him in the whole experience was that nothing made sense. He didn't relate to any of it—the religious rites and doctrine, the staged mourning, the ceremony and burial. I hadn't empathized with his character when I first read the novel, but now, with each passing hour, I did.

A luminescent green sign warned us that the Smith turnoff was thirty kilometres ahead. In forty-five minutes we would be there. Auntie turned to look at me.

Who the hell would do this—who would drive their mother's coffin around in a cargo van? What would they say—all my relations, and the white folks in Smith? *Geez, can't even afford a hearse, or is he too cheap? And to think his mother bragged about him being a teacher in Vancouver.*

I sighed and then mumbled, "Well, I guess things could be worse."

"Oh yeah? Whatcha mean?" Uncle Charlie took the bait.

"I read a story in school about an American family who had to take their mother's body halfway across their county in a horse-drawn wagon to bury her in her hometown. Took 'em nine days, and they almost lost the coffin twice—once while fording a river and then again in a barn fire. And to think they were flat broke—no money for embalming, and no ice or refrigeration. You can imagine the stench."

"*Wuh wah*... be awful, eh, Tairl! I guess we're lucky? Only a couple hours' drive. *Mah*—is that where you got the idea?" Auntie smiled.

The random stands of spruce trees around the picturesque cemetery confirmed it: we were entering Smith. Clusters of children with dark skin moved off the street to let us through—cousins for sure, even though they wouldn't know me. The cloud cover was thick, but I knew it wasn't going to rain.

Another whirlpool of memories.

LaFrance's General Store, now called something else: shopping with Mother for frozen hamburger and canned peas. Leonard, the LaFrance son, Smith's Prince Charming, never spoke a word to her and would shoo us kids away after we had spent our nickels and dimes on candy.

The three-storey Smith Hotel Café—Jack Mah, Mother's friend and former boss. She used to chuckle when recounting how she teased him about his calling out of the menu each day: "moosta meat a los-a-beef, a ham bone steak!"—or at the Dominion Day fair—"peanut, popcorn, clack-a-jack a jelly apple!" and how he in turn kidded her about *her* English pronunciation and mimicked her awkwardness when serving tea and pie to the who's who of Smith.

The night I ran to get Mother out of the bar because Uncle Andy was about to rape Debbie. The interminable seconds it had taken for the bartender to come to the door after I rang the buzzer.

We drove by the small wooden church, now painted blue with a simple white steeple. Mother had loved the original Gothic-style church, but it had burned to the ground the year after Greggie was raped. I still recalled Mother's terrified voice yelling, "The church is on fire!" at five in the morning, followed by a resounding *clang* when the huge bell hit the ground. She and Ned had speculated over coffee what a bad omen the fire was for Smith. Did the church burn because of Father Jal, I had wondered at the time—his foul mouth and bad behaviour? Mother had hated him. "*Kohkôs*—such a *pig*," she would say. "He went with my sister-in-law, and then bothered *me* after your dad died."

Tomorrow we would go to church. Tomorrow there would be a proper green hearse for Mother's coffin; tomorrow at this time it would all be over. Well, almost over—first the church, then the graveyard, then what? The longest night of my life, or would that be tonight—at the wake?

THE STAGE WAS set; people had done this before. The furniture had been cleared away from the living room, and the sheer curtains were tied back to reveal the long, dark wooden coffee table on which Mother's coffin would be placed. Rows of stackable plastic chairs were set up facing it. Cushions for kneeling sat in a straight line on the floor. Candles of different shapes and sizes flickered all around. How eerily familiar the scene felt. It was just like in *L'Étranger*.

Uncle Charlie directed how the coffin should be positioned. Odd music in the background—not the usual Johnny Cash or Loretta Lynn. When I recognized the *taa taa da-ta da taa taa taa* rhythm of Habanera from the opera *Carmen*, I was sure I had become delusional. The women were busy in the kitchen preparing sandwiches and coffee for the wake. The men—my cousins and uncles—were watching TV in the extra bedroom, their eyes glued to the screen. I sat with them. It wasn't an illusion: the chorus had rallied behind a voluptuous Carmen as she sang. *L'amour est un oiseau rebelle que nul ne peut apprivoiser.* I loved that line and remembered translating it for Milan: Love is a defiant bird that cannot be tamed.

"Why are you guys watching this?"

"Satellite's down," someone muttered.

Father Proulx opened the wake, looking tall and insipid in his full-length black cassock and three-peaked biretta cap with a pom-pom at the top. In one hand he carried a well-worn priests' missal and in the other a vial of holy water. A large pewter crucifix hung from his neck, askew.

"What's '*er* name?" he asked.

Auntie whispered close to his ear. "Father, it's Bertha. Remember, Bertha Dora. We called her Doris. You married her to Ned, Father. And you baptized her kids."

He flipped the book open, stared at the page for a moment and then started to recite a prayer in Latin.

Although I listened closely, I could only make out *our sister Bertha* at the end of each verse. Anger welled up in my chest at how mechanical and vacuous he seemed. Did he even have the correct prayer? Who would know?

Then he took the vial of holy water and sprinkled it over Mother in her coffin. I wiped drops of it from my forehead and stepped backwards before he could do it again. He gathered up his things and moved toward the door. I tried to compel him to look at me—to look me in the eye and acknowledge at least one of us. I wanted to bring him out of his trance, but it didn't work, so I stepped in front of him.

"*Merci d'être venu, Monsignor,*" I said. "*Je sais qu'il est tard. Maman vous respectait beaucoup.*"

"*Merci. Je suis désolé.*" He gave me a blank stare; I'm not sure it had even registered that we were now speaking French.

I held out my hand like Mother had taught me to, as a sign of respect. The priest extended his parrot claw. It was a small victory, but at that moment, when everything seemed surreal, it was an important one.

"What did you say to him, Darrel?" Maryann, Auntie Rosie's oldest girl, asked me.

I stepped outside and watched as my cousin Charlie Jr. helped the priest climb into the truck. I had come to loathe everything Catholic. My cousins remembered me from our early childhood together, and they loved me, but they didn't really know me. I had become an outsider on so many levels, like Meursault, and that could never change.

AUNTIE KNEELED AT the head of the coffin, with Maryann beside her; both stared straight ahead, their faces expressionless. Auntie Rosie's other children clustered around them. Our oldest cousin, Auntie Margaret's daughter, Chiq-iq, tired and morose, kneeled behind them. I recalled the story Mother used to tell about Chiq-iq being born on the trapline, and how every time Mother had cuddled her as a baby, Chiq-iq had latched onto Mother's bottom lip as a soother. A few of Chiq-iq's brothers and sisters, Chummy, Nancy, Beaver, Beatrice and Lady, were there too. I was grateful for their presence and for the respect they were showing for Mother—thankful too that no one asked why none of my siblings were there. With her hands in prayer pose, Auntie Rosie began threading a black rosary though her fingers, one bead at a time. She nodded at Maryann, who picked up her own rosary and pronounced each word deliberately in a monotone voice:

> *O my Jesus, forgive us our sins.*
> *Save us from the fires of hell...*

The words cut me to the core—there it was again, *hell*. Why was the Church so obsessed with hell—why did it need to instill terror into people's hearts?

As Maryann continued, our other cousins' voices echoed hers. I couldn't believe they had memorized all the prayers of the rosary. Mother had told me often about how she had struggled to learn the Hail Mary and other prayers in residential school, and how mean the Sisters had been when she made mistakes. I thought about Mother's medicine bundle. Gaylene had found it under the bed when packing up her place. I should have brought it with me.

I was in a daze when the fern-green hearse and matching limousine drove up to the house right on time. My white shirt and black dress slacks were wrinkled, but I couldn't do anything about that now. I pulled them on. The thought of entering an empty church and sitting through an hour-long mass filled me with dread. When two young cousins opened wide the double doors, I was astonished. The place was packed, and my sisters and brother were seated in the front row. Later, I would find out that people had come from Slave Lake, Calling Lake, Kinuso, High Prairie and Edmonton. Cousins, more aunts and uncles, Cree people I didn't recognize and a few white people.

I was relieved when the priest approached the coffin swinging the chain censer. The incense displaced the stale air and the funk of the pasty makeup the funeral home had caked onto Mother's face. I fidgeted as I thought about how much fun I had had with Mother when it was just the two of us at home. In spite of everything, I had always known she loved me, and that was part of the problem. All of my life, I had tried to make the conditions right for that love to shine through.

Unannounced, three elders began to sing, their warbling voices harmonizing "Amazing Grace" in Cree. Leathery brown faces framed by paisley scarves. It started quietly, then got louder as the other Cree speakers present joined in:

> *Kihci-kisewatisiwin e-ki-pimacihit*
> *Kise-manitow niki-miskak mekwac e-wanihoyan*

The song stirred powerful emotions within me, pride, sorrow, joy and a sense of validation, but I may have been the only one whose eyes were still dry when it stopped. My sisters' sobs made me even more determined not to cry.

Afterward, I went to stand in the doorway to thank people for coming. As they filed past, everyone shook my hand, and several seniors stopped to tell me what a good person Mother was. A man named Johnny Tait spoke about how Mother had invited the older bachelors and widowers in town to the house for turkey on Christmas day—he raved about her butter tarts and stuffing. He reminded me that one year she had even invited Ollie Andersen, the local eccentric, who had supposedly buried his parents on their property at the edge of town and had lived alone in an old shack there for years, surviving by collecting bottles and selling potatoes.

Another man told me that he had loved the way my mother and father harmonized and played guitar together. "She didn't even drink then, Darrel—used to drive your dad around in your grandpa's old Model T."

I lingered on the landing for a few minutes after everyone had left. Mother had touched all of these people in one way or another, and they hadn't held a grudge against her for the things she had done or the bad choices she had made. On the contrary, through their presence they showed they had forgiven her—given her absolution. But did people really know all that she had done, how horrific it had been for us? I was pretty sure they didn't. And they hadn't suffered the consequences my brother and sisters and I had.

THE GRAVEYARD WAS inviting—even in my dazed state I noticed the ochre-tipped Indian paintbrush scattered all around.

The harlequin-green outdoor carpet the undertakers had used to mask the stark hole in the ground looked out of place. A mound of clay and dark topsoil sat off to one side, waiting.

Crows, their obsidian feathers glossy and formal, were everywhere, flitting and hopping, cawing and rattling. They were there for a reason, and I welcomed them. I knew it was they who carried a soul through to the next phase, to the other side. These crows that I had feared and avoided all my life now made the notions of sin, absolution, heaven and hell seem frivolous and contrived. It was time for Mother to move to a higher plane, another dimension.

Chiq-iq handed me a scarlet rose she had broken off the spray that sat on the coffin.

The priest's voice: "We h'ar dust and h'unto dust we shall return."

Then the voices of Auntie Rosie, Maryann, Chiq-iq and a few other female cousins:

> *Hael Mareh, full of grace*
> *the Lord is with thee.*
> *Bles't art thou 'mongst all wimen,*
> *and bles't is the fruit of your womb—Cheezus. Amin.*

The crows flushed and flew off, cawing loudly.

"H'you may now lo-*her* the cof-*fin*." I heard the priest pronounce these words as I gazed toward the rolling hills in the distance—beyond the Athabasca. I was restless, anxious to escape to its shores. I wanted to wash away the heaviness of this foreign ritual. Tomorrow I would go down to the Athabasca alone. I would wade in and splash the water onto my arms and face.

Ekosi   etikwe

Acknowledgments

I OWE MY survival as well as my success and happiness to my great-grandfather, Mosom Joseph Powder, who is my hero and guide to this day; to my father, Sonny, who gave me strength from the spirit world; to my mother, Bertha Dora, who loved me with all her heart; to my sister Debbie, who took over the parenting role when Mother became incapacitated; to my brother/sister Greg/Trina for being a tireless champion and teacher of the harder lessons in life and to my younger sister Gaylene for always believing in me and urging me on.

I must acknowledge *dragi* Milan for walking alongside me for over thirty years, listening tirelessly to my capricious dreams and wishes, holding me up through many family tragedies and helping me to achieve and celebrate my successes. I give thanks to other dear friends who have supported me intensely over the years: Sandee and Joanne Mitchell, Yolande Levasseur, Sheila and John Vataiki, Frank Shannon, Dr. Kathy Absolon, Shelley Cardinal, Umit Kiziltan along with Kumru and Ekin, Dr. Margo Greenwood, Robin McLay and three very dear friends who are in the spirit world but live on in my heart: Shirley Joseph, Marion Roze and Ted Girdler.

I thank Betsy Warland for being gentle and inspiring yet demanding as a writing instructor, editor and mentor. Betsy's leit-motif, "trust the narrative, it knows where it needs to go," kept me writing even when I was unsure of my skill level or direction. Shaena Lambert provided brilliant, soul-stirring commentary at every stage of the development of this book and quickly became an energized champion; not a day goes by when I am not grateful for her teachings, inspiration and support. I thank Douglas Glover for rich advice in editing "Hail Mary, Full of Grace" and for referring me to his book *Attack of the Copula Spiders*—it has influenced every aspect of my writing. Barbara Pulling is a remarkable editor with an eye for both detail and structure. She proposed artful solutions for even the most challenging writing dilemmas, and I was awestruck by the final metamorphosis of *Mamaskatch* as a result of her sensitive and insightful approach.

My pre-readers Yolande, Joanne and Umit were generous with their time and wisdom, and I thank them.

Three schoolteachers took it upon themselves to intervene in my life, having a profound impact: Mrs. Earl, my Grade Four teacher; Mary Olsen, my junior high English and choir teacher; Judy Emmons, my beginning band teacher, and David Ferguson, my high school music teacher. My third-year French professor, Claire-Lise Rogers, and her husband, David, befriended me, taught me to speak French well and championed my teaching career.

Elder Catherine Bird, in one of our many visits, told me to write my life stories down. "Your stories will help people, Tairl," she admonished. Here's praying that her words prove true.

Ilja Herb

DARREL J. MCLEOD is Cree from treaty eight territory in Northern Alberta. Before deciding to pursue writing in his retirement, he was a chief negotiator of land claims for the federal government and executive director of education and international affairs with the Assembly of First Nations. He holds degrees in French literature and education from the University of British Columbia. He lives in Sooke, British Columbia.

The Editor's Circle of Milkweed Editions

We gratefully acknowledge the following individuals for their annual leadership support of the literary arts.

Anonymous
Mary Aamoth
Lynn Abrahamsen
Elizabeth Andrus Fund of
    The Minneapolis Foundation
Bill and Terry Ankeny
Meagan Bachmayer and Neal Meyer
Sarah and Michael Bauer
Mary and Keith Bednarowski
Barry Berg and Walter Tambor
Breyer Family Fund of The Minneapolis
    Foundation
Emilie and Henry Buchwald
Timothy and Tara Clark
Albert J. Colianni Jr. and
    Susan F. Colianni
Cassie and Dan Cramer
Christopher and Katherine Crosby
Lisa Dalke and Kurt Bachmayer
Edward and Sherry Ann Dayton
Wendy Dayton
Claire and Jack Dempsey
Arundhati Deo
Veena Deo
Mary C. Dolan—The Longview
    Foundation
Beth and Kevin Dooley
Kathy and Mike Dougherty
Margaret Driscoll and Robert Keeley
William Driscoll and Lisa Hoffman
Martha Gabbert
Charles and Barbara Geer
Daniel and Patricia Gerhan
Raeanna and Walter Gislason
Joanne and John Gordon
Geoff and Janny Gothro
Ellen Grace
Jeanne and William Grandy
John Gulla and Andrea Godbout
Elizabeth and Edwin Hlavka
William and Cheryl Hogle
Emily and George R.A. Johnson
Hart and Susan Kuller
Constance and Daniel Kunin
Chris Lawrence and Meghan McGrann
Jim and Susan Lenfestey
Kathleen and Allen Lenzmeier
Adam and Maryann Lerner
Ross and Bridget Levin
Amy and Mark Lucas
Ann and Chris Malecek
Walter McCarthy and Clara Ueland
Robert and Vivian McDonald

Lucy and Bob Mitchell—
    The Longview Foundation
Ann and Alfred Moore
Kate Moos and Valerie Arganbright
Betsy Moran and Brian Johnson
Sheila C. Morgan
Chris and Jack Morrison
Helen Morrison
Kelly Morrison and John Willoughby
Carolyn and Bob Nelson
Martha and Brock Nelson
Robin B. Nelson
Wendy Nelson
Emily and Will Nicoll
Christopher Pearson and Amy Larson
Margy Sather Peterson and
    Paul Peterson
Elizabeth Petrangelo and
    Michael Lundeby
Jörg and Angela Pierach
Patricia Ploetz
Janet Polli and Matt Ides
Margaret and Dan Preska
Melissa Raphan and Tom Rock
    Charitable Fund
Lewis and Connie Remele
Alicia and Rick Reuter
Paul and Mary Reyelts Foundation
Rickeman/Murphy Family Fund of
    The Minneapolis Foundation
Sandra Roe
Becky Rom and Reid Carron
Sharon and Bob Ryan
Caryn Schall and Jeff Davis
Linda and Jesse Singh
Daniel Slager and Alyssa Polack
Nell and Chris Smith
Stephanie Sommer and
    Stephen Spencer
Bruce and Julie Steiner
Cassidy and Andrew Steiner
Sarah Stoesz and David Foster
Tracey Thayer Breazeale and
    Jeff Breazeale
Ruth Travis
Rachel and Karl Ulfers
Joanne Von Blon
Kathleen and Bill Wanner
David Washburn and Meg Anderson
Greg and Ellen Weyandt
Eleanor and Fred Winston—
    The Longview Foundation
Margaret Wurtele

milkweed
editions

Founded as a nonprofit organization in 1980, Milkweed
Editions is an independent publisher. Our mission is to
identify, nurture and publish transformative literature,
and build an engaged community around it.

We are aided in this mission by generous individuals
who make a gift to underwrite books on our list.
Special underwriting for *Mamaskatch* was provided by
the Sommer-Spencer family.

milkweed.org